BOOKSHOPS

Jorge Carrión

BOOKSHOPS

Translated from the Spanish by
Peter Bush

MACLEHOSE PRESS
QUERCUS · LONDON

First published in the Spanish language as *Librerías* by
Editions Anagrama, Barcelona in 2013

First published in Great Britain in 2016 by MacLehose Press
This paperback edition published in 2018 by

MacLehose Press
An imprint of Quercus Publishing Ltd
Carmelite House
50 Victoria Embankment
London EC4Y 0DZ

An Hachette UK company

Esta obra ha sido publicada con una subvención del Ministerio de Educación,
Cultura y Deporte de España.

ISBN (MMP) 978 0 85705 446 3
ISBN (Ebook) 978 0 85705 435 7

10 9 8 7 6 5 4 3 2 1

Designed and typeset in Cycles by Libanus Press, Marlborough
Printed and bound in Great Britain by Clays Ltd, Elcograf S.p.A.

A bookshop is only an idea in time.

I do not doubt that I often happen to talk of things which are treated better in the writings of master-craftsmen, and with more authenticity. What you have here is purely an assay of my natural, not at all of my acquired, abilities. Anyone who catches me out in ignorance does me no harm: I cannot vouch to other people for my reasonings: I can scarcely vouch for them to myself and am by no means satisfied with them. If anyone is looking for knowledge let him go where such fish are to be caught: there is nothing I lay claim to less. These are my own thoughts, by which I am striving to make known not matter but me.

MICHEL DE MONTAIGNE, "On Books",
translated by M. A. Screech

A man recognises his genius only upon putting it to the test. The eaglet trembles like the young dove at the moment it first unfolds its wings and entrusts itself to a breath of air. When an author composes a first work, he does not know what it is worth, nor does the bookseller. If the bookseller pays us as he wishes, we in turn sell him what we are pleased to sell him. It is success that instructs the merchant and the man of letters.

DENIS DIDEROT, *Letter on the Book Trade*
translated by Arthur Goldhemmer

CONTENTS

Introduction inspired by a Stefan Zweig short story   9

I	Always a Journey	20
II	Athens: A Possible Beginning	34
III	The Oldest Bookshops in the World	45
IV	Shakespeare and Companies	61
V	Bookshops Fated to be Political	81
VI	An Oriental Bookshop	104
VII	America (I): "Coast to Coast"	122
VIII	America (II): From North to South	145
IX	Paris Without its Myths	173
X	Book Chains	192
XI	Books and Bookshops at the End of the World	209
XII	The Show Must Go On	222
XIII	Everyday Bookshops	241

Epilogue: Virtual Bookshops   259

Webography   281
Filmography   282
Bibliography   283
About the Author and Translator   304

Introduction inspired by
a Stefan Zweig short story

The way a specific story relates to the whole of literature is similar to the way a single bookshop relates to every bookshop that exists, has existed and will ever perhaps exist. Synecdoche and analogy are the two most useful figures of speech: I shall start by talking about all bookshops from the past, present and whatever the future may hold via one story, "Mendel the Bibliophile", written in 1929 by Stefan Zweig and set in Vienna in the twilight years of empire, and will then move on to other stories that speak of readers and books in the course of a frenzied twentieth century.

Zweig does not choose a renowned Viennese café for his setting, not the Frauenhuber or the Imperial, one of the cafés that were the best academies for studying the latest fashions – as he says in *The World of Yesterday* – but an unknown café; the story starts when the narrator goes to "the outer districts of the city". He is caught in the rain and takes shelter in the first place he finds. Once seated at a table, he is struck by a feeling of familiarity. He glances at the furniture, the tables, billiard tables, chessboard and telephone box, and senses that he has been there before. He scours his memory until he remembers with a sharp jolt.

He is in the Café Gluck, where the bookseller Jakob Mendel had once sat, each and every day from 7.30 a.m. to closing time, surrounded by heaps of his catalogues and books. Mendel would peer through his spectacles memorising his lists and data, and sway his chin and curly ringlets in a prayer-like rhythm: he had come to Vienna intending to study for the rabbinate, but antique books had

9

seduced him from that path, "so he could give himself up to idolatry in the form of the brilliant, thousand-fold polytheism of books". And thereby become the Great Mendel. Because Mendel had "a unique marvel of a memory"; he was "a bibliographical phenomenon", "a *miraculum mundi*, a magical catalogue of all the books in the world", "a Titan":

> Behind that chalky, grubby brow, which looked as if it were overgrown by grey moss, there stood in an invisible company, as if stamped in steel, every name and title that had ever been printed on the title page of a book. Whether a work had first been published yesterday or two hundred years ago, he knew at once its exact place of publication, its publisher and the price, both new and second-hand, and at the same time he unfailingly recollected the binding, illustrations and facsimile editions of every book [...] he knew every plant, every micro-organism, every star in the eternally oscillating, constantly changing cosmos of the universe of books. He knew more in every field than the experts in that field, he was more knowledgeable about libraries than the librarians themselves, he knew the stocks of most firms by heart better than their owners, for all their lists and card indexes, although he had nothing at his command but the magic of memory, nothing but his incomparable faculty of recollection, which could only be truly explained and analysed by citing a hundred separate examples.

The metaphors are beautiful: his brow looks "overgrown by grey moss", the books he has memorised are species or stars and constitute a community of phantoms, a textual universe. His knowledge as an itinerant seller without a licence to open a bookshop is greater than that of any expert or librarian. His portable bookshop, with its ideal location on a table – always the same one – in the Café Gluck, is now a shrine of pilgrimage for all lovers and collectors of books, as well as all the people who could not find the bibliographical references they had been looking for via more official routes. After an unhappy experience in a library, the narrator, a young university student, is taken to the legendary café table by a friend, a guide, who reveals to him a secret place that does not appear in guidebooks or on maps, one that is only known to the initiated.

Rabbi Jacob Mendel Morgenstern, rabbi of the Great Synagogue in Wegrow. He was the son of the rabbi of Sokolow. When the Nazis first entered Wegrow, they took him to the town square, made him clean the streets, and then bayoneted him to death.

One could include "Mendel the Bibliophile" in a series of contemporary stories that focus on the relationship between memory and reading, a series that might start in 1909 with "A World of Paper" by Luigi Pirandello and finish in 1981 with *The Encyclopedia of the Dead* by Danilo Kiš, by way of Zweig's story and the three Jorge Luis Borges wrote in the middle of the last century. The old meta-book tradition reaches such a level of maturity and transcendence in the world of Borges that we are duty-bound to consider what comes before and after each of his stories as precursors and heirs.

11

"The Library of Babel", from 1941, describes a hyper-textual universe in the form of a library hive devoid of meaning where reading is almost exclusively a matter of deciphering (an apparent paradox: in Borges' story reading for pleasure is banned). Published in *Sur* four years later, "The Aleph" is about how one might read "The Library of Babel" if it were reduced to the tiniest sphere that condenses the whole of space and time, and, above all, it is about the possible translation of such a reading into a poem, into language that makes the portentous *aleph*'s existence something *useful*. But "Funes the Memorious", from 1942, is undoubtedly the Borges story that most reminds us of Zweig's, with its protagonist who lives on the edge of Western civilisation, and who, like Mendel, is an incarnation of the genius of memory:

> Babylon, London and New York have overawed the imagination of men with their ferocious splendour; no-one in those populous towers, or upon those surging avenues, has felt the heat and the pressure of a reality as indefatigable as that which day and night converged upon the unfortunate Irineo in his humble South American farmhouse.

Like Mendel, Funes does not enjoy his amazing gifts of recall. Reading does not involve a process of unravelling plots for either of them, nor is it about investigating life patterns, understanding psychological states, abstracting, relating, thinking, experiencing fear and pleasure on their nerve-endings. Just as it is for Number 5, the robot in the film "Short Circuit" which appeared forty-four years later, reading for them is about absorbing data, myriad labels, indexing and processing information: desire is excluded. The stories by Zweig and Borges complement each other entirely: old man and young, the total recall of books and the exhaustive recall of the world, the Library of Babel in a single brain and the aleph in a single memory, both characters united by their poverty-stricken, peripheral status.

In "A World of Paper", Pirandello also imagines a reading scenario beset by poverty and obsession. A compulsive reader to the extent that his skin replicates the colour and texture of the paper, but deep in debt because of his habit, Balicci is going blind: "His whole world used to be there! And now he could not live there, except for that small area his memory brought back to him!" Reduced to a tactile reality, to volumes as disorganised as pieces of the Tetris, he decides to contract someone to classify his books, to bring order to his library, so that his world is "rescued from chaos". However, subsequently, he feels incomplete and orphaned, because he finds it impossible to read and hires a woman reader, Tilde Pagliocchini, whose voice and intonation annoy him so much that the only solution they can find is for her to read extremely quietly – that is, silently – so that he can imagine his own, ever-diminishing reading habit from the speed at which she covers lines and pages. His whole world, re-ordered in memory.

A world that can be encompassed and shrunk thanks to the metaphor of the library, a portable library or photographic memory that can be described and mapped.

It is not merely fortuitous that the protagonist of *The Encyclopedia of the Dead* by Kiš is, in fact, a topographer. His whole life has been determined in minute detail by a kind of sect or band of anonymous scholars who, from the end of the eighteenth century, have been pursuing an encyclopedic project – parallel to that of the Enlightenment – which includes everyone in history not to be found in all the other official or public encyclopedias available for consultation in any library. The story goes on to speculate about the existence of a Nordic library where one might find the rooms – each allocated a letter of the alphabet – of *The Encyclopedia of the Dead*, where every volume is chained to its shelf and is impossible to copy or reproduce, the object of partial readings that are immediately forgotten.

"My memory, sir, is like a garbage disposal," says Funes. Borges always speaks of failure: the three wonders he has conjured up amount to gestures in the face of death and the absurd. We know how foolish these lines are that Carlos Argentino was able to write with the inspiration of the incredible aleph, the possession of which he irrevocably squandered. And Borges' librarian, a persistent explorer of the library's nooks and crannies, lists in his old age all the certainties and expectations humanity has gradually discarded over the centuries, affirming at the end of his report, "I know of districts where the youth prostrate themselves before books and barbarously kiss the pages, though they do not know how to make out a single letter." We find the same elegiac tone in the stories I have mentioned: Pirandello's hero goes blind, Mendel is killed, the Library of Babel loses habitués to lung disease and suicide, Beatriz Viterbo has died, the father of Borges is ill and Funes dies of congested lungs, the father of Kiš's narrator also disappears. What links the six stories is an individual and a world in mourning: "Memory of indescribable melancholy: walking many a night along gleaming passageways and stairs and not finding a single librarian."

> So I was overcome by a kind of horror when I saw that the marble-topped table where Jakob Mendel made his oracular utterances now stood in the room as empty as a gravestone. Only now that I was older did I understand how much dies with such a man, first because anything unique is more and more valuable in a world now becoming hopelessly uniform.

His extraordinary nature, says Zweig, could only be recounted through examples. To describe the aleph, Borges has recourse to the chaotic enumeration of separate fragments of a body that is capable of processing the universal. Post-Borges, Kiš emphasises how each of the cases he mentions is but a small part of the material indexed by his anonymous sages. A table in a local café can be the tiny key to opening the doors to the superimposed layers of a vast city. And one man can have the key that gives access to a world that ignores geopolitical frontiers, that understands Europe as a unique cultural space beyond wars or the fall of empires. A cultural space that is always hospitable, because it only exists within the minds of those who walk and travel there. Unlike Borges, for whom history is unimportant, Zweig is keen to talk about how the First World War invented present-day frontiers. Mendel had lived his whole life in peace, without a single document to prove his original nationality or authorise his residency in the country where he was now living. The news that war has broken out never reaches his bookish world and the postcards he continues to send to booksellers in Paris or London – those enemy capitals – suddenly attract the attention of the censor (a reader who is central to the history of the persecution of books, a reader who spends his time betraying readers). The secret police discover that Mendel is Russian and therefore a potential enemy. He loses his glasses in a skirmish. He is interned in a concentration camp for two years, during which time reading, his most beloved, pressing, perpetual activity, is interrupted. He is released thanks to important, influential clients, book collectors who know the man is a genius. But when he returns to the café, he finds he has lost the ability to read as he once did and spirals irreversibly towards eviction and death.

It is significant that he is a wandering Jew, a member of the People of the Book, that he comes from the East and meets misfortune and his end in the West, even though this only happens after dozens of years of unconscious assimilation, of being respected and even venerated by the chosen few who are able to recognise that he is indeed exceptional. His relationship with printed information, Zweig tells us, caters for all his erotic needs. Like the ancient sages of Africa, he is a library man and his world is the non-material, accumulated energy that he shared.

The story is recounted by the only survivor from the old days, when the café had a different owner and staff and stood for the world that disappeared between 1914 and 1918: an old woman who remembered Mendel. She is the memory of an existence sentenced to oblivion (if it weren't for the fact that a writer listens to her and records a testimony he later transforms into a story). Thanks to this process of evocation and research, to the critical distancing of time, the narrator who is so like Zweig echoes like an epiphany:

> In him, I had come close for the first time to the great mystery of the way what is special and overwhelming in our existence is achieved only by an inner concentration of powers, a sublime monomania akin to madness.

*

He is racked by shame. Because he has forgotten a model, a teacher. And a victim. The whole story builds up to that *recognition*. And speaks obliquely of a great displacement: from the periphery in youth to a possible centre in maturity that has forgotten origins that should never have been forgotten. It is the story of a journey to those origins, a physical journey that encompasses another mnemonic and culminates in a homage. Generous and ironic, the narrator allows the illiterate old woman to keep the risqué volume that belonged to Mendel and represents one of the few palpable traces of his passage through this world: "And I was the one," the story ends, "who ought to know that you create books solely to forge links with others even after your own death, thus defending yourself against the inexorable adversary of all life, transience and oblivion."

By paying homage to an itinerant bookseller from a world that has disappeared, Zweig acts like a historian as understood by Walter Benjamin: a collector, a rag-and-bone merchant. In this respect, Georges Didi-Huberman wrote in his essay, "Before Time": "A remnant not only provides a symptomatic support for ignorance – the truth about a repressed period of history, but also the very place and texture of the 'content of things', of 'work on things'." Funes' memory is like a rubbish tip. The stories I have discussed, which might be taken to be about reading and memory, are in fact explorations of the relationship between memory and forgetfulness. A relationship expressed through objects, volumes that are *containers*, the result of a kind of handicraft we call books that we read as remnants, as ruins of the texture of the past, of their ideas that survive. Because it is the fate of what is whole to be reduced to parts, to fragments, chaotic lists and examples that are still legible.

Books as objects, as things, bookshops as archaeological sites or junk shops or archives that resist revealing to us the knowledge they possess, that by their very nature refuse to occupy their rightful

place in the history of culture, an often counter-spatial condition, opposed to any political organisation of space in terms of nations or states; the importance of inheritance, the erosion of the past, memory and books, non-material patrimony and its consolidation in materials that tend to decompose, Bookshop and Library as a two-faced Janus, or twin souls; police censorship, anti-frontier sites, bookshops as cafés and homes beyond the cardinal points of East and West, Orient and Occident; the lives and work of booksellers, whether sedentary or itinerant, isolated or members of a shared tradition, the tension between the unique and the serial; the power of encounters in a bookish context and their eroticism, latent sexiness; reading as obsession and madness but also as an unconscious drive or business, with its corresponding management problems and abuse of the workforce; numerous centres and infinite peripheries, the world as a bookshop and the bookshop as the world; irony and *gravitas*, the history of all books and specific books, with first names and surnames on jackets, of paper and pixels, bookshops at once universal and private: all that will be the subject of this book that until recently was in a bookshop or library or on a friend's bookshelf and now belongs, if only for a time, dear reader, to the library you call your own.

In other words, it has just left one *heterotopia* to enter another, with all the consequent changes of direction and differences in meaning. This book will *work* in this way: it will embrace the comfort of orderly reading and digressions and contradictions that disturb or threaten; it will re-create possible traditions and at the same time insist it only speaks of examples, exceptions from a map and a chronology of bookshops that it is impossible to re-create, that is made up of absence and oblivion, suggests analogies and synecdoche, a collection of glittering shards and leftover remnants from a future history or encyclopedia that can never be written.

COLONNESE
libri & altro

libri antichi
e moderni
esauriti
e rari
cartoline
gattofilia
stampe · fotografie
giornali · riviste
curiosità

32 - 33, via san pietro a majella - 80138 napoli
tel. 081.459858 - fax 455420

I

Always a Journey

Every bookshop is a condensed version of the world. It is not a flight path, but rather the corridor between bookshelves that unites your country and its language with vast regions that speak other languages. It is not an international frontier you must cross but a footstep – a mere footstep – you must take to change topography, toponyms and time: a volume first published in 1976 sits next to one launched yesterday, which has just arrived; a monograph on prehistoric migrations cohabits with a study of the megalopolis in the twenty-first century: the complete works of Camus precede those of Cervantes (it is in that unique reduced space where the line by J. V. Foix rings truest: "The new excites and the old seduces"). It is not a main road, but rather a set of stairs, perhaps a threshold, maybe not even that: turn and it is what links one genre to another, a discipline or obsession to an often complementary opposite; Greek drama to great North American novels, microbiology to photography, Far Eastern history to best-sellers about the Far West, Hindu poetry to chronicles of the Indies, entomology to chaos theory.

You need no passport to gain entry to the cartography of a bookshop, to its representation of the world – of the many worlds we call *world* – that is so much like a map, that sphere of freedom where time slows down and tourism turns into another kind of reading. Nevertheless, in bookshops like Green Apple Books in San Francisco, in La Ballena Blanca (the White Whale) in the

Venezuelan city of Mérida, in Robinson Crusoe 389 in Istanbul, in La Lupa (the Magnifying Glass) in Montevideo, in L'Écume des Pages (the Foam of Pages) in Paris, in the Book Lounge in Cape Town, in Eterna Cadencia in Buenos Aires, in La Rafael Alberti in Madrid, in Casa Tomada (House Taken Over) in Bogotá, in Metales Pesados (Heavy Metals) in Santiago de Chile, in Dante & Descartes in Naples, in John Sandoe Books in London, in Literanta in Palma de Mallorca – in all these places I felt that I was stamping some kind of document, accumulating stamps that attested to my journey along an international highway, the most important or significant, the best or oldest or most interesting or simply the nearest bookshop when it suddenly started raining in Bratislava, when I needed a computer connected to the Internet in Amman, when I was finally forced to sit down and rest for a few minutes in Rio de Janeiro or when I wearied of so many shrines in Peru and Japan.

I picked up my first stamp in La Librería del Pensativo (the Thinker's Bookshop) in Guatemala City. I landed there at the end of July in 1998 when the country was still reeling from the outcry over Bishop Gerardi, who had been viciously murdered two days after he, the visible face of the Bishopric's Human Rights Office, had launched the four volumes of the report "Guatemala: Never Again", which documented some 54,000 violations of basic human rights during almost thirty-six years of military dictatorship. They shattered his skull to the point that it was impossible to identify him by his facial features.

In those unstable months, when I switched abode four or five times, the cultural centre La Cúpula – comprising the gallery bar Los Girasoles (the Sunflowers), the bookshop and other shops – was most like home to me. La Librería del Pensativo sprang up in the next-door La Antigua Guatemala in 1987 when the country was still at war, thanks to the tenacity of a feminist anthropologist, Ana

María Cofiño, who had just returned from a long stay in Mexico. The familiar building on the calle del Arco had once been a petrol station and car-repair workshop. Distant shots fired by the guerrillas, army or paramilitary echoed around the volcanoes surrounding the city. As happened and happens in so many other bookshops, to a lesser or greater extent in bookshops throughout the world, the importing of titles hitherto unavailable in that central American country, support for national literature, launches, art exhibitions, and all that energy that soon linked the place to other newly inaugurated spaces, transformed El Pensativo into a centre of resistance. And of openness. After founding a publishing house for Guatemalan literature, they also inaugurated a branch in the capital that remained open for twelve years until 2006. Where I was happy – although nobody there knows that.

After it closed, Maurice Echevarría wrote: "Now, with the presence of Sophos, or the gradual growth of Artemis Edinter, we have forgotten how El Pensativo sustained our lucidity and intellectual alertness after so many brains had been devastated."

I look for Sophos on the Internet: it is undoubtedly the place where I would spend my evenings if I still lived in Guatemala City. It is one of those spacious, well-lit bookshops with a restaurant and a family air that have proliferated everywhere: Ler Devagar in Lisbon, El Péndulo in Mexico City, McNally Jackson in New York, 10 Corso Como in Milan, or the London Review Bookshop in London, spaces that welcome communities of readers and soon transform themselves into meeting points. Artemis Edinter already existed in 1998, had done so for over thirty years, and now has eight branches; there must be a book in my library that I bought from one of them, but I do not remember which. In El Pensativo in La Cúpula I first saw the shock of hair, the face and hands of poet Humberto Ak'abal and learned by heart a poem he wrote about the ribbon the Mayans still use to tie up the bundles they carry on their heads that are sometimes three times their own weight and size ("For/us/Indians/the sky finishes/where *el mecapal* begins"); I watched a man crouch down to speak to his three-year-old son and saw the butt of a pistol sticking out from the belt of his jeans; I bought *Que me maten si . . .* by Rodrigo Rey Rosa, in a house edition, poor-quality paper I'd never touched before, which still reminds me of the paper my mother used to wrap my rolls in when I was a child, the feel of the thousand copies printed in the Ediciones Don Quijote printworks on December 28, 1996, almost a week after the democratic elections; I also bought there "Guatemala: Never Again", the single-volume précis of the original report's four volumes of death and hate: *the militarisation of children, multiple rapes, technology at the service of violence, psychosexual control of soldiers,* all that is contrary to what a bookshop stands for.

I found I had a *mappa mundi* rather than a passport the day I finally spread out all those stamps on my desk (visiting cards, post-cards, notes, photographs, prints I had been putting in folders after each trip, anticipating the moment when I would begin this book). Or rather a map of my world. And consequently subject to my own life: how many of those bookshops must have closed their doors, changed address, multiplied, or must now be transnational or have reduced staff or opened a .com domain. A necessarily incomplete map criss-crossed by the length of my journeys, where huge areas remained unvisited and undocumented, where tens, hundreds of significant bookshops had yet to be noted (collected), though it nevertheless represents a possible overview of an ever-changing twilight scenario, of a phenomenon that was crying out to be analysed, written up as history, even if it would only be read by others who have also sat in bookshops here and thereabouts, so many embassies without a flag, time-machines, *caravanserai*, pages of a document no state can ever issue. Because bookshops like El Pensativo have disappeared or are disappearing or have become a tourist attraction in countries across the world, have opened a website or been subsumed into a bookshop chain with the same name and then inevitably transform, adapting to the vol-atile – and intriguing – signs of the times. And here, before me, lay a collage that evoked what Didi-Huberman has described in *Atlas. How to carry the world on your back*, where – just as in the passage-ways of a bookshop – "the *affective* as much as the *cognitive* element" has equal value on my desktop between "*classification* and *disorder*" or, if you prefer, between "reason and imagination" because "tables act as operational fields to *disassociate*, disband, destroy", and to "*agglutinate*, accumulate and set out" and, conse-quently, "they gather together heterogeneities, give shape to mul-tiple relationships": "where heterogeneous times and spaces continually meet, clash, cross or fuse".

The history of bookshops is completely unlike the history of libraries. The former lack continuity and institutional support. As private entrepreneurial responses to a public need they enjoy a degree of freedom, but by the same token they are not studied, rarely appear in tourist guides and are never the subject of doctoral theses until time deals them a final blow and they enter the realm of myths. Myths like St Paul's Churchyard, where – as I read in Anne Scott's *18 Bookshops* – the Parrot was one of thirty bookshops and its owner, William Apsley, was not only a bookseller but also one of Shakespeare's publishers, or the rue de l'Odéon in Paris which nurtured Adrienne Monnier's La Maison des Amis des Livres and Sylvia Beach's Shakespeare and Company. Myths like Charing Cross Road, the intergalactic avenue, London's bibliophile street *par excellence*, immortalised in the best non-fiction book I have read on bookshops, *84, Charing Cross Road* by Helene Hanff (where, as in any shop selling books, bibliophile passion is shot through with human feelings, and drama coexists with comedy), a first edition of which I was excited to see on sale for £250 in the window of Goldsboro Books, an establishment that specialises in selling signed first editions, very close to the same Charing Cross Road where nobody could tell me where I might find Hanff's bookshop. Myths like the bookshop *dei Marini*, later the Casella, that was founded in Naples in 1825 by Gennaro Casella and then inherited by his son Francesco, who at the turn of the twentieth century invited to his premises people like Filippo T. Marinetti, Eduardo de Filippo, Paul Valéry, Luigi Einaudi, George Bernard Shaw or Anatole France, who stayed in the Hotel Hassler del Chiatamone, but treated the bookshop as his front room. Myths like Moscow's Writers' Bookshop that in the 1900s and the early 1920s made the most of a brief interlude of revolutionary freedom and gave readers a centre of culture managed by intellectuals. The history of libraries can be told in minute detail, ordered by cities, regions and nations, respecting the frontiers that are sealed by international treaties and drawing on specialised bibliographies and individual library archives that fully document the development of stocks and cataloguing techniques and house minute-books, contracts, press cuttings, acquisition lists and other papers, the raw material for a chronicle backed by statistics, reports and timelines. The history of bookshops, on the other hand, can only be written after recourse to photograph and postcard albums, a situationist mapping, short-lived links between shops that have vanished and those that still exist, together with a range of literary fragments and essays.

When I was sorting out my visiting cards, leaflets, triptychs, postcards, catalogues, snapshots, notes and photocopies I came across several bookshops that did not fit any geographical or chronological criteria, could not be explained in terms of the stopovers and paths I was tracing for others, however conceptual and transversal these might be. I am referring to bookshops that specialise in travel, a paradox in itself, because every bookshop is an invitation to travel, and itself represents a journey. But the latter *are* different.

The word "specialise" points to their peculiarity. Like children's bookshops, comic shops, antiquarian bookshops and those trading in rare books. Their specialist focus is evident in the way they categorise their books: not by genre, language or academic discipline, but by geographical area. This principle is taken to an extreme in Altaïr, whose main shop in Barcelona is one of the most absorbing bookish spaces I know, where they also group poetry, fiction and essays according to country and continent, so you find them next to the relevant guidebooks and maps. Travel bookshops are the only ones where cartography outshines prose and poetry. If you follow the itinerary suggested by Altaïr, you pass by the window display to a noticeboard of messages posted by travellers. Behind that sits a collection of the shop's house magazines. Then come novels, histories and themed guidebooks on the subject of Barcelona in a pattern followed by most of the world's bookshops, as if the logic of necessity meant one must move from the immediate and local to what is most remote: the universe. Consequently the world is next, also arranged according to criteria of distance: from Catalonia,

Spain and Europe to the remaining continents, the world spreads across the two floors of the shop. Maps of the world are downstairs and beyond them, at the back, the travel agency. Noticeboard, magazines and all that reading matter can lead to only one outcome: setting out.

Ulyssus in Girona carries the secondary name of Travel Bookshop, and like the founders of Altaïr, Albert Padrol and Josep Bernadas, its owner, Josep María Iglesias, sees himself first and foremost as a traveller and secondly as a bookseller or publisher. Likewise Ulysses, the Paris bookshop, has Catherine Domain at the helm, a writer and explorer, who obliges her staff to travel with her every summer to the casino in Hendaye. By symbolic extension, this kind of establishment is usually full of maps and globes of the Earth: in Pied à Terre in Amsterdam, for example, there are dozens of globes that observe you on the sly as you hunt for guides and other reading matter. Its slogan could not be more insistant: "The traveller's paradise". Deviaje (Travelling), the Madrid bookshop, emphasises its character as an agency: "Bespoke travel, bookshop, travel accessories". The ordering does not alter the end product, because the truth is that travel bookshops throughout the world are also stores that sell practical travel items. Another Madrid shop, Desnivel (Uneven), specialising in exploration and mountaineering, sells G.P.S. trackers and compasses. The same is true of Chatwins in Berlin that devotes a good part of its display space to Moleskine notebooks, the mass-produced reincarnation of the artisan-made jotters that Bruce Chatwin used to buy in a Paris shop until the family in Tours that manufactured them stopped doing so in 1986, as he relates in *The Songlines*, a book published the following year.

Chatwin's funeral was held in a west London church, though in 1989 his ashes were scattered by the side of a Byzantine chapel in Kardamyli, one of the seven cities Agamemnon offers Achilles in return for the renewal of his offensive against Troy in the southern

Peloponnese, and near the home of one of his mentors, Patrick Leigh Fermor, a travel writer and member like him of the Restless Tradition. Thirty years earlier, a young man from the provinces by the name of Bruce Chatwin, without trade or income, had arrived in London to work as an apprentice at Sotheby's, unaware of his future as a travel writer, a mythomaniac and, above all, a myth in himself. Unaware he would give his name to a bookshop in Berlin. Two bookshops stand out among the many Chatwin might have discovered when he arrived in the city at the end of the 1950s: Foyles and Stanfords. One generalist and the other specialising in travel. One full of books and the other awash with maps.

In the middle of Charing Cross Road, Foyles' fifty kilometres of shelves make up the world's greatest labyrinth of print. In that period it became a tourist attraction because of its size and the absurd ideas put into practice by its owner, Christina Foyle, which turned the place into a monstrous anachronism in the second half of the twentieth century. Ideas like refusing to use calculators, cash registers, telephones or any other technological advances to process sales and orders, or arranging books by publishing house and not by author or genre, or forcing her customers to stand in three separate queues to pay for their purchases, or sacking her employees for no good reason. Her chaotic management of Foyles – which was founded in 1903 – lasted from 1945 to 1999. Her eccentricities can be explained by genes: William Foyle, her father, committed his very own lunacies before handing over to his daughter. Conversely, Christina must be credited for the finest initiative taken by the bookshop in all its history: its renowned literary lunches. From October 21, 1930 to this day half a million readers have dined with more than a thousand authors, including T. S. Eliot, H. G. Wells, George Bernard Shaw, Winston Churchill and John Lennon.

Black legends are now only part of the past (and of books like this): in 2014 Foyles was transformed into a large modern bookshop and moved to the adjacent building at 107 Charing Cross Road. The reshaping of the old Central Saint Martin's College of Art and Design was the responsibility of the architects Lifschutz Davidson Sandilands, who met the challenge of designing the largest book-shop to be built in Britain in the twenty-first century, creating a large, empty central courtyard suffused with bright white light, in turn reinforced by the huge lamps that punctuate the vast diaph-anous text, which is surrounded by stairs that go up and down like so many subordinate clauses. The cafeteria – which is always buzz-ing – is at the top, next to an exhibition room equipped for trans-media projects and the main presentation room. When you walk in you are greeted by this sign at ground level: "Welcome, book-lover, you are among friends." What would Christina say if she raised her head? Well, she would, in fact, see an entire wall commemorating her crowded lunches.

"Explore, describe, inspire" is the Stanfords' slogan, as I am reminded by the bookmark I keep as a souvenir of one of my visits. Although the business was founded in that same Charing Cross Road where Foyles still survives, its famous Covent Garden head-quarters in Long Acre opened its doors to the public in 1901. By then Stanfords had already forged a strong link with the Royal Geograph-ical Society by virtue of producing the best maps in an era when the expansion of British colonialism and an increase in tourism had led to a massive rise in the printing of maps. Although you can also find guidebooks, travel literature and related items on its three levels with floors covered by a huge map (London, the Himalayas, the World), cartography plays the lead role. Even the bellicose variety: from the 1950s to the 1980s the basement was home to the maritime and military topography department. I remember I vis-ited Stanfords because someone told me, or I read somewhere, that Chatwin bought his maps there, though there is no record of him ever having done so. The list of distinguished customers comprises everyone from Dr Livingstone and Captain Robert Scott to Bill Bryson or Sir Ranulph Fiennes, one of the last living explorers, not forgetting Florence Nightingale, Cecil Rhodes, Wilfred Thesiger or Sherlock Holmes, who ordered from Stanfords the map of the mysterious moor that enabled him to solve the case of *The Hound of the Baskervilles*.

Foyles has five branches in London and one in Bristol. Stanfords has shops in Bristol and Manchester, as well as a small space in the Royal Geographical Society that only opens for events. Chatwin missed by a couple of years the opportunity to experience Daunt Books, a bookshop for travelling readers, whose first shop – an Edwardian building on Marylebone High Street naturally lit by huge plate-glass windows – opened in 1991. This is a personal project pursued by James Daunt, the son of diplomats, so used to moving house. After a stay in New York he decided he wanted to dedicate himself to his two passions in life: travel and books. It is now a London chain with six branches. Au Vieux Campeur has sold maps, guide and travel books and hiking, camping and climbing equipment from 1941 and now owns a grand total of thirty-four establishments across France. Such is the way of Moleskine logic.

At the end of the nineteenth century and at the beginning of the twentieth many amateur and professional artists took up the habit of travelling with sketchbooks that had thick enough paper to cope with watercolours or Indian ink and sturdy covers to protect the drawings and paintings from the elements. They were manufactured in different parts of France and sold in Paris. We now know that Wilde, Van Gogh, Matisse, Hemingway and Picasso used them, but how many thousands of anonymous travellers also used them? Where might their *Moleskines* be? Chatwin gives them that name in the Australian book we mentioned and it was what encouraged Nodo & Nodo, a small Milanese firm, to launch five thousand copies of these Moleskine notebooks onto the market in 1999. I remember seeing some of them or the limited editions following on from that first printing in a Feltrinelli bookshop in Florence, a moment when I experienced an immediate surge of fetishist pleasure, the one that *recognition* brings. What any committed reader feels on walking into Lello in Oporto or City Lights in San Francisco. For years you were forced to travel to buy a Moleskine. It was not necessary to go to a Paris bookshop, though that did not mean you could find them in any bookshop in the world. In 2008 they were supplied to some 15,000 shops in over fifty countries. To cope with demand, production was moved to China, although the design remained Italian. Before 2009 I had to go to Lisbon if I wanted to visit Livraria Bertrand, the oldest bookshop in the world, which fleetingly opened a branch in Barcelona, the city where I live, and serial commercial expansion won yet another victory – its nth – over that old idea, now almost without a body to flesh it out: atmosphere.

II

Athens: A possible beginning

One can walk around and read Athens as if it were a strange souk of bookshops. Of course, the strangeness is a consequence of the decadent atmosphere and palpable feeling of antiquity rather than of the language in which shop names and shelf labels are written, not to mention book titles and author names. For a Western reader the East begins where unknown alphabets start to be used: Sarajevo, Belgrade and Athens. On the shelves of bookshops in Granada and Venice no trace remains of the alphabets of anyone who arrived in those cities from the East in a remote past: we read all that translated into our languages and have forgotten that theirs were also translations. The centrality of ancient Greek culture, philosophy and literature can only be understood if one considers its position astride the Mediterranean and Asia, between the Etruscans and Persians, opposite the Libyans, Egyptians or Phoenicians. Their situation as an archipelago of embassies. Or radial aqueduct. Or network of tunnels between different alphabets.

After a long search on the Internet, inspired by the card of one of the establishments I have kept from 2006, I finally find a reference in English to what I am looking for: Books Arcade, Book Gallery or Book Passage, a succession of twenty spaces with wrought-iron gates that are home to forty-five publishers, including Kedros and Publications of the National Bank. I made notes on the ways bookshops relate to libraries sitting on one of the many armchairs

in those passageways, under a ceiling fan that sliced through the heat in slow motion. Because the Pesmazoglou Arcade – which is another of its names, a reference to one of the streets giving access – is located opposite the National Library of Greece.

The Tunnel opposite the Building. The Gallery with no inaugural date opposite the Monument recorded in minute historical detail: neo-classical in style, financed from the diaspora by the Vallianos brothers. The first stone of the National Library was laid in 1888 and it was inaugurated in 1903. It conserves and houses some 4,500 ancient Greek manuscripts, Christian codices and important documents from the Greek revolution (it was not for nothing that the idea behind it apparently came from Johann Jakob Mayer, a lover of Hellenic culture and comrade-in-arms of Lord Byron). But any library is more than a building: it is a bibliographical collection. The National Library was previously lodged in the orphanage in Aegina, the baths in the Roman Market, the church of St Eleftherios and the University of Otto; over the next few years it will transfer to a grandiose new building, on the seafront, designed by architect Renzo Piano. The present Library of Alexandria is a far cry from the original: although its architecture is spectacular, although it converses with the nearby sea and 120 alphabets are inscribed on its reflective surface, although tourists will come from all over the world to gaze at it, its walls do not yet contain sufficient volumes for it to be the reincarnation of the building that lends it its mythical name.

The shadow of the Library of Alexandria is so powerful it has eclipsed every other previous, contemporary and future library, and has erased from collective memory the bookshops that nourished it. Because it was not born in a void: it was the main customer of book traders in the eastern Mediterranean in the third century BC. The Library cannot exist without the bookshop that has in turn been linked from the outset to the publishing house. The book trade had already developed before the fifth century BC; by this date – when the written was beginning to prevail over the oral in Hellenic culture – the works of the main philosophers, historians and poets we today think of as the classics were known in a large part of the eastern Mediterranean. Athenaeus quotes a lost work by Alexis, from the fourth century BC, entitled *Linos*, where the hero says to young Hercules:

"Take one of these beautiful books. Look at the titles in case one is of interest. Here you have Orpheus, Hesiod, Keralis, Homer and Epicharmus. There you'll find plays and everything you might want. Your choice will reveal your interests and taste."

In the event, Hercules chooses a cookery book and does not meet his companion's expectations. Because the book trade includes every kind of text and reading taste: speeches, poems, jottings, technical or law books, collections of jokes. And it also encompasses every level of quality: the first publishing houses comprised groups of copyists on whose ability to concentrate, to be disciplined and rigorous and on whose degree of exploitation depended the number of changes and mistakes in the copies that would eventually be put into circulation. To optimise time, someone dictated and the rest transcribed and thus Roman publishers were able to launch onto the market several hundred copies simultaneously. In his exile, Ovid consoled himself with the thought that he was "the most read writer in the world" since copies of his works reached the furthest boundary of the empire.

In his *Libros y libreros en la Antigüedad* (a shortened version of H.L. Pinner's *The World of Books in Classical Antiquity* that was only published after his death), Alfonso Reyes talks of "book traders" when he refers to the first publishers, distributors and booksellers, like Atticus, Cicero's friend, who was involved in every facet of the business. Apparently the first Greek and Roman bookshops were either itinerant stalls or huts where books were sold or rented out (a kind of mobile library) or spaces adjacent to the publishers. "In Rome bookshops were well known, at least in the days of Cicero and Catullus," writes Reyes. "They were located in the best commercial districts, and acted as meeting places for scholars and bibliophiles." The Sosii brothers, publishers of Horace, Secundus, one of the publishers of Martial, and Atrectus, among many other entrepreneurs, managed premises in the vicinity of the Forum. Lists were posted on the door advertising the latest books. And for a small amount one could consult the most valuable volumes, in a kind of fleeting loan. The same happened in big cities in the empire, like Rheims or Lyons, whose excellent bookshops surprised Pliny the Younger when he saw that they too sold his books.

The sale and purchase of beautiful copies increased as did the acquisition of volumes by weight so that wealthy Romans could cover a wall with a pretence to culture and boast about their libraries. Private collections, often in the hands of bibliophiles, were directly fed by bookshops and were a model for public collections, namely libraries, which sprang up in tyrannies, not democracies: the first two are attributed to Polycrates, the Tyrant of Samos, and Pisistratus, the Tyrant of Athens. Libraries are power: in 39 BC Gaius Asinius Polio founded the Library of Rome with booty from his campaign in Dalmatia. Greek and Roman titles were exhibited there for the first time publicly and together. Four centuries later there were twenty-eight libraries in the capital of the later Roman Empire. Now they are ruins like the library in Pergamum or the Palatine Library.

The Library of Alexandria was seemingly inspired by Aristotle's private library and was probably the first in history to have a cataloguing system. The dialogue between private and public collections, between the Bookshop and the Library, is therefore as old as civilisation itself, but the balance of history always inclines towards the latter. The Bookshop is light; the Library is heavy. The levity of the present continuous is counterpoised by the weight of tradition. Nothing could be more alien to the idea of a bookshop than heritage. While the Librarian accumulates, hoards, at most lends goods out for a short while – which thereby cease to be such or have their value frozen – the Bookseller acquires in order to free himself from what

he has acquired; he sells and buys, puts into circulation. His business is *traffic* and *transit*. The Library is always one step behind: looking towards the past. The Bookshop, on the other hand, is attached to the sinews of the present, suffers with it, but is also driven by an addiction to change. If history ensures the continuity of the Library, the future constantly threatens the existence of the Bookshop. The Library is solid, grandiose, is tied to the powers-that-be, to local authorities, to states and their armies: as well as despoiling the patrimony of Egypt, "Napoleon's army carried off around 1,500 manuscripts from the Austrian Lowlands and another 1,500 mainly from Bologna and the Vatican," writes Peter Burke in his *Social History of Knowledge*, in order to feed the voracious libraries of France. Conversely, the Bookshop is liquid, provisional, lasts as long as its ability to sustain an idea over time with minimal changes. The Library is stability. The Bookshop distributes; the Library preserves.

The Bookshop is in perpetual crisis, subject to the conflict between *novelty* and *stocks*, and precisely for that reason finds itself at the centre of the debate over cultural canons. Great Roman authors were aware that their influence depended on the public's access to their intellectual production. The figure of Homer is located in the two centuries prior to the consolidation of the book-selling business and his centrality to the Western canon is directly related to the fact that he is one of the Greek writers of whose work we have preserved the most fragments. That is, he was one of the most copied. One of the most disseminated, sold, gifted, stolen and purchased by collectors, general readers, booksellers, bibliophiles and library administrators. Our concept of cultural tradition, our list of writers and key titles depends on papyrus and parchments, rolls and codices from Greek and Roman bookshops, on the textual capital they put into circulation, provisionally confined in public and private spaces, the majority of which was destroyed in countless wars and fires and moves. The location of bookshops is fundamental to the structuring of these canons: there was a time when Athens and Rome were the centres of all possible worlds. We have built our entire subsequent culture on these lost, indemonstrable capitals.

SCRIPTORIUM MONK AT WORK.   (From *Lacroix*.)

The traffic in books shrank after the fall of the Roman Empire. Medieval monasteries continued the task of spreading written culture, through copyists, at the same time as, thanks to Islam, paper ended its long journey from China, where it was invented, to the south of Europe. Parchment was so expensive that texts were often erased so others could be put in their place: there are few metaphors as powerful as that of the palimpsest to represent the way culture is transmitted. In the Middle Ages, a book could have some hundred handwritten copies, be read by several thousands and listened to by many more, since orality was once again more important than individual reading. That does not mean that the bookselling trade came to a halt, since the noble and ecclesiastical classes needed to read, as did the students who relied on printed texts – in increasing numbers as the oldest European universities (Bologna, Oxford, Paris, Cambridge, Salamanca, Naples . . .) were founded between the eleventh and thirteenth centuries. As Alberto Manguel has written in *A History of Reading*:

> From roughly the end of the twelfth century, books became recognized as items of trade, and in Europe the commercial value of books was sufficiently established for money-lenders to accept them as collateral; notes recording such pledges are found in numerous medieval books, especially those belonging to students.

The pawning of books was a constant from that moment on until Xerox popularised photocopying in the middle of the last century. Photocopying shops coexist in the neighbourhood of the National Library of Greece and adjacent Academy of Athens, with universities, publishing houses, cultural centres and the most compact part of the souk of bookshops, because all these institutions feed on each other. I remember reading an edition of poetry by Cavafy that I was carrying in my rucksack in the spacious piano bar in the Ianos bookshop, a link in a *chain of civilisation*, with its mahogany-coloured shelves and white on apple-green labels, simply because I could not understand a single one of the volumes around me. I also remember spending hours between the dark wooden shelves in the Politeia bookshop, browsing, among the thousands of books in Greek, through the few hundred that had been published in English. Divided between two floors and a basement, the premises have four doors of entry. It is one of those over-lit spaces: countless rectangles of light, from barely six spotlights, make the covers, titles and floor gleam. *Politeia* means "community of citizens".

Finally I walked into the Librairie Kauffmann. Not only because it is the French bookshop in Athens and hence stocks books that I can read, but also because it is one of those bookshops where you must get a stamp on your imaginary bookshop passport. The black-and-white image of the shop's launch is striking: dated 1919, it shows a kiosk attended by a woman dressed in traditional fashion, her head partially covered, above her the words: "Librairie Kauffmann". Hermann Kauffmann thus began his business with a street stall selling second-hand French books. Ten years later he set up in premises on Zoodochos Pigis Street, which eventually grew into a kind of large apartment with views over the avenue, and he incorporated new titles into his shelves thanks to an agreement with Hachette the publishers. Soon it became the place to visit for the most enlightened people in Athens who came to stock up on French reading-matter whilst their children bought textbooks and course reading for their French-speaking schools and academies. A diploma granted to Kauffmann by L'Exposition Internationale des Arts et Techniques dans la Vie Moderne in Paris, 1937, hangs on the staircase wall next to photographs of Frida Kahlo and André Malraux. With Hachette's help, he created the Hellenic Distribution Agency. After his death in 1965, his widow took over the firm and was behind important initiatives, like the "Confluences" collection of Greek literature translated into French, or the publication of the *Dictionnaire français-grec moderne* – something that should always exist in a bookshop specialising in a foreign language: a dictionary that is at least bilingual.

The Kauffmann web page no longer works. There is no sign on the web that the bookshop is still open. After several futile searches, I salvage the orange card from that trip, with a tree embossed above Greek and Latin characters, like a murky archipelago at the bottom of the sea. And I dial the number. Two or three times. Nobody picks up the telephone. As I wander from one search engine to the next

I finally find photographs I did not want to see. One shows the Pesmazoglou Arcade – or Book Gallery – burnt to the ground during the riots at the beginning of 2012 because it was home to private enterprises, including a branch of the National Bank's Publishing House. On the other hand, although the international press had initially reported that the library had also been burned down, it was not attacked or ravaged by fire: public and ancient, with an inaugural date and plans to move, its past and future guaranteed as much as anything can be, it remains standing.

III

The Oldest Bookshops in the World

As well as being old, a bookshop must look the part. When you go into the Livraria Bertrand, at 73 rua Garrett in Lisbon, very close to the Café Brasileira and its Fernando Pessoa statue in the heart of the Chiado, the B on the red background of the logo proudly displays a date: 1732. Everything in the first room points to the venerable past that this date highlights: the display cabinet of extraordinary books; the extending steps or wooden ladders that give access to the highest shelves of some of the ancient bookcases; the rusty plaque that dubs the place where you stand "Sala Aquilino Ribeiro", in homage to one of its most distinguished customers, a regular like Oliveira Martins, Eça de Queirós, Antero de Quental or José Cardoso Pires; and above all the certificate from the Guinness World Records that attests to it being the oldest functioning bookshop in the world.

A function that has been uninterrupted and is well documented. Books have been sold intermittently since 1581 at number 1 Trinity Street, Cambridge, with famous customers like William Thackeray and Charles Kingsley, but for long stretches the premises were exclusively the seat of Cambridge University Press, with no direct sales to the public. Conversely, caught in a quagmire of the absence of reliable documents, we find Matras in the city of Kraków – still called Gebether and Wolff by elderly locals – the mythical origins of which go back to the seventeenth century (when the book dealer Franz Jacob Mertzenich opened a bookshop in 1610 that did

not close until 1872), and which was the site of a renowned literary
salon at the turn of this century and now hosts important literary
events within the framework of a U.N.E.S.C.O. city of literature.
That is why the Librairie Delamain in Paris that opened its doors in
the Comédie Française in 1700 or 1701 – according to sources – and
did not move to rue Saint-Honoré until 1906 may genuinely be
the world's oldest bookshop, though I imagine it cannot prove
such a felicitous uninterrupted period of bookselling. Winchester's
P&G Wells bookshop does appear to be the oldest bookshop in the
United Kingdom and quite possibly the oldest in the world with
single premises that are emphatically independent (it opened a

branch at the end of the twentieth century, in the University of Winchester). Receipts from 1729 for the purchase of books have been preserved and constant bookselling activity in the shop on College Street appears to date back to the 1750s. In 1768, Hodges Figgis began to deal in books. The oldest bookshop in Ireland and still active, it is also the largest with a stock of 60,000 books. It is equally the most Dubliner of bookshops, because it appears in that most Dubliner of books which is not Joyce's *Dubliners* but *Ulysses*, ("She, she, she. What she? The virgin at Hodges Figgis' window on Monday looking in for one of the alphabet books you were going to write."). Hatchards, which opened its doors in 1797 and has never shut them since, is London's oldest bookshop, in its aristocratic building at 187 Piccadilly with the portrait in oils of its founder, John Hatchard, that gives the establishment a suitably antique patina. It now belongs to the Waterstones chain but it hasn't lost any of its plush-carpet identity: unlike more commercial bookshops, it still sells novels on the first floor and reserves the ground floor for hardback history books, biographies and current affairs, which have always been purchased by its customers on their way to the Royal Academy or their Jermyn Street tailors. In recent years it has initiated a subscription service that, in our era of algorithms, employs three expert readers to study the tastes of subscribers and dispatch to them a selection of books on a regular basis. Mary Kennedy, who was my guide to the shop's history and hidden corners, told me proudly, "They all have the right to return the titles they don't like but we have only ever had one return."

The only really important nineteenth-century bookshop I have visited is perhaps the Librería de Ávila – opposite the church of San Ignacio and very close to the Colegio Nacional de Buenos Aires – apparently founded in 1785, the year when a shop was established on that same corner selling food, alcohol and books. If P&G Wells printed books for Winchester College, its contemporaneous bookshop in Buenos Aires was linked to the nearby educational institution even by name: Librería del Colegio. There are no documents extant relating to the Librería del Colegio at the same address until 1830 when it is frequently mentioned in the press, since it hosted conversations led by Sarmiento with Estrada, Hernández, Alberdi, Aristóbulo del Valle, Groussac, Avellaneda, Perito Moreno and other intellectuals who now have streets named after them. The present building on this corner was not built until 1926, where thirteen years later the Editorial Sudamericana was founded, which existed side by side with the Librería del Colegio until 1989. It was shut for four years before Miguel Ángel Ávila bought the business and renamed it after himself. The names of these shops changed much less than those of the two streets where they shared a corner: San Carlos and Santísima Trinidad, Potosí and Colegio, Adolfo Alsina and Bolívar, at the last count.

It says "*Antiguos Libros Modernos*" on the façade. On my first visit to Buenos Aires in July 2002 I bought a few copies of the magazine *Sur* in its basement. Touching old books is one of the few tactile experiences that can connect you to a distant past. Although the concept of the antiquarian bookshop belongs to the eighteenth century as a result of the corresponding growth of disciplines like history and archaeology, in the previous two centuries it had been developed by book binders and sellers who worked as much with printed books as hand-written copies. The same can be said of the catalogues of printers and publishers that evolved from simple lists of publications to small but sophisticated books. I have never so much as touched one of these relics. Or even a book that was not printed.

Sven Dahl in his *A History of the Book* states that manuscripts prevailed over printed books in the first years of printing, by virtue of a veneer of prestige, as was the case with papyrus over parchment, or in the 1960s with handmade books over ones that were machine set. In the beginning the printer was the publisher: "But itinerant sellers soon appeared who went from city to city offering books they had bought from printers." They hawked the titles they were carrying on the streets and in the taverns where they stayed and set up a nomadic market. Some also had permanent stalls in big cities. From the sixteenth century copies of the same book could be bought in the thousands and their readers were in the hundreds of thousands: more than a hundred thousand different printed books began to flood Europe over the next hundred years. A double system of classifying and displaying books was developed: using filing boxes and cards or bookcases, because it was usual for the books to be unbound so customers could choose the kind of binding they wanted for their individual copy. Hence those whimsical collections of books that only have in common the covers their owners selected. Some can be found intact in the basement of the Librería de Ávila and in the second-hand bookshops on the Avenida de Mayo.

MESS.ʳˢ LACKINGTON ALLEN & C.ᵒ
TEMPLE OF THE MUSES, FINSBURY SQUARE.

What were the bookshops in the eighteenth century like, when Bertrand Livreiros, Hatchards and the Librería del Colegio opened their doors in Lisbon, London and Buenos Aires respectively? As one can see from the seventeenth- and eighteenth-century engravings studied by Henry Petroski in *The Book on the Bookshelf*, a detailed history of how we arrange our books and the evolution of the bookshelf, the bookseller sat behind a large desk to manage his business, which was often physically linked to the printers or publishers on which it depended, surrounded by a display from a large archive of sewn, though not bound, folders that were the bookshops. The boxes were often part of the counter, as one can see in a famous engraving of the Temple of the Muses, perhaps the most legendary and beautiful eighteenth-century bookshop, located in Finsbury Square and run by James Lackington, who refused to destroy the books that were not sold and sold them off cheaply, in accordance with what he understood as his professional mission. He wrote: "Books are the key to knowledge, reason and happiness, and everyone, no matter what their economic background, social class or sex, has the right to have access to books at cheap prices."

Goethe's is one of the finest written testimonies to bookshops; on September 26, 1786, he jotted in his *Italian Journey*:

> At last I have acquired the works of Palladio, not the original edition with woodcuts, but a facsimile with copperplate engravings published by Smith, an excellent man who was formerly English consul in Venice. One must give the English credit for having so long appreciated what is good and for their munificence and remarkable skill in publicizing it.
>
> On the occasion of this purchase, I had entered a bookshop which, in Italy, is a peculiar place. The books

are all in stitched covers and at any time of day you can find good company in the shop. Everyone who is in any way connected with literature – secular clergy, nobility, artists – drop in. You ask for a book, browse in it or take part in a conversation as the occasion arises. There were about half a dozen people there when I entered, and when I asked for the work of Palladio, they all focused their attention on me. While the proprietor was looking for the book, they spoke highly of it and gave me all kinds of information about the original edition and the reprint. They were well acquainted with the work and with the merits of the author. Taking me for an architect, they complimented me on my desire to study this master who had more useful and practical suggestions to offer than Vitruvius, since he had made a thorough study of classical antiquity and tried to adapt his knowledge to the needs of our times. I had a long conversation with these friendly men and learned much about the sights of interest in the town.

The first sentences tell of the fulfilment of a wish: the aim of every visit to a bookshop. The final sentences, the acquisition of knowledge that is not to be found in the books themselves, but in the people in their vicinity. What most surprises the erudite German traveller is the fact that all the books are bound and accessible, so visitors can establish dialogues as much with the books as among themselves. Binding didn't become standard in Europe until the requisite machines began to function around 1823, when bookshops slowly began to look like libraries, because they offered finished products and not half-made books: what surprises Goethe are the handmade bindings. In *A Sentimental Journey Through France and Italy* (1768) Laurence Sterne enters a bookshop on the Conti quayside to buy "a collection of Shakespeare" but the bookseller tells him he does not have one. The traveller indignantly picks up a copy on the table and asks, "And what about this?" And the bookseller explains that it is not his, that it belongs to a count, who has sent it to be bound: he is an "*esprit fort*", he explains, "fond of English books" and hobnobbing with islanders.

When Chateaubriand went to Avignon in 1802 after being tipped off about pirated copies of four volumes of *The Genius of Christianity*, as he recounts in his memoirs, "By going from bookshop to bookshop, I unearthed the counterfeiter, to whom I was unknown." Every city had many and we have preserved no record of most. We tend to think of literature as an abstraction when the truth is that it is an infinite network of objects, bodies, materials and spaces. Eyes that read, hands that write and turn pages and hold tomes, cerebral synapses, feet that seek out bookshops and libraries, or vice versa, biochemical desire, money to purchase, paper and cardboard, stocked shelves, pulped timber and vanished forests, more eyes and hands that drive lorries, load boxes, order volumes, browse, peer and leaf, contracts, letters, numbers and photographs, warehouses, premises, square metres of cities, characters, screens, wonders in ink and pixels.

The word "*poiein*" that in ancient Greek meant "making" is the linguistic root of "poetry". In *The Craftsman* Richard Sennett the sociologist has explored the intimate relationship between hand and eye: "Every good craftsman conducts a dialogue between concrete practices and thinking; this dialogue evolves into sustaining habits, and these habits establish a rhythm between problem solving and problem finding." He focuses especially on carpenters, musicians, cooks, luthiers, people we generally understand to be *craftsmen*, but the truth is his reflections can be extended both to the endless craftsmen who have always collaborated in the making of books (paper-makers, typographers, printers, binders, illustrators) and the actual bodies of readers, their dilating pupils, ability to concentrate, bodily posture, digital memory (in their fingertips). Writing itself, inasmuch as it is calligraphy – that is, manufacture – is even subject to a discipline of perfection in civilisations like the Arab and Chinese. And the step from writing by hand to keying in is still very recent in the history of culture. Although he does not intervene directly in the creation of the object, the bookseller can be understood as the *craftsman reader*, that person who after the 10,000 hours that according to various studies are necessary to become expert in a practical skill is able to combine work with excellence, manufacture with poetry.

Romano Montroni, who for decades worked in Feltrinelli's in the Piazza di Porta Ravegnana, Bologna, writes in "The Bookseller's Decalogue" that "the customer is the most important person in the enterprise", and places dust at the centre of activity in a bookshop: "One must dust every day and everyone must do it!" he exclaims in *Soul Selling. The Bookseller's Trade.* "Dust is a vitally important issue for a bookseller. He dusts up and down and clockwise in the first half-hour every morning. While doing so, the bookseller memorises where the books are and gets to know them *physically*."

Some of the world's bookshops carefully nurture their tactile dimension, so that paper and wood bear witness to a tradition of craftsman readers. In England, for example, the three branches of Topping and Company were furnished with shelving made by local carpenters, and the small signs labelling the sections and the cards recommending titles are handwritten. The Bath branch's well-stocked poetry section shows how important it is for a bookshop to cherish and develop the interests of the local community. "People here have a great fondness for poetry," Saber Khan, one of its staff, told me, "and we stock the largest selection of poetry in the country." Readers, like carpenters, are different in each locality: the branches of Topping and Company "have their own identity, like brothers and sisters, but in every one coffee is free, because you can't deny anyone their cup of coffee". I saw readers who sat for hours on wooden chairs at wooden tables. And the bed and bowl for the dog who roamed around the shop, his home and ours. Its slogan, "A proper old-fashioned bookshop", could be read as "a genuine period bookshop", or "a bookshop *comme il faut*, fallen out of fashion".

As José Pinho, the Alma Mater of Lisbon's Ler Devagar, told me, a bookshop can regenerate the social and economic fabric of an area, because it is the present pure and simple, and a speedy engine of change. That is why we should not be surprised if many bookshops are part of greater social projects for change. I think of those in Latin American cities that are linked to Eloísa Cartonera, inspired by her original shop in Argentina, with its books bound by the unemployed workers who collect paper and cardboard from the streets. I think of La Jícara, a restaurant serving the tastiest of local food wedged between a double bookshop, for both children and adults, which only sells books from independent presses in Oaxaca, Mexico. I think of Housing Works Bookstore Café, which is run exclusively by volunteers and gives all its profits from the sale of books, the renting of space and the cafeteria to help those most in need in New York. They are bookshops that hold out a hand to create human chains. There could be no better metaphor for the book tradition, because we read as much with our hands as with our eyes. I have often heard the same story on my travels. When the time came to change premises, it was the customers, now friends, who offered to help with the move. That human chain uniting the old premises of Auzolán in Pamplona with the new. Or RiverRun's in Portsmouth. Or Robinson Crusoe's in Istanbul. Or Nollegiu's in the Poblenou district of Barcelona.

At the very least from the time of ancient Rome, bookshops have been spaces for establishing contact, in which textuality becomes more physical than in the lecture theatre or library, because they are so dynamic. And it is the readers who are most on the move, who bring the copies on display to the counter, interact with the booksellers, take out coins, notes or credit cards and exchange them for books, and who, as they move around, observe what other people are looking for and buying. Books, booksellers and bookshops stay relatively still in comparison with customers who are constantly coming and going, and whose role inside is precisely to circulate. They are travellers in a miniature city whose aim is to provoke the letters – still inside the book – into motion as long as the reading (and its recollection) lasts, because, as Mallarmé wrote: "The book, which is a total expansion of the letter, must derive its mobility from the letter." Nonetheless, the bookshop itself, with or without buyers or browsers, has its own cardiac rhythms. Not only the rhythms involved in unwrapping, arranging, returning and re-ordering. Not only those involved in changes of staff. Bookshelves also enjoy a relationship of conflict with the premises that lodge and partially define them, but do not constitute them. And with their own names, which often alter with successive owners. Inside and out, bookshops are portable and changeable. That's why the Guinness World Record for the Oldest Bookshop in the World is held by the Livraria Bertrand, because it is the only one that can demonstrate its longevity. Usually bookshops change names when they change hands, at the very least. The oldest in Italy is a case in point: the Libreria Bozzi was founded in 1810 and is still open on a down-at-heel corner in Genoa, but its first owner, a survivor of the French Revolution, was Antonio Beuf; it was not purchased until 1927 by Alberto Colombo, father of the first wife of Mario Bozzi, who gave the establishment, now managed by Tonino Bozzi, its current name. Another good example is the Lello bookshop in Oporto. The establishment was opened under the name of Livraria Internacional de Ernesto Chardron, on rua Dos Clérigos; in 1881 José Pinto set it up

on rua do Almada; thirteen years later it was sold on by Mathieux Lugan to José Lello and his brother António, who renamed it Sociedade José Pinto Sousa Lello & Irmão. And if those were not changes enough, after the building of the present edifice – a neo-Gothic and art deco hybrid – in 1906, the bookshop was given its definitive name in 1919: Livraria Lello & Irmão. An article by Enrique Vila-Matas still hangs in a corner of the shop, where he describes it as the most beautiful bookshop in the world. The card I retain from my 2002 visit is made from elegant, slightly crinkly paper, with the logo and address printed in purple ink. Under the logo it says: "Livraria Lello". "Prólogo Livreiros, S.A." is the name of the company that runs it.

Another internationally renowned, contemporary bookshop, the Luxemburg, in Turin, tells a similar story: although it was founded in 1872 – if we accept that changes of owner, premises and even name do not destroy a bookshop's identity – like Ávila, it had a different name for most of its existence. Owned by Francesco Casanova, an important Piedmontese publisher, the Libreria Casanova was a pre-eminent cultural centre in the final decades of the nineteenth century and the first of the twentieth. The Neapolitan chronicler Matilde Serao, the decadent Antonio Fogarrazo and the creator of *verismo* Giovanni Verga were some of its habitués. Casanova forged a close friendship with Edmondo De Amicis, whose *Gli*

azzurri e i rossi he published in 1897. If the premises succeeded in catching the spirit of the times under his management, when the project was taken over in 1963 by activist and writer Angelo Pezzana, who renamed the bookshop Hellas, the new owner also knew how to connect with the times. Given that he was the founder of Fuori!, Italy's first gay rights group, it is hardly surprising that on February 12, 1972 the bookshop should launch the countercultural, psyche-delic magazine *Tampax* that later engendered another, *Zombie International*. Together with Fernanda Pivano, the great promoter of American literature in Italy, Allen Ginsberg visited the book-shop five years earlier and gave a reading in the basement. When Ginsberg returned to Turin in 1992, he read a continuation of "Hum Bom!", the poem he had begun in 1971, with Bush and Saddam as characters (I'm listening to it on YouTube as I write: an echo of the beat that bookshop had in the 1970s). Pezzana changed the name of the shop again in 1975: Luxemburg Libreria Internazionale. It continued its political and cultural activity: it was behind the inception of the International Gay Association, the Italy-Israel Foundation and the creation of the Turin Book Fair. Under wooden stairs at the back of the first floor, the bookseller's small office is decorated with Italian and Israeli flags, and the Jewish section is almost as well stocked as that of international magazines in the entrance or books in other European languages on the floor above. There is a black-and-white photo of the beat poet and a yellow-ing press cutting testifying to his visit. One glass cabinet displays invoices and orders made by Francesco Casanova. Pezzana himself, his spectacles teetering on the last millimetre of his nose, takes the money for the copy of Alessandro Baricco's latest novel that I have bought as a present for Marilena. Access to the basement is shut off.

A Bertrand Livreiros catalogue has been preserved from 1775, the year of the Lisbon earthquake. In it, the French brothers list almost two thousand titles, a third of which are history books, a third sciences and art, and a third law, theology and literature. The majority are written in French and were published in Paris. Many Italian and French booksellers in the Portuguese capital had resumed their activity a few months after the earthquake, and although we do not have Bertrand Livreiros catalogues from those years, there do exist order forms for titles sent to the Holy Office and to the censorship body that took over its role. In one of the public auctions of land devastated by the 1775 earthquake they bought the bookshop's definitive premises, in what was then called rua das Portas de Santa Catarina. It remained a family firm until 1876, the year when it was sold on by the last direct descendant, João Augusto Bertrand Martin, to the firm Carvalho & Cia. It became one of the many commercial enterprises that have enjoyed ever since a brand name that incorporated the date 1732 into the initial B, so nobody could question its antiquity.

It says: "*Fondata nel 1872*" on the card Pezzana gave me before we said goodbye.

IV

Shakespeare and Companies

I shall begin this chapter with a quotation from *L'Histoire par le théâtre* (1865) by Théodore Muret, recorded by Walter Benjamin in his unfinished *The Arcades Project*:

> There were, first, a great many milliners, who worked on large stools facing outwards, without even a window to separate them; and their spirited expressions were, for many strollers, no small part of the place's attractions. And then the Galeries de Bois were the centre of the new book trade.

The association between weaving and writing, between thread and text, between seamstress and artist, is a constant in the history of literature and art. The attraction to artisans and their bodies is related in Muret's lines to cultural consumption. He emphasises the absence of glass, in an era when all bookshops begin to have windows, a transparent display of their merchandise they share with toy or clothes shops. When Zweig describes the return of Jakob Mendel to Vienna, after being interned for two years in a concentration camp, he refers to "window displays of books" in the city, because that is how the inner experience of bookshops is projected outwards, and with it, the exuberance of urban cultural life. The following jotting by Benjamin surely derives from the association of ideas:

Julius Rodenberg on the small reading room in the Passage de l'Opéra: What a cheerful air this small, half-darkened room has in my memory, with its high book-shelves, green tables, its red-haired *garçon* (a great lover of books, who was always reading books rather than taking them to others), its German newspapers which every morning gladdened the heart of the German abroad (with the exception of the *Kölnische Zeitung* which on average made an appearance only once every ten days). And when there is any news in Paris, it is here that one can receive it.

Salons, reading rooms, athenaeums, cafés or bookshops act as second homes and political spaces for the exchange of informa-tion, as one can see in *The Traveller of the Century* by Andrés Neuman, who also described bookshops as momentary homes. Local and foreign presses enter a dialogue in the *extraterritorial* brains of travellers and exiles, who move from one European cap-ital to another as the Grand Tour dies out. Europe becomes a great space where books flow thanks to their industrial production, which is accompanied by proliferating bookshop chains, the promotion of serial fiction as the main form of commercial novel, an exponential increase in literacy and the transformation of the Continent into a vast tangle of railway tracks. In parallel the insti-tutions that look after the production and sale of books become stronger. In Germany, for example – as Svend Dahl reminds us – the Association of Booksellers was created in 1825, and twenty-three years later it succeeded in getting censorship abolished and in 1870 in establishing a norm for the whole country that meant that an author's copyright remained in place for thirty years after his death. By then a system of commission and intermediary wholesalers was in place. Like other consumer goods, books are also subject to the rules of labour legislation, competition, publicity or scandal-mongering.

It was no coincidence that the two major literary scandals of the nineteenth century took place simultaneously in Paris (with apologies to Oscar Wilde, who died, poverty-stricken, in the French capital). The 1857 prosecutions for offences against public morality and propriety brought against Charles Baudelaire, for his masterpiece, *Les Fleurs du mal*, and against Gustave Flaubert, for his work of genius, *Madame Bovary*, constitute a perfect nexus of controversy with which to illustrate the changes that were taking place in the book industry and the history of literature. Possible answers to questions like: to what extent is a writer responsible for what he writes? And what if it is fiction? Is censorship legitimate in a democratic society? To what degree can a book really influence individuals? What is a publisher's legal relationship with his books? And the printer's, distributor's and bookseller's? Questions with distinguished precedents. After being denounced by his parish priest Diderot was prosecuted in 1749 for his *Letter on the Blind* and imprisoned in the fortress of Vincennes, until associated booksellers managed to get him released, arguing that if the *Encyclopédie* project continued in abeyance, the nation's industry would be the main victim of the damage. When *The Origin of the Narrator*, which brought together the proceedings of both trials, was published, Daniel Link astutely reinterpreted the volume's title: "Above all it concerns the (modern) notion of author: his simultaneous appearance and disappearance from the scene (of the crime) and the way in which (penal and ethical) responsibility allows specific statements to be related to specific proper names." Baudelaire lost his case (a fine and the suppression of six poems); Flaubert won his. The proceedings reveal that the main protagonist of both trials was Ernest Pinard the prosecutor. Strangely enough, it was in the case that he lost that he showed himself to be an excellent literary critic. We owe to him the interpretation of the novel that still remains in vogue today. Every reader is a critic, but only those who make their opinions about their reading in some way public become literary critics. Pinard was one of the latter, and rightly so, as can be seen from the proceedings.

The poet spent his whole life wanting to write "a history of *Les Fleurs du mal*", in order to demonstrate that his book was "deeply moral" (although it had been found guilty of immorality). What happened to the book *physically*? Poulet-Masset, its publisher, continued to sell the unexpurgated edition at double the price, and even sold mutilated copies with pages missing. And in 1858 he brought out a second edition, now complete again, which sold out in a few months. Unlike Wilde's, which was a genuine tragedy, the scandals provoked by Flaubert and Baudelaire had no serious repercussions. However, they still frame the reading of both masterpieces in the present century – and of the books that followed.

Because of its social impact, the reading of literature is conditioned by countless critical and micro-critical agents. That a critic could be a prosecutor, and that we can pursue the process through the texts he wrote is extraordinary, as much as if a bookseller were to reveal himself in a similar way. Nonetheless, the two most important Paris booksellers of the first half of the twentieth – perhaps in the world and of the century – did publish memoirs that enable us to glimpse how key bookshops functioned critically and related to the culture in general. A parallel reading of *Rue de l'Odéon* by Adrienne Monnier and *Shakespeare and Company* by Sylvia Beach allows us to speak of twin projects. Even, by chance, in their initial financing, because Monnier was able to open La Maison des Amis des Livres in 1915 thanks to compensation her father received (as a result of a railway accident) and Beach's mother lent her all her savings so she could invest them in a business that opened its doors at a nearby address in 1919 and moved to l'Odéon two years later. The most important aspect of the trade for both women was the opportunity it afforded to mix with writers who were their customers and who also became their friends. Most of their respective books are dedicated to celebrating their distinguished visitors: Walter Benjamin, André Breton, Paul Valéry, Jules Romain or Léon-Paul Fargue, amongst others, in the case of La Maison des Amis des Livres; Ernest Hemingway, Francis Scott Fitzgerald, Jean Prévost, André Gide, James Joyce or Valéry Larbaud, in the case of Shakespeare and Company. If such a division is even possible, because visiting the rue de l'Odéon meant paying a visit to both bookshops and the clientele and friendships of the two booksellers meshed as much in their cultural activities as in their personal lives. While Monnier maintains a degree of balance and devotes similar amounts of space to all her favourite authors, Beach comes down overwhelmingly on the side of Joyce, whom she considered to be "the greatest writer of our era" even before she met him. The entire Joyce family linked up with Shakespeare and Company from the start: youngsters Giorgio and Lucia carried boxes when the bookshop moved from its original premises on rue Dupuytren to its definitive base on l'Odéon, which acted as post office and bank for the whole family, and later Lucia was the lover of Samuel Beckett, her father's assistant, and of Myrsine Moschos, who helped Beach in her bookshop. The story behind the publication of *Ulysses* is the central thread of her book and its author's personality permeates the text, for good or for evil, like a cloud of black-and-white butterflies. I do not think it is pure chance that that book and author are key: *literary bookshops* shape their discourse by creating a sophisticated taste that prefers *difficulty*. As Pierre Bourdieu says in *Distinction: A Social Critique of the Judgement of Taste*: "The whole language of aesthetics is contained in a fundamental refusal of the *facile*, in all the meanings which bourgeois ethics and aesthetics give to the word."

Monnier talks of "the beautiful visits: by authors and well-read fans", Beach of the "pilgrims" who come from the United States attracted by the aura given to the city by the presence of Picasso, Pound or Stravinsky. In fact, she becomes a genuine "tourist guide" when visitors like Sherwood Anderson – one of many – ask her to take them to the residence of Gertrude Stein, and she documents such activity in her pilgrims' sanctuary thanks to the collaborations of Man Ray, whose photographs festoon the establishment. Both places were also lending libraries (in *A Moveable Feast*, Hemingway comments that there was no money to buy books in those days). And Shakespeare and Company also had a guest bedroom. So they acted as art gallery, library and hotel. And embassy: Beach boasts about buying the biggest United States flag in the whole of Paris. And cultural centre: readings and lectures were given periodically in both, and La Maison was home to the first public performance of "Socrate" by Erik Satie in 1919, as well as the first reading of *Ulysses* two years later. Music and literature that were *difficult* and *distinguished*.

Beach decided to keep the bookshop open during the Occupation, but her nationality and Jewish friendships came to the attention of the Nazis. One day in 1941 "a high-ranking German officer" turned up and in "perfect English" told her that he wanted to buy the copy of *Finnegans Wake* that was in the window. She refused to hand it over. He came back a fortnight later and threatened her. And the intellectual decided to close her business and store all the material in a flat in the same building, above where she herself was living. She spent six months in an internment camp. She remained in hiding on her return to Paris: "I visited the rue de l'Odéon daily, secretly, and heard the latest news of Adrienne's bookshop, saw the latest volume of the clandestine Éditions de Minuit." Hemingway was the soldier in the Allied Armies who in 1944 liberated the street with the mythical bookshops (and then he went to the bar at the Ritz to *liberate* that as well). La Maison continued to be open until 1951, four years before the death of Monnier, who committed suicide after eight months of hearing noises inside her head.

During those decades Léon-Paul Fargue was the bridge between that Anglo-Saxon-French Paris and Latin American Paris. Alejo Carpentier describes him as astonishingly erudite and a brilliant poet, always dressed in navy-blue, the ultimate wanderer in the night addicted to the metropolis and averse to travelling. Despite his random urban itineraries and lack of punctuality, he was apparently faithful to the Lipp beer-house, the Café de Flore – where he would meet up with Picasso – the rue de l'Odéon and Elvira de Alvear's house, where he hobnobbed with Arturo Uslar Pietri and Miguel Ángel Asturias. Another fetish poet and bridge between the two shores was Paul Valéry, whom Victoria Ocampo met on her 1928 visit, a crucial visit since she was in the process of preparing the great project of her life, the magazine *Sur*, the first issue of which would be published three years later. Over several months she got to know philosophers, writers and plastic artists. She visited the Russian Lev Shestov in the company of José Ortega y Gasset. She didn't survive her encounter with Pierre Drieu La Rochelle unscathed: they escaped to London embroiled in an adulterous passion. After meeting Monnier and Beach, who introduced her to the work of Virginia Woolf, Ocampo crossed the Channel again in order to meet her in 1934 and returned once more in 1939, accompanied by Gisèle Freund, who took photographs of Woolf that were to become more famous than the ones Man Ray took of Ocampo. The bookselling couple also introduced her to Valéry Larbaud. And Monnier drank tea more than once in the house that Alfonso Reyes and his wife rented in Paris during the previous decade. Nevertheless, to judge by their articles, letters and books, none of these Latin American names resonated in the memories of the Parisian pair of booksellers.

Without a doubt both were radically committed to the literature of their time: the owner of Shakespeare and Company risked her economic well-being to publish the masterpiece of one man and the owner of La Maison des Amis des Livres risked hers to publish her own literary magazine, *Le Navire d'Argent*. However, Monnier had a more visible profile as a critic than Beach and a greater desire to intervene in contemporary debates. Included in her book is a close reading of the poetry of Pierre Reverdy. Beach recounts an after-dinner conversation with Joyce and Jules Benda where Monnier argued about the best contemporary French writers. In terms of the avant-garde, she states: "We were all very conscious that we were heading towards a renaissance." And on the function of a bookshop with regard to the literary present she says:

> It is truly indispensable that a house devoted to books be founded and directed conscientiously by someone who unites with an erudition that is as vast as possible a love for the spirit of what is new, and who, without falling into the wrongheadedness of any kind of snobbery, is ready to assist the new truths and forms.

To keep both majority and minority happy it is necessary to perform genuine feats of organisation and, above all, to keep the space to a minimum. La Maison was a small bookshop and, consequently, it is hardly surprising that its offering was limited. Many of the writers who paid a visit looked to see whether their books were displayed, or gave them to the library, so it is understandable that the circle of friends and supporters influenced what was for sale, especially if the owner was defending them aesthetically in her interventions in the cultural sphere. In this way the bookshop is transformed into an anomalous place, where exceptional works that, according to Mallarmé, didn't find an opening in modern

bookshops are both on sale and find subscribers, investors, translators and publishers.

Monnier writes: "And what discoveries are possible in a book
shop, through which inevitably pass, amid the innumerable
passers-by, the Pleiades, those who among us already slightly
resemble 'great blue persons', and who, with a smile, justify what
we call our greatest expectations." The bookseller, critic and cultural activist includes herself in the elite. Beyond the difficulties
they have finding a publisher or even subsisting, they are the best
writers of the period. They possess the aura of recognition: they
are *recognised* by those who see them in person, because they may
not have read them, but they have seen them in photos, as might
have happened with the Eiffel Tower. Chateaubriand says in
Memoirs from Beyond the Tomb:

> I was in a happy mood; my reputation made my life easy:
> one dreams endlessly in the first intoxication of fame, and

one's eyes are first filled with the joys of the light that breaks through; but when this light goes out, it leaves one in darkness; if it persists, the habit of seeing it soon makes one insensitive to it.

The key word is, of course, *reputation*. Another that is equally crucial depends on it, *consecration*. From the birth of modernity a highly complex literary system has been articulated through sites of consecration: publication by particular houses, praise from specific critics or writers, translation into certain languages, the winning of awards, prizes, important recognition first locally then internationally, knowing the right people and visiting key cafés, salons and bookshops. Paris during the nineteenth century and the first half of the twentieth constituted the world's pre-eminent republic of letters, the centre where a large slice of world literature was legitimised. When Goethe describes a bookshop in his *Italian Journey* he counterposes three cultural influences: the German he carries with him (and the language in which he is writing his book), the English (the much praised English edition of the book he buys) and the Italian (Palladio and the bookshop itself). As Pascale Casanova has reminded us, Goethe spoke in his work about both a *world literature* and a *world market for cultural goods*. He was fully aware that modernity would be based on the transformation of cultural and artistic objects into merchandise that moves in two parallel markets, the symbolic one (the aim of which is prestige and distinction) and the economic one (the goal of which is the earning of profits for work done, that is part craft and part art).

As is the case with most biographies, essays and most cultural critiques, Casanova's *The World Republic of Letters* does not mention the important role of bookshops in an atmosphere of progressively more international literary geopolitics. Shakespeare and Company is referred to once in relation to Joyce, and La Maison des Amis des Livres appears a few pages earlier in a paragraph on the topic of the writer as a passer-by with no certified fatherland:

> This improbable combination of qualities lastingly established Paris, both in France and throughout the world, as the capital of a republic having neither borders nor boundaries, a universal homeland exempt from all profession of patriotism, a kingdom of literature set up in opposition to the ordinary laws of states, a transnational realm whose sole imperatives are those of art and literature: the universal republic of letters. "Here," wrote Henri Michaux with reference to Adrienne Monnier's bookshop, one of the chief places of literary consecration in Paris, "is the homeland of all those free spirits who have not found a homeland." Paris, therefore, became the capital for those who proclaimed themselves to be stateless and above political laws: in a word, artists.

In the 1969 article that gives the title to *Extraterritorial*, George Steiner speaks of post-modern authors like Borges, Beckett or Nabokov, representatives of a "multilingual imagination", of "internalised translation", the inspiration for their remarkable work. Friedrich Nietzsche was impressed by the existence of trilingual bookshops in Turin when he lived there. Further north, in another polyglot frontier city, Trieste, the Librería Antiquaria, in the interwar period, was the place where the great writers of Trieste, like Umberto Saba, the poet who ran the bookshop, or his friend Italo Svevo, conversed with writers from other countries, like James Joyce. Consequently, changes of abode and language led to a state of artistic extraterritoriality, but as citizens artists continued to be subject to formal laws and as authors to the rules of the game in their respective literary fields. Although writers in Paris could cultivate a fiction of freedom, it was perhaps easier to do that in relation to geopolitics than in relation to the mechanisms of literary consecration. As well as being a bookseller, Monnier was a literary critic: she judged and she reported. Her important role as a consecrator was recognised by her contemporaries: in 1923 she was accused publicly of exerting a powerful influence with her book recommendations in *Histoire de la littérature française contemporaine* by René Lalou (according to an article in *Les Cahiers Idéalistes* she "ignored those books that weren't on her shelves"). In her defence, the bookseller argued that she simply stocked titles that were not available in other bookshops, and, by listing them, she shaped a canon.

The Monnier and Beach duo constituted a doubly anti-institutional site: respectively, opposing the big local legitimising platforms (daily newspapers, magazines, universities, government bodies), and as a clandestine cultural consulate, opposing the big U.S. legitimising platforms (especially publishers). From Paris they foiled the American censors and made it possible to publish Joyce's work in New York: an accomplice of Beach's ferried copies of *Ulysses* from Canada hidden in her trousers. That anti-national oppositional-space emphasis hardened during the Nazi Occupation when it became a bunker for symbolic resistance.

In 1953 Monnier wrote a piece entitled "Memories of London" in which she recalls her first trip to the English capital in 1909 when she was seventeen. It is striking that she does not mention a single bookshop. Perhaps she had not yet found her vocation, although people tend to reinforce myths about themselves in retrospective accounts. I think there may be a more straightforward explanation: at the beginning of the last century, it was difficult to find any awareness of belonging to a tradition. In fact, the strong tradition of conceptually related independent bookshops (Shakespeare and Companies) was born in that transition between

Library and Bookshop that was a revelation for Sylvia Beach:

> One day at the Bibliothèque Nationale, I noticed that one of the reviews – Paul Fort's *Vers et prose*, I think it was – could be purchased at A. Monnier's bookshop, 7 rue de l'Odéon, Paris VI. I had not heard the name before, nor was the Odéon quarter familiar to me, but suddenly something drew me irresistibly to the spot where such important things in my life were to happen. I crossed the Seine and was soon in the rue de l'Odéon, with its theatre at the end, reminding me somehow of the colonial houses in Princeton. Halfway up the street on the left was a little grey bookshop with "A. Monnier" above the door. I gazed at the exciting books in the window, then, peering into the shop, saw all round the walls shelves containing volumes in the glistening "crystal paper" overcoats that French books wear while waiting, often for a long time, to be taken to the binder's. There were also some interesting portraits of writers here and there. At a table sat a young woman. A. Monnier herself, no doubt. [. . .] "I like America very much," she said. I replied that I liked France very much. And, as our future collaboration proved, we meant it.

The book was published in 1959 and its natural readership was Anglo-Saxon (hence the comparison with Princeton), as she was fully conscious of the fact that her bookshop was an inevitable reference point and the re-creation of its origins would be of interest to literary history. Her tale of discovery is a reader's journey and implies that a frontier must be crossed (the Seine) to reach the unknown. Through the shop window (the second frontier), Beach is linked to Goethe's sense of surprise: businesses still existed that didn't bind their bundles of paper, so the reader could choose the binding to match his or her own taste. The desire in the gaze is concerned as much with the (*attractive*) books on display as with the (*interesting*) portraits of writers, which to this day continue to provide the usual bookshop decor. Their alliance would be finally sealed by a statement of tastes that, with the passage of time, was re-interpreted as a declaration of intent. And of love: Monnier and Beach were a couple for almost fifteen years, although their private relationship does not surface in the books they wrote (nor does the fact that they were among the first women booksellers in the world to be completely independent of male power or investment). That alliance was the first stone of their myth to be laid. Beach knew she was arriving on the scene four years later and positioning herself in a line initiated by La Maison des Amis des Livres. What she could not know when she published her book was that both bookshops were already part of a tradition connecting the lost generation to the beat generation. Moreover, Beach wrote about the former: "I can't think of a generation less deserving of this name."

The second Shakespeare and Company opened its doors at 37 rue de la Bûcherie in 1951, under the name of Le Mistral, and was not renamed after its admired predecessor until 1964, following Sylvia Beach's death. George Whitman was little more than a scruffy Yankee tramp with some army experience when he arrived in Paris. After graduating in 1935 in science and journalism, he spent several years travelling the world, until the United States's entry into the Second World War led him to a medical clinic in Greenland, north of the Arctic Circle, and later to the military base in Taunton, Massachusetts, where he opened his first, rudimentary bookshop. It was there he discovered that personnel were needed in France and he volunteered to help in a camp for orphans, but was attracted to the capital, moved there and signed up for a course at the Sorbonne. He bought a few English books with the idea of earning a little from a small lending fee, and suddenly saw his rented bedroom invaded by strangers in search of reading matter; he soon made sure that bread and hot soup were available for those who came to his incipient business. That was the Communist embryo of his future bookshop.

Because Whitman was always an uncomfortable figure by U.S. standards. He sold banned books in Paris, like *Tropic of Cancer* by Henry Miller, to soldiers from his country. His American dream followed, as Jeremy Mercer noted, the Marxist principle "Give what you can, take what you need"; and he always saw his project as a kind of utopia. From the very first day in Le Mistral he installed a bed, an oven to warm up food, and a lending library for people who could not afford to buy books. The melding of bookshop and hostel continued for decades: to that end Whitman sacrificed his privacy and continually lived with strangers. In sixty years some hundred thousand people have lodged in Shakespeare and Company in exchange for a few hours worked in the bookshop and spent reading and writing, because new and second-hand books live together, and the presence of sofas and armchairs invites you to use the building as if it were a large library. The presiding motto is written above one of the thresholds within the labyrinth: "Be not inhospitable towards strangers lest they be angels in disguise." An amateur poet, Whitman stated on several occasions that his great work was the bookshop: each of its rooms "was like a different chapter of the same novel".

On one of the windows of Shakespeare and Company it says: "City Lights Books". And above the entrance to City Lights in San Francisco, probably hand-painted by Lawrence Ferlinghetti himself on the green background: "Paris. Shakespeare + Co.". Twinned with its Parisian prototype, conscious that it walks the same path, after the four years the beat poet spent studying at the Sorbonne, when he befriended Whitman in his rented room full of books and the smell of simmering soup, the mythical bookshop on the West Coast was born a mere two years after he returned in 1953. It immediately became a publishing house, bringing out books by Ferlinghetti and poets like Denise Levertov, Gregory Corso, William Carlos Williams or Allen Ginsberg. The list was not focused on beat poetry, but many of the books emerged from that orbit: from stories by Bukowski to political texts by Noam Chomsky. The publishing house and its publisher entered literary history in autumn 1955, when Ginsberg gave a reading in the city's Six Gallery: Ferlinghetti suggested publishing *Howl*. He did so, and it was very soon withdrawn from circulation by the police who accused an employee of the bookshop and the publisher of fomenting obscenity. The case received lots of media attention and the verdict, found in favour of City Lights, still constitutes a reference point in the legal history of the United States in matters of freedom of expression. "Books not Bombs" greets you in graffiti on paper hanging in the stairwell. The bookshop defines itself on its walls: "A literary meeting place"; "Welcome, have a seat and read."

Public readings and performance have been a constant from the very start in the Parisian and Californian bookshops. In a famous recital in City Lights in 1959, Ginsberg said he had concentrated hard in order to capture a rhythm to write what he was about to declaim and that, from then on, he improvised with the help of something very similar to *divine inspiration*; he also led readings opposite Shakespeare and Company drunk on red wine. Both shops are committed to agitation and libraries, to hospitality and openness to the new. Both have well-stocked sections of fanzines that continue to be one of the means of expression of the same counterculture that emerged in the 1950s. Whitman witnessed the events of May 1968 from the balcony of Shakespeare and Company. It is not by chance that both have their poetry and reading room at the top of their respective buildings, if one bears in mind their vagabond, beatnik, protest character – neo-Romantics in a word. Constant renewal is guaranteed in the Paris bookshop by dint of the continual flow of young, temporarily bohemian bodies.

As Ken Goffman writes in *Counterculture Through the Ages*, French artistic society at the beginning of the twentieth century linked the search for artistic originality with bohemian life:

> In the first four decades of the twentieth century, this Parisian artistic bohemia really exploded into something that bordered on a mass movement. Literally hundreds of artists, writers, and world historic characters whose innovative works (and, in some cases, challenging personas) still resonate today, passed through the portals of what literary historian Donald Piece has labelled "The Paris Moment"... As Dan Franck, author of the historical work *Bohemian Paris: Picasso, Modigliani, Matisse and the Birth of Modern Art*, wrote, "Paris ... [had] become the capital of the world. On the pavements, there would no longer be a handful of artists but hundreds, thousands of them. It was an artistic flowering of a richness and quality never to be rivalled.

The saturation of Paris has its end date: 1939. During the Second World War cultural life in the city was partially frozen, while the territory of the United States and its intellectual activity remained intact. Once the 1940s and their political and military myths passed, cracks opened up in the 1950s that allowed an incipient bohemian life in at bebop pace. A first quantitative broadening out takes place from the beat to the beatnik world. Ferlinghetti recounts how busloads of beatniks began to draw up outside the doors of City Lights in the 1960s, as part of their pilgrimage in the tracks of Kerouac, Snyder, Burroughs and the rest. But it is the hippy movement that really turns the new version of bohemia into a mass movement, now entirely stripped of the recherché, distinguished impulses of the first dandies. A genuinely new mass culture, because there is such a level of literacy and sophistication in the West after the Second World War that several cultural masses can coexist, each with perfectly defined features, and only partially incompatible.

A consensus must be reached and consequently there have to be followers and readers before a literary generation can be canonised. The last two generations in North American literature – the lost and the beat – entered the canon thanks, among many other factors, to the activity of the first Shakespeare and Company and its interplay with La Maison des Amis des Livres on the rue de l'Odéon; and to City Lights and the other cultural nuclei of the San Francisco Renaissance, the period of cultural splendour the West Coast city enjoyed in the 1950s. It is no coincidence that 'renaissance' is a French word.

V

Bookshops fated to be political

A poster of Cicciolina, the then porn actress and future Italian politician, with her bright red lips and swooping neckline, and next to it a poster of the neighbouring Baroque district. A healthy supply of new books and magazines from various countries, on stained walls, under useless, fused bulbs. I discovered that kind of contrast at the start of the century in La Reduta, a bookshop on Bratislava's Palacky Street, close to what was a quiet park, despite the sparks thrown up by passing trams. That feeling of being between two waters, between two historical moments, shared by those in every place that has been touched by Communism. The buyers devoted as much space to Slovakian literature as to Czech, though new books in Slovakian were thicker, as if proudly under- lining the state of play within the context of an extremely slow transition.

The whole of Berlin communicates a similar sense of waters parting. Walking from Alexanderplatz down that wide boulevard, built according to a socialist aesthetic, once called Stalin Avenue, and later Karl-Marx-Allee, so broad a whole army could parade down it flanked by several tanks, you are surprised that in that site of megalomania, that perfect scenario for political intimidation, so much emphasis is given to culture. Firstly you find the Teacher's House's huge mural, with its colourful, didactic exalting of the world of work. A little further on, on the left, you see the façade of Kino International that from 1963 was the venue for the premieres of the D.E.F.A. (Deutsche Film A.G.). After that come Café Moskau, Bar Babette, the D.S.A. Bar before you reach the Karl Marx Buchhandlung, the old Communist bookshop that since its closure in 2008 has housed a film production company, and on its left the old Rose-Theater. Two years before it shut, the bookshop acted as the set for the end of "The Life of Others", a film that essentially is about reading.

Stasi captain Gerd Wiesler, who signs off his reports as "H.G.W. X.X./7", spends his whole time reading (listening in on) the daily lives of writer Georg Dreyman and his partner, actor Christa-Maria Sieland. At a key moment in the action, the spy removes a book by Bertolt Brecht from Dreyman's library, a narrow strait through which he timidly verges on the dissident. If in this way the book becomes a symbol of dissenting reading, a typewriter smuggled over from the West – since the secret services controlled every typewriter in the German Democratic Republic – stands out as the symbol of oppositional writing. It is when Dreyman, a supporter of the regime, now disillusioned by the persecution of his friends and the infidelity of his girlfriend (who decides to sleep with a military man in order to avoid being ostracised), types out an article on the extremely high level of suicides that the government is keeping quiet. It can be published in *Der Spiegel* because Wiesler has begun to feel favourably towards the couple and protects them by writing reports that omit any mention of the suspicious activities being carried out in their house. Thanks to him, the typewriter is not found during a raid and Dreyman is spared the consequences of his *treachery*, although Christa-Maria accidentally dies during an inspection. As his superior intuits – rightly but without proof – that the spy has switched sides, he reduces him in rank to a purely reading role in the postal service: opening letters of suspects, reading the private correspondence of individuals who might be sending information to the enemy or conspiring to overthrow the regime. After the fall of the Wall, the writer has access to the Stasi archives and discovers that the informer existed and grasps his role in events he had not been able to understand previously. He seeks him out. He is now a postman. He goes from one house to the next delivering envelopes sealed in accordance with the right to privacy. He decides not to say anything. Two years later Wiesler walks past the Karl Marx Buchhandlug and stops when he recognises Georg Dreyman on a poster advertising the publication of his latest book. He goes in. The book is dedicated to "H.G.W. X.X./7". "Is it a present?" asks the cashier. "No, it's for me," he replies. The film ends with that response, in this bookshop that is now a large office though I recognise its shelves both from the film and my visits in 2005. I take a photograph of the mural of Karl Marx with his purplish bearded face, tucked away at one end of the premises. Those traces.

In his novel *Central Europe*, William T. Vollmann enters the brain of one of those spies who acted as perpetual readers of the lives of human beings who, in their eyes, were genuinely literary characters. A critical, censorious brain. His responsibilities include the control of Akhmatova's movements and he writes, choosing a metaphor that was turned into reality by the Stalinist apparatus: "From my point of view, the correct thing to do would have been to erase her from the picture and then blame the Fascists." Alluding to the sending of subversive material that is much more important than the article written by Dreyman in the film, the spy declares, "For instance, had he been left to me, Solzhenitsyn never could have smuggled his poisonous *Gulag Archipelago* to the other side." Vollmann describes the frantic activity of the bookstalls on the Nevsky Prospect, the cultural artery of St Petersburg, in whose Sytin bookshop Lenin bought his books. Together with bookseller Alexandra Komikova, who sent books to Siberia ordered by revolutionary militants confined there, he created the Marxist newspaper that the cause needed in order to spread the word. For *The Development of Capitalism in Russia*, Lenin secured a contract for 2,400 copies, and with the accompanying advance he was able to buy the books he needed for his research in Komikova's shop.

With an honesty one doesn't find that often in literary endeavours, Vollmann recognises *A Tomb for Boris Davidovitch*, by Danilo Kiš, as the model for his work, where political conflict is taken to extremes in dictatorships of the proletariat, being social constructions based on the existence of legions of readers of ordinary lives. And on eminently textual negotiations. Banned books, censorship, translations that are authorised or rejected, accusations, confessions, forms, reports: writing. Based on suspicion, born from horror: writing. In the final struggle between Novski the prisoner and Fedukin his torturer, who tries to drag a full confession from Novski's innards, Kiš captures the essence of all such relationships between intellectuals and repressors that are repeated, like racist jokes, in every community suffering from systematic suspicion. As in *The Encyclopedia of the Dead*, the Serbian writer takes Borges as

his starting point but in this instance, he does so in order to politi-
cise him, enriching his legacy with a commitment that is absent
from the original:

> Novski lengthened the hearing in an attempt to introduce
> into the document of his confession, the only record that
> would remain after his death, a few clarifications that
> might soften his definitive fall from grace and, at the same
> time, provide a lead for any future researcher, through
> cleverly fashioned contradictions and exaggerations, to
> the fact that the entire fabrication of that confession was
> based on a lie, wormed out of him, of course, by torture.
> Consequently, he struggled tenaciously for every word, for
> every formulation. [. . .] In the last instance, I think that
> both acted for motives that went beyond any narrow,
> selfish end: Novski struggled in his death, in his fall, to
> hold on to his dignity, as any revolutionary would; Fed-
> ukin was attempting, within his investigation of the fic-
> tion and conjectures, to hold on to what was strictly
> consistent with revolutionary justice and with those who
> created that, for it was better to sacrifice one man's or a
> tiny organism's truth, than to put into question on their
> behalf principles and interests that were much more
> sublime.

If the Karl Marx was the most emblematic bookshop in East Berlin,
Autorenbuchhandlung was and still is the most influential in West
Berlin. Charlottenburg was the centre of the federal half in the
divided city and the shop is a few steps away from Savignyplatz,
close to the street where Walter Benjamin based himself to write
One Way Street, the urban manual that – like Italo Calvino's *Invisible Cities* – helps one finds one's bearings in any metropolitan

psycho-geography in the world. The bookshop was inaugurated in 1976 by Günter Grass, but to signal clearly that its mission was not entirely solemn, Ginsberg turned up a few weeks later – and yet again in this bookshoppy book – to re-inaugurate it with a poetic performance. Until the fall of the Wall, it was a focus for debates about Communism and democracy, repression and freedom, with invited speakers like Susan Sontag or Jorge Semprún, but in the 1990s it concentrated on cultural reunification, paying great attention to literature from East Germany and championing it. Its main distinguishing feature – as its name suggests – was that it was set up by a group of writers, who took it upon themselves to disseminate the German literature they were producing and reading. The bookshop physically resembles Laie in Barcelona, Eterna Cadencia in Buenos Aires or Robinson Crusoe 389 in Istanbul: sober, elegant and classical. It is fitting that the protagonist of Cees Nooteboom's *All Souls' Day*, a novel with clearly European ambitions, buys his books there.

The axis articulating *Central Europe* is Germany and Russia. In Nooteboom's novel we read:

It was as if those two countries professed mutual nostalgia for each other that could barely be understood by an Atlantic Netherlander, as if that boundless plain that seemed to begin in Berlin exercised a mysterious power of attraction, from which sooner or later something must again emerge, something that cannot be understood at this point in time but that, despite all appearances to the contrary, would give another twist to European history, as if that huge landmass could thus turn, twist and drop its western edge like a sheet.

The regimes of Hitler and Stalin were atomic bombs with lethally similar content that exploded simultaneously in two geographical areas condemned to dialogue, at least after Karl Marx the Prussian Jew developed his political ideas. During his period in a seminary, the young Stalin sought freedom to read in the bookshop of Zakharyh Chichinadze, afraid that the books he borrowed from the public library might be checked and lead to reprisals. At that time imperial censors ruled with an iron hand in St Petersburg and encouraged the production in Moscow – concentrated in Nikolskaya Street and its vicinity – of *lubki*, the Russian equivalent of chapbooks or pamphlets – that exalted the figure of the Tsar, retold great battles or reproduced popular stories, much to the indignation of pre-revolutionary intellectuals who accused them of being reactionary, anti-Semitic and pro-Orthodox. After the 1917 Revolution they were airbrushed from history. The Great Encounter took place in Chichinadze's bookshop: Stalin had access to Marx's texts. In retrospect, the mytho-maniac transformed the experience into an adventure: according to his account, he and his companions surreptitiously entered Chichinadze's premises and, hard up, took it in turns to copy the banned books, as described by Robert Service in his biography of the Soviet genocidal leader:

Chichinadze was on the side of those who opposed the Russian establishment in Tbilisi. When the seminarians visited his premises, he surely greeted them warmly; and if copying took place, it must have been with his express or implicit permission. The spread of ideas was more important to the metropolitan elite than mere profit. It was a battle the liberals could scarcely help winning. Chichinadze's was a treasure house for the sort of books the youngsters wanted. Josef Dzhughashvili was fond of Victor Hugo's *The Year Ninety-Three*. He was punished for smuggling it into the seminary; and when in 1896 an inspection turned up a copy of Hugo's *The Toilers of the Sea*, Rector Gemorgen meted out "a lengthy stay" in the solitary cell. According to his friend Iremashvili, the group also got hold of texts by Marx, Darwin, Plekhanov and Lenin. Stalin recounted this in 1938, claiming that each member paid five kopecks to borrow the first volume of Marx's *Capital* for a fortnight.

When he won power, Stalin developed a convoluted system of controlling texts, partly thanks to these personal experiences that had made him realise that all censorship has its weak points. Books have always been key elements in maintaining control of power and governments have developed mechanisms for censoring books, just as they have built castles, fortresses and bunkers that – inevitably – are in the end seized or destroyed, as if unaware of the comment by Tacitus: "On the contrary, the standing of persecuted talent grows, and neither foreign kings nor any that operated with similar fury managed to produce anything but dishonour for themselves and glory for them." It was of course with the printing press that countries began to experience serious problems when they tried to curb the traffic in banned books. And it was under modern dictatorships that the greatest political credit was gained from the public burning of books, at the same time as huge amounts of the national budget were allocated to subsidise *organs of reading*.

In the first centuries of the modern era Spain pioneered not only the massive systems for spying on and repressing readers (if not, what else was the Holy Inquisition?) but also routes for importing slaves, concentration camps, schemes for re-education and strategies for extermination. It is hardly surprising that Franco's great rhetorical model for his state was Imperial Spain, the National-Catholic paraphernalia of the conquest of America. The Málaga bookseller, Francisco Puche, has written about the symbols that were counterposed to the Francoist ones:

> All booksellers who suffered Francoist censorship, police persecution, and fascist bomb attacks were marked for ever by this period and have always believed that a bookshop is more than just a business. We picked up the torch from the last man executed by the Inquisition, a bookseller from Córdoba who was condemned in the nineteenth century for introducing books banned by the Church. And this period made it quite clear, once again, that that reflex action dictatorships have of burning books is no coincidence but the product of two incompatible realities. And it also clearly demonstrated how important independent bookshops are as instruments of democracy.

However, one cannot consider the problematic relationship between aristocratic, dictatorial and fascist regimes and the free circulation of written culture from a Manichaean stance that completely exonerates parliamentary democracies, although fortunately many of them do not have to resort to physical punishment or the death penalty. The United States is the prime example of how freedom of expression and reading have been perpetually besieged by mechanisms of control and censorship. From the 1873 Comstock Law, which focuses on obscene and lascivious books, to the present proscription of books enforced by thousands of bookshops, educational institutions and libraries, for political or religious reasons, or the ways in which the Treasury Department's Office of Foreign Assets Control boycotts the diffusion of works from Cuba and other regions in the world, one can see the history of North American democracy as an endless round of negotiations in the fragile area of intellectual freedom. In our era when any sensational news story is immediately broken, book-burning catapults onto front pages. As Henry Jenkins has shown in *Convergence Culture*, the books that caused most controversy in the first decade of this century was the Harry Potter series that in 2002 was at the centre of more than five hundred different court cases throughout the U.S.A. In Alamogordo, New Mexico, the Christ Community Church burnt thirty copies together with Disney films and C.D.s of Eminem, because according to Jack Brock, the church's pastor, they were Satanic masterpieces and instruments for self-education in the black arts.

However, it was at the end of the 1980s when the publication of *The Satanic Verses* by Salman Rushdie not only illustrated for the umpteenth time the United States' problematic relationship with direct or indirect censorship, but also placed on the agenda a much more crucial issue: the geopolitical migration of threats to freedom of expression. Because if they were concentrated for half a century mostly in Eastern Europe and Asia, from the 1990s they would shift to the Arab world, with the difference that changes in economic relationships and above all the media meant that domestic or national polemics could no longer be hurriedly buried by the powers-that-be. From *The Satanic Verses* onwards, the damnation of which coincided with the fall of the Wall, the violence in Tiananmen Square and the unstoppable expansion of the Internet, whenever freedom of expression and reading were under attack, the consequences would automatically be global.

In his memoirs *Joseph Anton* Salman Rushdie recounts the details of his case. Initially publication followed its usual course in the West, he went on the obligatory promotional tours and was Booker Prize shortlisted, while in India the circulation of *The Satanic Verses* slowly ground to a halt, as a result of being spotlighted in *India Today* ("It will necessarily unleash an avalanche of protest") and the decision by two Muslim Members of Parliament to take up the attack on the book as a personal matter (without having read it). All that led to a decision to ban the book. As so often happened in the United States, in India this decision fell to the Treasury Department, guided by the Customs Law. Rushdie wrote in protest to Rajiv Gandhi, the prime minister. In their turn, fanatics responded by sending a death threat to Viking Press, the publishing house, and another to the place where the writer was going to do a reading. Then the novel was banned in South Africa. An anonymous message was sent to his house in London. Then Saudi Arabia and many other Arab countries banned the novel. And the telephone threats started. And copies of *The Satanic Verses* were publicly burnt in Bradford and the next day "WHSmith, the main British chain of bookshops, withdrew the book from its shelves in its four hundred and thirty shops," while in an official press release, they asked not to be considered "censors". The novel won the Whitbread Prize. A mob attacked the U.S. Centre for Information in Islamabad and five people died as a result of the shooting while the crowd shouted, "Rushdie, you're a dead man!" Then there was Ayatollah Khomeini and his fatwa and two bodyguards night and day and a farm in a remote corner of Wales and the threat to boycott all Penguin books on sale in the entire Muslim world and number 1 in the *New York Times'* best-seller list and a lot of bomb threats and a real bomb that exploded in Cody's bookshop in Berkeley destroying shelves, the remains of which are preserved as a reminder of barbarism, and multiple death threats to publishers and foreign translators and the Archbishop of Canterbury, and the Pope's solidarity with the injured feelings of the Muslim people and the Declaration of Support by Writers Throughout the World, then Iran broke off diplomatic relations with Britain and many institutions refused to allow events in support of the writer for security reasons and conflicts escalated ("Those small battles between lovers of books seemed like tragedies in an era when the very freedom of literature was being attacked so violently") and the periodic house moves and a false name ("Joseph Anton") and fire bombs in Collet's and

Dillon's bookshops in London and in Abbey's in Australia and in four branches of the Penguin chain and the International Rushdie Defence Committee and daily life conditioned, shot through, shaken by the constant shockwaves from security measures and the first anniversary of the book burning in Bradford and the ratification of the fatwa and the murder of the Japanese translator Hitoshi Igarashi and the ratification of the fatwa and the stabbing of the Italian translator Ettore Capriolo and the ratification of the fatwa and the attempted assassination of the Norwegian publisher William Nygaard and the ratification of the fatwa and the death of thirty-seven people in another protest and eleven years in hiding, eleven unable to stroll along the streets, have dinner quietly with friends in a restaurant, or check that his books were properly displayed in a bookshop. And that his books, on the shelves of a bookshop, should blamelessly lead to so many corpses. So very many.

At the core of Rushdie's description lies an awareness that his book belongs to a tradtion of persecuted literature:

> When friends asked what they could do to help, he often pleaded, "Defend the text." The attack was very specific, yet the defence was often a general one, resting on the mighty principle of freedom of speech. He hoped for, he often felt he needed, a more particular defence. Like the quality defence made in the case of other assaulted books, *Lady Chatterley's Lover*, *Ulysses*, *Lolita*; because this was a violent assault not on the novel in general or free speech per se, but on a particular accumulation of words [. . .] and on the intentions and integrity and ability of the writer who had put those words together.

However, unlike its predecessors which scandalised a world where news was not spread instantly, *The Satanic Verses* fell victim to a new international context. A context in which the pole of Islamic intransigence sends the other pole into a state of extreme tension, the democracies that in one way or another are heirs to the French Revolution. However, if we see the French Revolution as the first definitive step towards modern democracy, we should remember that alongside the massive number of executions and the sacking of the property of the aristocracy, the people accumulated a huge amount of capital in terms of books that they did not really know how to handle. Alberto Manguel, in *A History of Reading*, reminds us how at the end of the eighteenth century, when an antique book was much cheaper than a new one, French and German collectors benefited from the revolution, purchasing by weight thousands of bibliographic jewels, naturally through French intermediaries. As the literacy levels of ordinary people were very low, the books that were not sold or destroyed did not find too many readers in the public libraries where they were sent. Nor did the opening of public galleries lead to immediate cultural consumption: the most important consequences of collective education are always long-term. The redistribution of books would bear fruit several generations later. In a large number of Islamic countries they are now working to consolidate systems for repressing reading in order to ensure a future without plurality, dissension and irony.

In the history of Foyles, the prestigious London bookshop, we find another triangle, two sides of which are to be found in Germany and Russia, through the same dynamic that has been repeated from time immemorial: wars, revolutions, political changes of a radical nature as moments that encourage huge quantities of books to change side and owner. When Hitler began massively burning books in the 1930s, the first thing that William Foyle thought to do was to send him a telegram offering him a good price for those tons of inflammable printed material. Shortly before that he had sent his daughter Christina, then in her twenties, to Stalinist Russia in search of bargains. The Russian expedition was a success, but not the German sortie: Hitler continued to burn books and had no intention of selling them. Once war broke out and London fell victim to the Nazi bombing raids, the old books from the cellar, were mixed with sand and filled the bags that protected the walls of his shop whilst, apparently, Mr Foyle covered the roof with copies of *Mein Kampf*.

There were certainly copies of *My Struggle*, the English edition published by Hurst & Blackett and translated by Edgar Dugdale, a Zionist activist who did so with a view to denouncing Hitler's plans. Unfortunately, both the English and North American publishers (*My Battle*) yielded to the demands of Eher-Verlag, which compelled them to cut out the many xenophobic and anti-Semitic rants in the original. As Antoine Vitkine explains in his history of the book, as soon as it appeared in Britain in 1934 18,000 copies were sold, but by that time it had been read by Churchill, Roosevelt, Ben-Gurion and Stalin who had unexpurgated translations made by their intelligence services. *Mein Kampf* not only turned Adolf Hitler into *the* best-selling author in the Germany of the 1930s, and a millionaire thanks to his royalties, it also made him think of himself as a *writer*, which is how he describes himself in the corresponding section of his income tax returns for 1935. There is no doubt that the fact he was the country's political leader helped his sales, though the writing myth (prison) and his Messianic will also helped spread the word at a dizzying rate, conveniently backed by advertisements in the main newspapers of the day. Rather than a typical bookshop launch, Hitler decided on the Bürgerbräukeller to promote the work of his life:

> It is a clumsy and contrived argument, but he convinces his audience. In order to struggle against the shades of Marx, a Nazi Marx is needed or, in other words, Hitler

himself, the author of *Mein Kampf*. By presenting himself as a writer, Hitler changes his image and emerges from the mud where he had operated until then. He is no longer simply a beer-house braggart, a loudmouth, a failed putschist: now he covers himself with the prestige that comes with letters and appears as a new theorist. When he leaves the room, Hitler's men hand out promotional leaflets advertising the publication of his book and even specifying the price.

His fame as a book burner eclipsed his fame as a book collector: by the time of his death the exterminator had amassed a library of more than 1,500 volumes. After leaving school, in the shift from adolescence to young man that was accompanied by lung problems, Hitler devoted himself to the life of the artist and intellectual, drawing and reading compulsively. He never gave up on the second activity. August Kubizek, his only friend from the Linz years, relates how he used to go to the Popular Educational Society bookshop on Bismarkstrasse, and several lending libraries. He recalls him surrounded by piles of books, especially the "Sagas of German Heroes" collection.

Some fifteen years later, on the other side of the world, while Hitler was staging his first mass rally and setting the Nazi propaganda machine in motion, another future perpetrator of genocide, Mao Tse-tung, was opening a bookshop and publishing house in Changsa which he dubbed the Cultural Society of Books. Business was so brisk he soon had six employees, thanks to whom he could spend his time writing political articles that brought him to the attention of leading Chinese intellectuals. He fell in love and married in the same period. In previous years he had worked as a librarian, assistant to Li Dazhao, one of the first Chinese Communists, in whose study group he was introduced to the basic texts of Marxism-Leninism, but it was in 1920, when he became a bookseller, that he began to call himself a Communist. Forty-six years later he spurred on the Cultural Revolution, one of whose fronts was the burning of books.

As the world's principal Communist regime, China supports state chains that open vast bookshops in the country's main cities, oversee public morality and abundantly stock the Studies of Success sections, in order to foment hard work and the surpassing of individual expectation, the basis of collective endeavours. The Shinhua chain is probably the biggest and owns monsters like the Beijing Book Building, at the junction of two metro lines, with 300,000 volumes spread over five floors. But the titles selected by the government coexist on its shelves with best-selling literature, school textbooks and some books in English. However, in the University of Military Science, the School of the Central Party, and the University of National Defence bookshops, official output isn't covered by layers of pretence: they publish works of statistics and forecasts written by officers in the People's Army, doctoral theses and studies that reveal the hard core of Communist thought, undisguised by the camouflage of official communiqués intended for the foreign press. Fortunately, the Book Worm bookshop in Beijing, beneath its glamorous veneer and distinction as being one of the most beautiful bookshops in the world, has over the last few years offered its customers banned or dissident books like those by the artist Ai Weiwei.

The last time I went to Venezuela, a very young soldier smelled the twenty-three books I was carrying in my luggage one by one. I asked him whether drugs now travelled inside literature and he gave me a puzzled look before replying that they mixed them with glue, in the binding, you know what they're like. He also sniffed the two volumes from the Biblioteca Ayacucho that I had bought in a Librería del Sur, the bookshop chain run by the Ministry for the Popular Power of Culture of the Bolivarian Government of Venezuela. When he finished his inspection, he grasped my iPad, relaxed his tone of voice and asked me if I had bought it in the United States and how much it had cost. Apart from Maiquetía they have scrutinised the books in my luggage in two other airports – title by title and running a thumb across the pages: in Tel Aviv and in Havana. Israeli spies are very young and are often doing compulsory military service; while they hold one of your books they ask you if you are planning to visit Palestine, or if you have been there and brought something back, and who you know in the country, where you will stay or have stayed, why you have come, and transfer the information to a label they stick in your passport that evaluates the level of danger you represent. Venezuelan soldiers dress exactly like their Cuban counterparts and are equally unsophisticated; they are in fact copies of that original Cuban style.

It was in the Communist bookshop on calle Carlos III in Havana that future commander and repressor Fidel Castro bought the two key books of his life: *The Communist Manifesto* and *State and Revolution*. When he was in prison, he devoured all manner of reading matter, from Victor Hugo and Zweig to Marx or Weber, volumes that were presents from people who visited him in prison; he had bought many others in the same bookshop on Carlos III. In *Un seguidor de Montaigne mira La Habana* (*A Follower of Montaigne Looks at Havana*), Antonio José Ponte remembers how you could once buy books in Russian on calle Obispo in the old city:

> I found an old photograph in an encyclopedia from the beginning of the century: a street with shops and awnings on both pavements, it looks like a souk, an Arab market seen from on high. Some time ago I wrote it is rather beachy. It begins with the bookshops and ends by opening out into the square and the port. One of the bookshops then sold books in Russian. Soviet ships passed through the port. Obispo was framed by two notices in Cyrillic: the title of a book and the name of a boat.

But it is in *La fiesta vigilada* (*The Fiesta under Surveillance*) where Ponte traces more precisely the tortured topography of Castro's city, capital of "the theme park of the Cold War". He evokes Comandante Guevara in all his complexity: revolutionary soldier and professional photographer, political leader and writer by vocation, a keen reader. "From his military headquarters in La Cabaña," he tells us in one masterly sentence, "Ernesto Guevara managed a magazine, the camp's military band, the army's film unit and the execution squad." The Revolution provoked, and still provokes, wave after wave of revolutionary tourists. At one point in his book, Ponte recalls the experiences of Jean-Paul Sartre and Susan Sontag, his firmness and her doubts, how Nicolás Guillén's chilling words echo in the wake of their footsteps: "Any investigation is counter-revolutionary". In the last section, the narrator moves to Berlin, where he meets his translator who has just got hold of the Stasi file on him: "Thanks to a neighbour who spied on his movements, he was able to revisit a day in his life from thirty years ago." That trip allows Ponte to transform his life as a writer under surveillance in Havana into a universal experience.

It was a long journey that brought Che from Buenos Aires to Cuba. And a reverse journey, from north to south, ended in a laundry in El Señor de Malta public hospital, Valle Grande, his corpse before the lens of Freddy Alborta. I met Freddy by chance in his photography shop in La Paz, shortly before his own death, and he told me the story of that other journey: its result, photographs of the illustrious corpse in a glass cabinet alongside rolls of film and frames. On sale like postcards. In one of the best known, Bolivian military officers pose next to the body, as if it were an improvised anatomy lesson, and one touches the stiff body with his index finger, gesturing towards it, demonstrating that myths are also made of flesh, of matter in a constant process of putrefaction.

Would the books of Ernesto Guevara the writer be on sale in the Librería Universal? I don't think so. In the same year that the revolutionary was appointed President of the National Bank and Minister of the Economy, counter-revolutionary Juan Manuel Salvat abandoned the island via Guantánamo. Five years later he and his wife opened what was to become one of the cultural focuses of the exiled community on 8th Street in the city of Miami, with its literary conversations and editions of books in Spanish. In a report by Maye Primera, prompted by the closure of the Librería Universal on June 20, 2013, Salvat declared that the first generation of exiled Cubans, the one that read most, was dying out and the "new generation, our children, although they feel Cuban, have no experience of Cuba, don't have the accoutrements of nationality, and their first language is English, not Spanish." A law of life.

On May 2, 1911 Pedro Henríquez Ureña wrote a letter from the Cuban capital to Alfonso Reyes in which he said: "But don't think for one minute that there are good second-hand or new bookshops here: the Havana bookshops aren't much better than those in

Puebla." It is possible that for a Mexican visitor the city's bookshops did not seem anything special at the beginning of the last century, but calle Obispo – in whose Hotel Ambos Mundos Hemingway liked to stay – and the Plaza de Armas were the heart of the book trade, where the citizens of Havana had reading supplies in the decades when they were unable to travel. When I visited the island in the last days of 1999, I only bought books on the stalls in the Plaza de Armas, because the state shops had very few titles on offer, and filled up all those square metres of space with dozens and dozens of copies of the same title. In doorways, garages and entrance halls second-hand books were on sale: people were offloading family heirlooms for a fistful of dollars. But La Casa de las Américas, once the powerful bastion of Latin American culture, displayed only a few volumes by writers who were officially approved. Jorge Edwards, who at the end of the 1960s was a jury member for its prestigious annual prizes, recounted in *Persona non grata* the brutal turn made by the regime at the beginning of the 1970s. The Chilean writer gives many examples of these changes, unfortunately inscribed in the D.N.A. of the very idea of a Communist revolution, and very similar to those related by Kiš and Vollmann in their stories about paranoia in the Soviet orbit, though one is particularly telling. The rector of the University of Havana informs him, "We in Cuba don't need critics, because it is very easy to criticise, you can criticise anything, the difficult thing is to build a country and what that needs is creators, builders of society." So much so that they wonder whether to suppress a magazine whose name suddenly seems highly subversive: *Pensamiento Crítico*. And Raúl Castro conspires to subject theoretical studies of Marxism to army control. I read that book, and also *Before Night Falls* by Reinaldo Arenas, in those days at the turn of the century, part of an archive of the degeneration that had been gathering pace for over thirty years. As if all the work carried out then – which one can imagine, for example, when reading Cortázar's letters – had been drained away and the shelves of Rayuela, the Casa de las Américas' bookshop, were the end result of that draining away.

I can think of few images that are sadder than an almost empty bookshop or the remains of a bonfire on which books have been burnt. In the sixteenth century the Sorbonne decreed that 500 books were heretical. At the end of the eighteenth 7,400 titles were listed in the *Index of Banned Books* and, when the revolutionaries took La Bastille, they found a mountain of books that were about to be burnt. In the 1920s the United States Postal Service burnt copies of *Ulysses*. Until the 1960s it was impossible to publish legally without charges of obscenity in Britain and the United States D. H. Lawrence's *Lady Chatterley's Lover*, or Henry Miller's *Tropic of Cancer*. In 1930 the Soviet Union banned private publishing and official censorship lasted until Perestroika. Eugenio Pacelli, the future Pius XII, read *Mein Kampf* in 1934 and persuaded Pius XI that it would be better not to include it in the *Index*, to avoid infuriating the Führer. Books were publicly burnt by the most recent dictatorships in Chile and Argentina. Serbian mortars tried to destroy the National

Library of Sarajevo. Periodically puritan, Christian and Muslim demonstrators appear and burn books just as they burn flags. The Nazi government destroyed millions of books by Jewish writers at the same time as it was exterminating millions of Jewish human beings, homosexuals, political prisoners, gypsies or sick people; though it preserved a few – the rarest or most beautiful – intending to put them on display in a museum of Judaism that would only open its doors after the Final Solution had reached a definitive conclusion. We have often been reminded of how the Nazis in charge of the death camps were fond of classical music; people rarely consider, on the other hand, how those who designed the biggest systems of control, repression and execution in the contemporary world, who showed themselves to be the most effective censors of books, were also individuals who studied culture, writers, *keen* readers, in a word: lovers of bookshops.

VI

An Oriental Bookshop

Where does the West end and the East begin?

Of course, there is no answer to this question. Perhaps there was in more distant days: in Flaubert's time, maybe, or much earlier, in Marco Polo's, or much, much earlier, in Alexander the Great's. Nevertheless Western thought in ancient Greece was created in dialogue with philosophies from the other shores of the Mediterranean, so it was already in itself thought that encompassed an abstraction known as *the Oriental*, even though later rereadings tried to efface that. But this chapter must start somewhere, as previous ones have in Athens or in Bratislava, and will begin in Budapest, one of those cities – like Venice, like Palermo, like Smyrna – that seem to be adrift between two different waters that are less in contradiction than in conversation.

It was a summer's day at the beginning of this century and on my strolls through the city I finally became infatuated with a hand-painted wooden box that was peculiar: it did not open and hence seemed completely useless. A green wooden cube with filigree decorations. It was on display, alongside other souvenirs, on one of the stalls on the banks of the Danube. It clearly had a lid but no keyhole. The stallholder waited a while until she could see I was desperately turning that hermetic object round in my hands, then she came over and whispered, "It is a magic box." A few movements by her fingers laid bare loose pieces in the wooden structure, parts that slid one way and another to reveal a keyhole and indeed, the crevice where the key was hidden. The device had entranced me. She realised that immediately. The haggling began.

The dichotomy between fixed prices and haggling could be one of the axes that today polarise East and West. Another could be the material and the oral. These are uncontrollable, slippery points of opposition, but they can help us to decide whether categories like "the Western reader" or "the Oriental bookshop" have any meaning. In Marrakesh's Djemaa el-Fna Square the library is non-material and inaccessible to those who don't know the local languages: the snake charmers, ointment-sellers and, above all, the storytellers, construct a story that you cannot understand out of thin air, the story accompanied by hypnotic gestures, illustrations using human bodies or drawn maps. In *The Voices of Marrakesh*, Canetti links that lack of understanding with a degree of nostalgia for more artisan ways of life that have died the death in Europe, ones that give more credence to the oral transmission of knowledge. No doubt there is wisdom and the greatest value in the oral traditions that flow into that dusty, rather caravanserai-like square that every afternoon turns into a huge, informal, steaming, open-air diner. However, to idealise it is to return to an Orientalist mentality, to the clichés and simplifications in relation to the Arab and Asian worlds that we so-called *Westerners* like to traffic in. Just like that image of an Egyptian bookseller I photographed in a small village on the shores of the Red Sea. After all, the Arab and Asian worlds are worlds of calligraphy and books with ancient, powerful texts that are closed to us unless we partially betray them through translation.

Because Tangier was so close to the end of Europe, the city soon began to be Orientalised by European writers and painters, particularly the French. Delacroix was the first to turn the Moroccan city into a landscape that represented a huge abstraction. His repertoire of *djellabas* and horses, young boys and carpets, against a simple white architectural backdrop where a glassy sea often appears

comprises the clichés that will be repeated time and again in the representation of North Africa. Eighty years later, as part of the same tradition, Matisse gave geometrical form to the city and its inhabitants: he modernised it. Among the Spanish painters, Mariano Fortuny, Antonio Fuentes and José Hernández gradually added different shades to that pictorial landscape. The latter, a member of the city's Hispanic community, exhibited in the Librairie des Colonnes, perhaps its most important cultural centre over the last sixty years, and where the writer Ángel Vázquez worked. He won the Planeta Prize in 1962 and fifteen years later published his great novel about the city, *La vida perra de Juanita Narboni*. People tend to remember the roll-call of American and French artists who made the International City one of the key focal points of twentieth-century culture, but nonconformist figures from many parts of the globe hovered around them, like the Spaniards I have mentioned, or Claudio Bravo, the Chilean hyper-realist painter who lived in Tangier from 1972 until his death in 2011, or the Moroccan artists who participated in the creation of the myth, like Mohamed Hamri the painter, or the writers Mohamed Choukri, Abdeslam Boulaich, Larbi Layachi, Mohammed Mrabet or Ahmed Yacoubi.

The official narrative of what could be called the *Tangier myth* credits 1947, when Paul Bowles arrived in the city, as the year it began. The following year his wife Jane settled down with him. Tennessee Williams, Truman Capote, Jean Genet, William Burroughs (and the rest of the beat generation) or Juan Goytisolo would appear later. Beyond numerous parties in private homes and certain cafés that became daily points of encounter, two main meeting places emerged for the motley band of artists and numerous other characters who came and went, tycoons and adventurers, dilettantes and musicians interested in African rhythms, actors like Hungarian Paul Lukas (who appeared with Elvis Presley in "Fun in Acapulco" and in the version of "Lord Jim" directed by Richard Brooks, and died in Tangier while he was looking for a place to spend the last years of his life), film directors like Bernardo Bertolucci and rock groups like the Rolling Stones. These two meeting places were, on the one hand, Paul Bowles himself, who became a tourist attraction similar to Gertrude Stein or Sylvia Beach in Paris in the inter-war years; on the other, the Librairie des Colonnes, founded in the period when the Bowleses settled in Tangier, and which has survived them both.

The Belgian couple, Robert – architect and archaeologist, friend of Genet, André Gide and Malcolm Forbes – and Yvonne Gerofi, a librarian by training, with the indispensable collaboration of her sister, Isabelle, took the helm of the Librairie des Colonnes from its founding in 1949. It was Gallimard, the owner of the business, who offered them the post. Their marriage was paper-thin. The couple had got together for convenience as both were homosexuals and Tangier at that time was the ideal place for that kind of family set-up, so similar to the one being lived by the Bowleses. While the Gerofi sisters assumed control of the bookshop, and even became two genuine celebrities in the cultural sphere, Robert devoted himself to design and architecture. Among other projects, he was responsible for reshaping the Arab palace where Forbes, the publisher and owner of the famous magazine, housed his collection of 100,000 toy lead soldiers. In a Magnum Agency photograph an old man appears, looking at the camera, holding a white jacket and white hat, as "manager of the Forbes Estate". The Gerofis and the Bowleses were in close contact as one can glean from the writers' correspondence. As far as Paul was concerned the Gerofis' constant presence went without saying: they were as much a part of the daily scene as the Zoco Chico or the Straits of Gibraltar. On the other hand, Yvonne was a close friend of Jane's, when she wasn't being her nurse, since Jane depended on her during the long periods when she was psychologically unstable. On January 17, 1968 Jane walked into the Librairie des Colonnes not recognising anyone, her mind a complete blank, and asked to borrow two dirhams; then she took two books, and, despite being spoken to by Aicha her servant, she left without paying for them.

Whenever Marguerite Yourcenar passed through Tangier, she would drop in at the bookshop to greet her friend Robert, and whenever an American writer – like Gore Vidal – or a European intellectual – like Paul Morand – or Arab – like Amin Maalouf – visited the white city, they inevitably ended up between its shelves that over time came to stock a varied selection of Arab, English and Spanish titles, as well as the wealth of French books one would expect. Not for nothing was it a bastion of anti-Francoist resistance which encouraged publications by and organised meetings of exiles. The most renowned Spanish writer linked to the Librairie des Colonnes is Juan Goytisolo who began to inhabit Arab culture in the mid-1960s, in that very city. As soon as he arrived he wrote to Monique Lange, as we read in *In Realms of Strife*: "I feel happy, I walk around for ten hours a day, I'm seeing Haro and his wife, I'm not going to bed with anyone and I look at Spain from afar, full of intellectual excitement." And that will inspire *Count Julian*: "The idea I'm working on is based on the vision of the Spanish coast from Tangier: I want to start off with this image and write something beautiful that will go beyond anything I have written so far." He takes detailed notes, sketches out ideas and reads Golden Age literature profusely in his rented room. Although he later decides to settle in Marrakesh, Goytisolo will spend most of his summers in Tangier and become a supporter of its most important bookshop. In one of his most recent novels, *A Cock-Eyed Comedy*, where he gives a turn of the screw to the camouflaged homosexual tradition in Spanish literature, he has the colourful père de Trennes declare:

> Do you know whether Genet still stays at the Minzeh or has he set up in Larache? I've heard great things about an autobiography by one Choukri, translated into English by Paul Bowles. Have you read it? As soon as we arrive I'll track it down in the Librairie des Colonnes. You're a friend of the Gerofi sisters, I suppose? Who doesn't know the Gerofi sisters in Tangier? What! You've never heard of them? *Pas possible!* Doesn't an honorary Tangerine like you go to their bookshop? Allow me to say I don't believe you. They're the engine driving the city's intellectual life!

The case of Eduardo Haro Ibars is less well known, but perhaps more emblematic given his affinity with bisexuality, drugs and the destructive inertia that permeated the intellectual climate in

Tangier. The son of exiles, born in fact in Tangier in 1948, he infiltrated the beat circle as an adolescent who accompanied Ginsberg and Corso on their nocturnal wanderings. "I grew up rather a roamer, between Madrid, Paris and Tangier," he wrote; but it was surely the spatial vector Tangier–Madrid that really marked his life, because he took to the Spanish capital a nonconformist injection of beat which as a militant homosexual he used to nourish *la movida*, writing poems and songs and experimenting with all kinds of hallucinogenic drugs. In the spring of 1969, after four months in prison with Leopoldo María Panero, he returned to the family home in Tangier. And on another occasion, he boarded a night train that took him to Algeciras, crossed the straits, lodged in the house of Joseph McPhillips – a friend of the Bowleses' – and was helped by the Gerofi ladies who let him do a few jobs in their bookshop. He

The word is electric star in the fog

defined himself as "homosexual, drug addict, delinquent and poet". He died of Aids at the age of forty.

Bookshops tend to survive the writers who fed their mythology and their owners. After the Gerofis, between 1973 and 1998, the business was looked after by Rachel Muyal. As we can read in *My Years in the Librairie des Colonnes*, as a Tangerine and neighbour of the bookshop from 1949, she brought to the cosmopolitanism she inherited her added interest in the Moroccan nature of Tangier:

> A person who honoured me with his visits was Si Ahmed Balafrej. He liked to browse through the interior design and architectural magazines. Si Adelkebir el Fassi, a resistance hero, used to accompany him. It was in the course of one of their conversations that Si Ahmed looked me in the eye and said, "Only God knows that I have done everything to ensure Tangier preserves its special status whilst remaining part of the Kingdom of Morocco."

Like other great booksellers who have appeared or will appear in these pages, Muyal lived within a stone's throw of the shop and often organised cocktail parties and fiestas linked to the launch of books or cultural events, and like them she also became a point of reference, an ambassador, a link: on a weekly basis three or four people would ask her to put them in contact with Paul Bowles, who didn't have a telephone; she'd ask for appointments via messengers and he almost always granted them.

Later Pierre Bergé and Simon-Pierre Hamelin arrived and the magazine *Nejma*, which has devoted its pages to the memory of the international myth, to that map where so many Moroccan writers found paths to translation and recognition outside Tangier. The Straits of Gibraltar have always been a place of transit between Africa and Europe, so it is only natural that the bookshop should have played a privileged role in the cultural communication between the two shores. Muyal declared in a lecture she gave to the city's Rotary Club:

> I could feel myself in the centre of the city and even in the centre of the world in that mythical place that is the Librairie des Colonnes. That is why, I told myself, it was absolutely necessary to make the institution participate in the cultural movement in Tangier, a city that symbolises better than any other in the world the meeting of two continents, two seas, two poles: East and West and also three cultures and three religions constituting a single, homogeneous population.

I still have the hand-woven paper card of the Librairie Papeterie run by Mademoiselle El Ghazzali Amal in Marrakesh, on which she has proudly embossed: "Since 1956", and I remember how disappointed I was by the scant number of books on sale and by the fact they were all written in Arabic. The Librairie des Colonnes, on the other hand, can only enthuse a European writer, because it is like any great bookshop here, but is on the shores of Africa and possesses all the necessary notes of local colour. It sells fixed-price books in French, English and Spanish, without the option of haggling that is amusing initially but soon becomes trying and wearisome, and that gives us a feeling of security. The same is the case with the other two Moroccan bookshops I have got to know recently: the Ahmed Chatr, also in Marrakesh, and in particular the Carrefour des Livres in Casablanca, with its stridently coloured canvases and large stock of titles in Arabic and French (it has direct links with the Librairie des Colonnes, since it sells the same small white-and-tangerine books from the Khar Bladna house that I have been collecting over the years). You feel at ease. I have rarely had such a feeling of suffocation as in that other Marrakesh bookshop, which was dedicated exclusively to religious books, entirely in Arabic, without a single breathing space. We travel to discover but also to recognise. Only a balance between those two activities can give us the pleasure we are seeking. Bookshops are almost always a sure-fire bet in that respect: their structures are soothing, because they always seem familiar; intuitively we understand the orderliness, the layout, what they have to offer, but we need at least one section where we recognise an alphabet we can read, an area of illustrated books we can leaf through, a scattering of information that in its precision – or simply by chance – we can decipher.

That was exactly what occurred in the Book Bazaar in Istanbul: among thousands of incomprehensible covers I found a volume about Turkish travellers published in English and illustrated with photographs, *Through the Eyes of Turkish Travellers, Seven Seas and Five Continents*, by Alpay Kabacali, in an exquisite cased edition published by Toprakbank. As I needed that piece of the puzzle in my collection of historical travels – accounts by Turkish travellers – I was determined to buy it. Right away I was reminded of the seller of magic boxes on that Budapest street stall, where I had gone day after day, keeping firmly to my offer – a third of the asking price – until she yielded on the last day with a feigned smile of resignation. I bought two, to give to my brothers. The very minute she handed them over, wrapped in grey paper, an American tourist, holding an identical box, was asking how much they cost. The lady doubled the initial price. Without objecting, her customer also asked for two and put his hand in his pocket and, highly amused, with a wink that begged me not to say a word, she agreed a sale the same as mine, but six times more expensive. So I asked the Turkish shop assistant who was listening to the radio behind the counter for the price of the cased volume, though it turned out that he was only keeping an eye on the merchandise, because he immediately shouted to a clean-shaven, middle-aged man who looked me in the eye and said it cost $40. I think 25 would be a fairer price, I replied. He shrugged and went back by the route he had come.

He had come round one of the corners of the Sahaflar Carsisi that is Turkish for "Book Bazaar". Located in an old courtyard, boxed in between the Beyazit Mosque and the Fesciler entrance to the Great Bazaar, close to Istanbul University, it occupies approximately the same number of square metres enjoyed by the Charto-prateia that was Byzantium's market for paper and books. Perhaps because in the centre of the courtyard sits a bust of Ibrahim Müteferrika, accompanied by the titles of the first seventeen books published in Turkish thanks to the printing house he ran from the beginning of the eighteenth century, I thought I might be able to secure the anthology of travel writers employing the same tactic I had used in Budapest. Because Müteferrika hailed from Transylvania and we don't how he came to Constantinople or why he converted to Islam and in my eyes his Turkish journey was linked with my incursions in the Balkans and along the Danube. I soon got into the habit of going there every day and upping my offer by $5 on each visit.

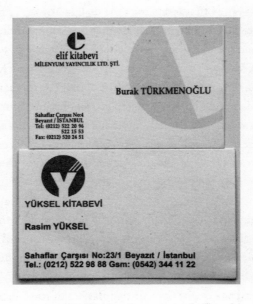

I also adopted the habit of reading in the afternoons on the terrace of the Café Pierre Loti, with its views over the Marmara, and strolling at nightfall along the Istiklal Caddesi or Independence Avenue, the other great book centre in the city. Like Buda and Pest, the two banks of Istanbul separated by the Galata Bridge have their own idiosyncratic character which could be summed up by the two different focuses on writing: the Bazaar and the Avenue. Merchants from Venice and Genoa established themselves around the latter; there are beautiful arcades and bookshops with the price of each book printed on a white label stuck on the back cover. I looked in vain for the travellers' anthology in places like Robinson Crusoe 389, where conversely I bought two books by Juan Goytisolo translated into Turkish. The photographs included in the edition of *Ottoman Istanbul* do not include any of the old or modern bookshops, because they have never featured in travel literature or cultural history. I searched for a bibliography on the Armenian genocide and, at the end of the avenue that looks over the Galata Tower, I finally found a bookseller who spoke perfect English – with a London accent – who referred me to the two volumes of *The History of the Ottoman Empire and Modern Turkey* by Stanford J. Shaw and Ezel Kural Shaw. Their index of topics left no room for doubt: "Armenian nationalism, terrorism; Armenian revolt; the Armenian question; war with Turkish nationalists". Equally shocking but less comprehensible is the fact that the historical summary offered by *Lonely Planet Turkey* also avoids mention of those systematic massacres that took the lives of a million people, the first of the genocides of the twentieth century.

In premises close to the bust of the first Turkish printer – who was Hungarian – I had several conversations with a bookseller who spoke good English and who – as the days went by – became less and less wary. Orhan Pamuk, who had just won the Nobel Prize, was, so he said, a mediocre writer who had made the most of his foreign contacts. And the Armenian genocide was an episode in history that really did not deserve that name, because one should separate out facts from propaganda. I cannot work out if his name was Burak Türkmenoğlu or Rasim Yüksel, because I have kept his card as well as one from the middle-aged, always freshly shaven man, who on the day I took the night bus to Athens sold me the blue-cased volume for $40. However, I do remember very clearly the way his eyes shone like silver paper reflecting flames in the half-dark of his premises.

There is an abundance of denial literature in Turkey, as there is of anti-Semitic material in Egypt or anti-Islamic books in Israel. In the Madbouly bookshop on Talaat Harb Square in Cairo I saw three copies of *The Protocols of the Elders of Zion*, though they also had the complete works of Naguib Mahfouz on display, the only Egyptian writer who emulated Stein or Bowles and transformed himself into a tourist attraction in his lifetime, as a regular customer at the Fishawi or Café of Mirrors. In Sefer Ve Sefel in Jerusalem, which was founded in 1975 with the idea of offering books in English and had to close down during the intifada, or in Tamir Books, on the same Jaffa Road, where they only sell books in Hebrew, and all the different political and historical tendencies, including the indefensible kind, coexist: generalist bookshops tend to be a micorcosm of the wider society: radical minorities are represented on shelves that are also in themselves minimal. But I went to fewer bookshops in Jerusalem than in Tel Aviv, a city less obsessed by religions and thus more tolerant, and the bookshop I visited daily during my stay in Cairo was the one in the American University that is apolitical and secular, and deliberately so. There I bought one of the most beautiful books I have ever given as a present: *Contemporary Arabic Calligraphy* by Nihad Dukhan.

I have never seen an Arabic calligrapher in action, though I have seen a Chinese one. I visited dozens of bookshops, as is my wont, in the main cities of China and Japan, but I must say I was less interested in those big, perfectly ordered stores from which I was driven by the characters I couldn't understand, than in another kind of space and style that attracted me as a traveller with their magnetic Oriental power. I was surprised to discover in Libro Books in Tokyo that Haruki Murakami had published several volumes of cybernetic correspondence with his fans. In Shanghai's Bookmall I liked leafing through the Chinese translation of *Don Quixote*. However I particularly sought out a mixture of discovery and recognition in the Hutong tearooms on Philosophy Way, in a few gardens, in antique shops, in an old calligrapher's workshop. Perhaps it was because I could not understand their voices when they spoke to me, but I liked to hear the musical rhythms of Zhongyuan or Rui'an. Perhaps because I was denied any possible access to Japanese literature in the original language, I fell in love with the paper they used to wrap books, boxes of sweets, glasses or plates, their extraordinary, refined art of paper-making.

*

I had another – memorable – tussle with the practice of haggling in an antiques shop in Beijing. After reviewing the dusty shelves packed with lovely objects, I was set on buying a teapot that seemed more affordable than the engravings, tapestries or vases. As we did not understand one another, the adolescent attending to me grabbed a toy calculator with huge letters and keyed in the price in dollars: 1,000. I snatched the device and keyed in my counter-offer: 5. He immediately went down to 300. I went up to 7. He asked the owner for help, an impassive, very old man with an alert gaze who sat down opposite me and with a couple of whirls of his hands indicated that it was now serious bargaining: 50. I went up to 10. He asked me for 40, 30, 20, 12. That was what I paid and I was so pleased with myself. He wrapped my teapot in white silk paper.

It was when I saw the American tourist in Budapest paying three times more for the same box that I understood the value of my own box and, above all, my would-be value as a tourist. It was in a Beijing market the day after my new purchase that I saw a hundred teapots identical to mine but gleaming, without a speck of dust, mass-produced, on a carpet on the floor, priced at $1, and realised that aura has to do with context (or was reminded of that yet again). Comparison and context are also basic factors when it comes to valuing the importance of a book, the text of which is tied to a specific moment of production. That is what literary criticism is doing continually: establishing comparative hierarchies within a specific cultural field. The framework of a bookshop is the physical place where we readers compare most. But to make that comparison we must understand the language in which the books we are looking at are written. And that is why, for me and so many other Western readers, the cultural ecosystems that we call the Orient, and the bookshops in which they are given material form, constitute a parallel universe that is at once fascinating and frustrating to navigate.

Paper was invented in China at the beginning of the second

century AD. Apparently a eunuch, Cai Lun, was responsible: he made the pulp from rags, hemp, tree bark and fishing nets. Because paper was less exalted than bamboo and silk, it took centuries for it to establish itself as the best support for the written word and it wasn't until the sixth century that it travelled beyond the Chinese frontiers and until the twelfth that it reached Europe. In France its production coincided with the production of linen from flax fibre. By that time Chinese printers were using movable type, but the thousands of characters in the language stopped printing from really constituting a revolution, as would occur with Gutenberg four hundred years later. Nonetheless, as Martyn Lyons has noted in *Books: A Living History*, China had produced more books than the rest of the world put together by the end of the fifteenth century. Each volume: an object. A body. Matter. Secretions and silk worm paper. Gutenberg had to perfect oil-based indelible ink, by experimenting with soot, varnish and egg-whites. Forging type with alloys made from lead, antimony, tin and copper. In the following centuries a different combination was reached: nutshells, resin, linseed and turpentine. Though industrial production of paper was later standardised through the use of pine or eucalyptus wood, together with hemp or cotton, its manufacture from cotton rags, pure cellulose free of any bark, was still synonymous with quality in the eyes of the experts. Books depended on the rag-and-bone man until the eighteenth century; then modern systems were developed to extract paper from wood pulp and the price of books was halved. Rags were cheap, but the process was expensive. In his studies on Baudelaire – as we have seen – Benjamin highlights the figure of the rag-and-bone man as a collector, as the archivist of everything the city has reduced to bits and pieces, flotsam from the city's shipwreck. As well as the analogy between fabric and the syntax of writing, between the rags used and the ageing of what is published, the circle being closed is important: recycling, the reabsorption of rubbish by industry, so the information machine doesn't grind to a halt.

The idea endured for centuries in the Orient that the best way to absorb the contents of a book was by copying it manually: that intellect and memory work with words in the same manner as ink does with paper.

VII

America (I): "Coast to Coast"

The classic route for the coast-to-coast ride begins in New York and ends in California. As this is a classic essay, a bastard child of Montaigne, this chapter will tease out the route, despite scant intermediate stops; a route that will inevitably develop into a journey as textual as it is audio-visual – though it is anchored quite firmly in particular bookshops that are *exemplary* in their way – through myths of American culture, a culture that is surely characterised above all by its creation of contemporary myths.

Nevertheless, most of them are individual and generally linked to significant spaces that often have collective connotations. Elvis Presley is a unique body in movement, and hence an itinerary, a biography, but he *is* also Graceland and Las Vegas. And Michael Jackson expressed himself spatially in Neverland, as Walt Disney did before him in his first theme park in California. Similarly, one can visit the cultural history of the United States in the twentieth century by focusing chronologically on certain emblematic places, *examples* of a complete picture one could never encompass. The 1920s saw the famous lunches at the restaurant in the Algonquin, the New York hotel, where writers, critics and publishers like John Peter Tooley, Robert Sherwood, Dorothy Parker, Edmund Wilson or Harold Ross argued about aesthetics and the national and international publishing industry; in the 1930s the Gotham Book Mart established itself in the same city, specialised in the dissemination of experimental writers, organised all manner of lectures and literary parties and gradually became a rendezvous for avant-garde artists exiled from Europe; during the 1940s Peggy Guggenheim's New York Art of This Century gallery was the decisive launch pad for abstract expressionism as *the* form adopted by the nation's avant-garde; in the 1950s, the City Lights Bookshop in San Francisco brought onto the market some of the most representative books of that period and promoted them with launches and readings; under the leadership of Andy Warhol, the Factory in Manhattan stood out in the 1960s as a film studio, art workshop and home to druggy parties, and in the 1970s and early 1980s the nightclub Studio 64 picked up the baton.

Obviously, these are key places for their times. Especially on the East Coast, although one cannot understand the culture of the United States without the perpetual Coast to Coast movement: "I love Los Angeles. I love Hollywood. They're so beautiful. Everybody's plastic, but I love plastic. I want to be plastic," said Andy Warhol. If I had to choose a single building to symbolise, if only tangentially, intellectual life in the United States in the twentieth century, it would be the Chelsea Hotel, inaugurated in 1885 and still going strong. The list of its celebrities and important moments could begin with Mark Twain and end with Madonna (photographs of room 822 appear in "Sex"), not forgetting a few survivors of the *Titanic*, Frida Kahlo and Diego Rivera, Dylan Thomas's suicide in 1953, the writing of *2001: A Space Odyssey* by Arthur C. Clarke, the composing of "Blonde on Blonde" by Bob Dylan, the performing of "Chelsea Hotel" by Leonard Cohen and some scenes in "9 1/2 Weeks". The hotel is like a bookshop. It is equally central to the history of ideas, as a meeting place for migrants, as a site for intense, solitary reading – which Edward Hopper portrayed so well – for writing and creation and the interchange of experiences, contacts and fluids. It is also at a crossroads between uniqueness and cloning, independence and chain, with a museum-like vocation. And it falls outside the institutional circuit and hence has a history hewn from discontinuities. Although more than a hundred and thirty years in New York guarantees the possibility of a chronologically structured narrative, as it has been visited – bombarded – by the biographies of hundreds of artists, the Chelsea Hotel and the other hotels where hundreds of artists have lodged on their endless travels, can only be recounted through a constellation of stories and dates.

The beat generation had to experience in the flesh their fetish, the Beat Hotel in Paris, that city which, in Burroughs' words, "is a disgusting hole for anyone without a dime", full of French people, "genuine pigs", but where he managed to finish *The Naked Lunch* and work on his cut-ups thanks to the facilities provided in fact by a Frenchwoman, Madame Rachou, who ran that hotel without a name (9 rue Gît-le-Cœur) where he stayed with Ginsberg, Corso and other friends. When the movement transformed into the beat trend, the beat fashion, all things beatnik, that Paris hotel was christened the Beat Hotel. The same city that had watched the birth of Cubism half a century earlier via the brushes of Juan Gris, Georges

Braque and Pablo Picasso now welcomed the postmodern éclosion of cut-ups and literary montage. After Tangier and Paris they continued to take drugs and create in the Chelsea Hotel in New York. Burroughs wrote that it was a place that "seemed to have specialised in the deaths of famous writers". The shooting of "The Chelsea Girls", Warhol's experimental film, can be seen as another turning point: the end of a particular way of understanding Romanticism, a wild, vagabond style, the start of serial production and the spectacular showcasing of contemporary art.

Were the beats good bookshop customers? They weren't, if one believes the legend. It is much easier to imagine them borrowing or stealing books, taking them for a while from the shelves of Shakespeare and Company rather than buying them. Indeed Whitman's bookshop – to judge by the copious correspondence – was above all a source of income: "The bookseller here, who is a friend of Ferlinghetti's, has fifty copies of my book in the window and sells several every week." The big book thief was Gregory Corso, who often tried to sell the next morning the books he had stolen the previous night. They were no doubt keener on second-hand than new. And on the reading of originals, addicted as they were not only to chemical substances but also to the epistolary art, automatic writing, lyrical rhapsody and jazz rhythms. However, legends mainly exist to be disproved: in Paris, for example, they took advantage of their access to Olympia Press books to acquire works by banned French and American authors. "Ferlinghetti sent me $100 yesterday, so we ate, I paid Gregory's 20 dollar back rent he's moved in with us temporarily," Ginsberg writes to Kerouac in a letter dated 1957. "We bought Genet and Apollinaire dirty book and a paper of junk and a matchbox of bad kief and a huge quart expensive bottle of perpetual maggi seasoning-soy sauce. While they lived in the Chelsea Hotel they went to New York bookshops like the Phoenix that mimeographed copies of Ed Sanders' magazine *Fuck You* and was behind a poetry collection in the form of chapbooks that included titles by Auden, Snyder, Ginsberg and Corso. Sanders himself opened the Peace Eye Bookstore in 1964 in an old kosher butcher's. It sold books as well as articles for counterculture fetishists, like a collection framed by the pubic hair of sixteen innovative poets or Ginsberg's beard. It quickly became a site for political activism and defended the legalisation of marijuana amongst other things. On January 2, 1966 the police raided the shop and arrested its owner accusing him of stocking obscene literature and lewd prints. Although he won his case, they never returned the confiscated material and that was why he was forced to close the bookshop.

If the abstract expressionists became heirs to the European avant-garde in the 1950s through a complex cultural, economic and political operation driven by institutions as different as the Museum of Modern Art and the C.I.A., it was thanks to a confluence of new sociological forces, new ways of understanding life and travel, music and art, as performative as the brushstrokes of Jackson Pollock, that the beat generation were to become the heirs to the lost generation and the French surrealists, namely, the usual suspects on the rue de l'Odéon. Until the Second World War, Gotham Book Mart was the United States equivalent of the original Shakespeare and Company. As we read in Anaïs Nin's diary, Frances Steloff's bookshop played the same role as Sylvia Beach's in Paris. The same infectious enthusiasm, the same support for more nonconformist poetics: the shop lent Nin $100, offered her all the publicity possible so she could self-publish *Winter Artifice* and celebrate it with a launch party. But immediately after Hiroshima Frances Steloff couldn't accept or refused to acknowledge the power of the beats and her renowned bookshop stayed anchored in the pre-war literary world. Art was a different matter: she found Duchamp an artisan able to make the prototype of his famous suitcase-museum, and her shop window displayed an installation by him on the occasion of the launch of a book by André Breton and together with Peggy Guggenheim he designed another with the Art of This Century in mind. But the gesture that most emphatically defines the bookshop belongs to 1947 and was the founding of the James Joyce Society, the first member of which was T. S. Eliot. Almost a decade later, when the Irish writer was still alive, Steloff dedicated an ironic shop-window display to *Finnegans Wake*, in the form of a wake in sync with the mood of the present. However, linking the bookshop to a dead author now afforded it a dangerously premature museum status, even if it was still a relatively young establishment (it opened in 1920 and did not disappear until 2007) when its Alma Mater was under fifty and destined to be a hundred-year-old bookseller.

One only has to read *In Touch with Genius*: *Memoirs of a New York Bookseller* to realise that, although the Gotham Book Mart always defended small reviews and fanzines, it supported young writers and high-quality literature, and the memoir remains faithful to its own roots and champions a particular kind of literature from the first half of the last century, the roll-call of which was defined by the publication of the anthology *We Moderns: 1920–1940*. The memoirs were published in 1975 and are reminiscent of Beach's: it was no coincidence that both booksellers were born in 1887 and devoted their lives to promoting the same authors, with James Joyce leading the way. The bookseller emulates her predecessor and assumes an observer's role ("I never approached my customers unless they looked as if they needed help") and is a collector of distinguished visitors. She met Beach in Paris and they coincided on several occasions, she relates, and ends on this note: "Our bookshops were often thought of as similar projects, but I never enjoyed the advantages she had."

In the 1920s and 1930s the Gotham Book Mart became primarily the focus for spotlighting books banned in the United States, an island where treasures could be found like books by Anaïs Nin, D. H. Lawrence and Henry Miller, and this was the literary horizon that sealed its reputation and concentrated all its energy in terms of promotion. We find allusions to it in the private correspondence of these writers. For example, in a letter from the author of *Tropic of Cancer* to Lawrence Durrell:

> Naturally the sales weren't very high, neither for *The Black Book* nor for *Max*. But they are selling slowly all the time. I myself have bought out of my own pocket a number of your books, which friends asked for. And now that the ban is off them, in America, we may get somewhere – through the Gotham Book Mart at least. In the next ten days or so I ought to have some interesting news from them, as I have written to them about the state of affairs. Cairns may not have had time to see you, his boat left the day after he arrived. But he has a high opinion of you and all of us – a staunch fellow, full of integrity, somewhat naive, but on

the right side. I count him a good friend and perhaps my best critic in America.

Gotham Book Mart and its famous slogan "Wise men fish here" appear in the graphic memoir *Are You My Mother?*, by Alison Bechdel. "This bookshop has been here for ever, it's an institution." Culture has always circulated as much through alternative networks as established market channels and writers have always been the biggest shareholders in these parallel poetics. Nonetheless, it is worth underlining Miller's reference to Huntington Cairns to explore the complex relationships that exist between art and political power in the United States, given that the latter was both an excellent reader and a lawyer who advised the Treasury on the matter of the importing of publications that might be considered to be pornographic. In other words, he was a censor. Probably the most important one of his time. The letter, dated March 1939, ends on this rather startling note: "I'm a Zen right here in Paris, and I've never felt better or more lucid, secure and focused. Only a war could distract me from this." In another letter from that time that he wrote to Steloff offering her the most recent first editions of *Tropic of Cancer* and *Black Spring*, he elaborates the idea even further: "My decision isn't based on fear of a war. I don't think there will be one this year, nor do I think there will be next year." Just as well he devoted himself to reading and not futurology.

In 1959 Gay Talese reported on the case of *Lady Chatterley's Lover*, a novel banned from the country until that year. A federal judge diluted the definition of obscenity that the Supreme Court had formulated two years before in the case of Samuel Roth against the United States of America for dealing in pornography:

> The liberation of the novel had actually been initiated by the courtroom efforts of a New York publisher, Grove

Press, which had filed and won its case against the U.S. Post Office, which until then had assumed broad authority in banning "dirty" books and other objectionable materials from being mailed in America. The courtroom triumph of Grove Press was immediately celebrated by advocates of literary freedom as a national victory against censorship and an affirmation of the First Amendment.

That was how one more of the infinite chapters of censorship in the history of culture was closed, as if we hadn't already had access to Diderot's words from the eighteenth century in his renowned *Letter on the Book Trade* (1763), a systematic dissection of the way the publishing system works from royalties to the writer's relationship with his printer, publisher and bookseller that, *toutes proportions gardées*, can be applied to a good number of areas into which the book trade is still divided legally and conceptually. Diderot, the driving force behind *L'Encyclopédie*, was himself forced to sell his library in order to provide his daughter's dowry. He was the author of other famous letters, like those to Sophie Volland or *Letter on the Deaf and Mute*, and was possibly a lover of the Empress of Russia. After his death one of the great novels of the modern era, his *Jacques the Fatalist*, was published. He wrote the following on the circulation of banned books:

> Please name one of those dangerous works that were banned, then clandestinely printed either abroad or in the kingdom that did not within four months become as available as any book which had been granted the *privilège*. What book is more contrary to good morals, to religion, to conventional ideas of philosophy and administration, in a word, to all vulgar prejudices, and, consequently, more dangerous, than *The Persian Fables*? Is there anything

worse? Yet there are a hundred editions of *The Persian Letters* and any student can find a copy for twelve sous on the banks of the Seine. Who doesn't own a translation of Juvenal or Petronius? There are countless reprints of Boccaccio's *Decameron* or La Fontaine's *Fables*. Is it perhaps beyond French typographers to print at the foot of the front page "By Merkus, in Amsterdam" like the Dutch printers? Multiple editions of *The Social Contract* are on sale for a crown by the entrance to the sovereign's palace. What does this mean? Essentially that we have always managed to secure these works; we have paid abroad the cost of labour that a more indulgent magistrate with better policies could have spared us rather than abandoning us to the black marketeers, who, taking advantage of our double curiosity, tripled by prohibition, have expensively sold on to us the real or imaginary danger which they exposed themselves in order to satisfy that curiosity.

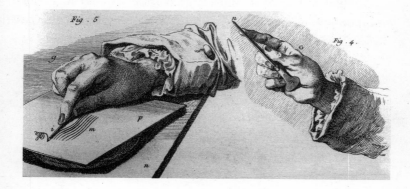

While small, often short-lived, bookshops nourish the literary fiction that is outside the mainstream, bookshops that pride themselves on their huge size remind us that the publishing industry is not based on sophisticated books for a minority, but on mass production, just like the food industry. The New York bookshop equivalent to the Chelsea Hotel, in terms of independence, long life and symbolic importance, is possibly Strand, with its "eighteen miles of books", founded in 1927 by Benjamin Bass, who left it to his son Fred, who in turn bequeathed it to Nancy, his daughter, who handed the business on in 2006 to her own children, William Peter and Ava Rose Wyden. The expression "family business" must have been coined with them in mind. Four generations and two premises: the original in "Book Row" on 4th Street, where in the good old times there were up to forty-eight bookshops, of which Strand is the only survivor, the current one being on 12th and Broadway. José Donoso wrote eloquently about its importance in an article entitled "A New York Obsession":

> I don't go to the big bookstores: I inevitably head to the Strand Bookstore on Broadway, corner of Twelfth Street, that cathedral of second-hand books where it is possible to find or order everything, and where on Saturday afternoon or Sunday morning one can see celebrities from the world of literature, theatre or cinema, in jeans and without make-up, looking for something with which to feed their obsessions.

I am interested in the insistence on the word "everything": the idea that there are bookshops like the Library of Babel, as opposed to those like Jakob Mendel's table in Café Gluck. Strand boasts that it houses one and a half million titles. The record size, quantity and extent are advertising tools that suit a large number of bookshops in the United States, a naturally megalomaniac country. And neighbouring Canada: the World's Biggest Bookstore is in Ontario and was previously a big bowling alley. Its twenty kilometres of shelves were immortalised, in a manner of speaking, by the memory machine, the reader on automatic pilot Number 5, in the sequence of "Short Circuit", when its voracious need for data provokes mayhem in the bookshop. On this side of the frontier, if we are to believe the hype, the biggest academic bookshop is in Chicago. In the months that I lived in Hyde Park I was a fan of the Seminary Co-op Bookstore on 57th Street, the best refuge when it was snowing, and close to the university library. Its main distinguishing feature was "The Front Table", a coloured leaflet that reviewed the main new titles, though there was also a selection of other free cultural publications. It is one of those eminently subterranean bookshops, in whose rooms one can spend long periods browsing in complete solitude. However, the main base was not in 57th Street but where the cooperative was founded, in the basement of the Theology Seminary in the middle of the campus which is now home to the Becker Friedman Institute for Research in Economics. The University of Chicago has good reason to be proud of the twenty-four Nobel Prize winners in economics among its professors, guest researchers and ex-alumni, but nobody could give me many clues as to the movements of Saul Bellow and John Maxwell Coetzee through

its corridors and neo-Gothic lecture theatres. On the other hand, in the digital magazine *Gapers Block*, I do find the account of a bookseller, Jack Cella, who remembers that Saul Bellow used to love leafing through books that had just arrived, as they were being unpacked: the latest members of the community.

Conversely, Prairie Lights did find a way to benefit from the nearby, most famous creative writing programme in the country at the University of Iowa. Its web page lists the seven Nobel Literature Prize winners who have visited them: Seamus Heaney, Czesław Miłosz, Derek Walcott, Saul Bellow, Toni Morrison, Orhan Pamuk and J. M. Coetzee. It was the personal project of Jim Harris, a graduate in journalism who decided to invest a small inheritance in the book trade and open the bookshop in 1978. The present premises, now managed by his former employees, coincidentally occupy the space that in the 1930s housed a literary society where Carl Sandburg, Robert Frost and Sherwood Anderson used to meet. One of the former students of the renowned Writers' Workshop, Abraham Verghese, has written in the chapter about Prairie Lights in *My Bookstore*: *Writers Celebrate Their Favorite Places to Browse, Read and Shop*, that his booksellers were also in a way teachers: shaping sensibilities and treating him as a serious writer even when he had less confidence in his own potential. In the same volume Chuck Palahniuk focuses on Powell's City of Books and waxes ironic about the circuits for the launch of the latest books: Mark Twain died of stress on a reading tour.

The next stop on our coast-to-coast bookshop ride could be Tattered Cover in Denver, since that is where all the important authors on tour in the United States stop, including Barack Obama. This project has been led from 1973 by the activist Joyce Meskis, a genuine civil rights leader, who is so appreciated by her neighbours and customers that 200 of them have helped the bookshop on its moves, transporting boxes of books to nearby premises. Meskis applies a small profit margin, from 1 to 5 per cent on the price of the book, in order to be able to compete with the bookshop chains and show a customer that he or she is the great protagonist, the one who most profits. Her pleasant approach is not restricted to personal and economic fields, it is also translated into dozens of armchairs that, according to the owner, are an attempt to remind the visitor that he is in somewhere like his own front room. Tattered Cover has always been characterised by its defence of civil rights, but in 2000 that struggle became national news when, by appealing to the afore-mentioned First Amendment, it succeeded in persuading the Supreme Court of Colorado to decide in its favour, after the police tried to force Meskis to inform on the customer who had bought a particular book, which, according to them, was a manual on how to manufacture meta-amphetamines. In the end it turned out to be a handbook on Japanese calligraphy.

Two thousand kilometres further on – leaving Las Vegas and Reno to our left – we would come to another North American bookshop that no writer on tour can afford to miss out, Powell's in Portland that must appeal to Palahniuk because it is so like a ca-sino: countless interconnected rooms, a labyrinth in which each of the nine rooms has its own name (Golden, Pink, Purple), like the characters in "Reservoir Dogs", or like a vast brothel. As in the Strand or other megalomaniac bookshops, quality is a treasure to be sought out among layer after layer of quantity. No less than a million and a half books. Visiting this shop is a journey you under-take with a map of the establishment as a guide: the aim may be to find the Rare Books Room, with its eighteenth- and nineteenth-century volumes, or simply to go to the café, and take a breather and rest. Because Powell's in Portland is so famous owing to its size (it may *really* even be the biggest in the world) it has become a tourist attraction and, as such, is constantly explored by visitors from the whole of this enormous country.

California is in the south. To reach Los Angeles, where Quentin Tarantino's first film was shot, where so many fictional bookshops have been filmed and even built, you still have to cross Berkeley and San Francisco. It is really worth one's time visiting Moe's Books in the small university city, a building with 200,000 new, second-hand and old books; a bookshop with over half a century of history. It was founded by Moe Moskowitz in 1959, and consequently established itself as a cultural project in the political years of the 1960s with their protests against the Vietnam War. In 1968 the bookseller was arrested for selling shocking material (like Robert Crumb's comics and Valerie Solanas's books). After his demise in 1997 his daughter Doris took the helm, which she now shares with Eli, her own son, a third generation of independent booksellers. And in neighbouring San Francisco four important Californian bookshops await us: the oldest in the state (Books Inc.), the country's most famous one (City Lights), perhaps the most fascinating one I know (Green Apple Books) and one of the most interesting that I have visited in terms of art and community (Dog Eared Books).

The history of the first goes back to the middle of the nineteenth century at the height of the Gold Rush when in 1853 the Swabian traveller Anton Roman started selling books and musical instruments to miners in Shasta City at the Shasta Book Store opposite the El Dorado Hotel. Its horizons were soon broadened by the addition of Roman's Picture Gallery: it was, after all, a desert where everything had to be created, culture, history, music, the frontier imagination. Four years later it moved to San Francisco, where the trade in texts and images was extended further to include its own printing and publishing business. It has changed place and name so often since then that all that remains is a slogan: "The oldest independent bookshop in the West". We have already mentioned the establishment that is still run by Lawrence Ferlinghetti, and that was in terms of the French connection we find time and again in the history of North American culture. Naturally, it is based in the centre of the city next to Chinatown, Little Italy and most of the tourist icons. Green Apple Books, on the other hand, is off the beaten track, one could say: on the main roadway through the hybrid district of Clement. It appears in the novel, *The Royal Family*, by William T. Vollmann, as it really is: the place to go in search of answers. The character in the novel opens the Buddhist Scriptures and reads: "Things do not come and do not go, neither do they appear and disappear; therefore, one does not get things or lose things." However, on my first visit to San Francisco, I went on a devout pilgrimage to City Lights because I still believed in my invisible passport; when I returned ten years later and they took me to Clement Street, I felt I was gaining something I would never lose.

Green Apple Books unequivocally demonstrates its vocation as a traditional neighbourhood bookshop in the balance it strikes between new and second-hand books, in its calculated improvisation, in its dozens of passageways, uneven surfaces, connecting doorways and stairwells, in the dozens of handwritten reviews to guide readers and customers in their imminent choices, and its wooden floor. A bookshop is defined above all by what stands out: the posters, the photographs, the books recommended or displayed to draw attention. In Green Apple Books they have framed the "Open Letter" by Hunter S. Thompson, who came to San Francisco in the mid-1960s attracted by the magnetic power of the hippy movement. The stairs are dominated by a huge map of the United States, but there is also a section in the entrance called "Read the World", where new translations are recommended and displayed. And the right-hand-side wall in the basement is a genuine museum of African and Asian masks, the work of Richard Savoy, who opened the business in 1967, when he was barely twenty-five, his only work experience being as a radio engineer with American Airlines. But above all, it is about reading. In the labyrinthine bookshop on Clement Street you find them crouching down, almost hidden, as if confined within the cells of a Buddhist monastery or in the catacombs of the early Christians, of all ages and conditions, standing, squatting or sitting down: readers. And that is priceless.

A bookshop is a community of believers. This idea is nowhere better illustrated than in Dog Eared Books, which since 1992 has created a real atmosphere of empathy with the inhabitants of Mission District. As well as magazines, books and graphic art, we find in the window on that street corner the perfect expression of the bond of love and respect a bookstore must create with its reader customers: an altar to the dead that artist Verónica de Jesús updates weekly. Anonymous neighbours, personal friends, writers and pop stars come together here. Famous readers or complete unknowns united by death and paid homage in a bookshop that, above all, feels itself to be part of a neighbourhood.

Somebody had stuck on a bookshelf in Green Apple Books the photograph of Marilyn Monroe reading *Ulysses*. The Hollywood Body reading the Mind of an Irish Writer exiled in Trieste or Paris. The United States reading Europe. In the old film "Funny Face" that kind of opposition had experienced an interesting twist. Under instructions from the editor of the magazine where he is employed, a fashion photographer played by Fred Astaire has to find models who harness beauty and thought, who "think as well as they look". The bookshop Embryo Concepts in Greenwich Village – invented in a Hollywood studio – is the place where the hunt-and-capture operation is carried out: there Fred Astaire meets Jo Stockton, a beautiful amateur philosopher (with the face and skin of Audrey Hepburn), and persuades her to accompany him to a fashion show in Paris. She accepts not because she is attracted by possible photograph shoots, but because it might enable her to attend the classes of a philosopher who is an expert on "empathicalism". The inversion of traditional roles is striking in a film from 1957: he represents superficiality and she intellectual depth. However, in the end, as is only right in a musical, they kiss and the kiss erases, or at least freezes, all previous friction. In "Notting Hill" there is an opposite starting point: he (Hugh Grant) runs an independent bookshop specialising in travel and she (Julia Roberts) is a Hollywood actress. While she browses upon entering his shop for the first time (the fictional Travel Book Company is in reality a shoe shop now called Notting Hill), he catches a book thief and is politely explaining the options of buying or returning the book hidden in his trousers. The thief recognises the famous actress and asks her for an autograph; thebookseller, on the other hand, simply falls in love with her.

As an erotic space, every bookshop is the supreme meeting place: for booksellers and books, for readers and booksellers, for readers on the hoof. The familiar features shared by bookshops throughout the world, their nature as refuges or bubbles, means that encounters are more likely there than elsewhere. The strange sensation of knowing by the title that that book, published in Arabic or Japanese, is by Tolstoy or Lorca, or else by the author's photo or some kind of intuition. That shared experience of a re-encounter in some bookshop in the world. It is scarcely surprising that falling in love in a bookshop is a well-established literary and cinematic theme. In "Before Sunset", the sequel to "Before Sunrise", the story of the nine delicious hours the two protagonists shared in Vienna nine years earlier, while they were both travelling through Europe by train, they meet up again in Shakespeare and Company. True serendipity: he has become a writer and that is the place where American writers launch their books in Paris. The moment when he recognises her has all the magic of a classic erotic performance. While he tells his audience the plot of a story he would like to write, a book made from a minimum present and maximum memories, which would endure for as long as a pop song, by way of flashbacks we enter the coded story of what that other superficial story would in fact retell, fragments of the preceding film, of that night in Vienna. Then he turns to his right and notices her. He recognises her immediately. He becomes extremely agitated. They only have a few hours to pick up the thread they dropped almost a decade before. What prevails is a romantic attitude to the idea of the bookshop: it is a symbol of communication, of friendship, of love, as one detects in other products of popular culture, from novels like *The Shadow of the Wind* and *Seaglass Summer* to the romantic comedies "Remember Me" and "Julie & Julia", both with scenes shot in Strand, and above all, "You've Got Mail", where an independent bookshop is threatened by the branch that a chain has opened around the corner while, simultaneously, the person running the first (Meg Ryan) and the manager of the second (Tom Hanks) are engaged in an epistolary relationship, though they do not know each other's names or faces.

Platonic love: love of knowledge. In an episode of the first series of the television series "The West Wing" we are shown the police operation that is necessary whenever President Bartlett feel likes buying the antiquarian books that are a real love of his. The majority of volumes he collects are from the nineteenth century or the beginning of the twentieth and are quite eccentric: on bear hunting, skiing in the Alps, Phaedrus and Lucretius. In contemporary fiction a bookshop signifies a space for the kind of knowledge that can't be found in official institutions - the library or university – because as it is a private business it avoids issues of regulation and because booksellers are even freakier than librarians or university lecturers. This is why fantasy and horror genres have made the bookshop run by an atypical sage who hoards banned or esoteric knowledge an alternative to the antiquarian shop with a secret room or basement. Several comics from the twenty-first century have as refrain the idea of the bookshop as a clandestine archive, for instance *The Boys* by Garth Ennis and Darick Robertson, where the basement of a comics shop protects the real memory of the super-heroic world, or *Neonomicon*, by Alan Moore, in whose bookshop you can buy all kinds of magic and sadomasochistic titles. This passage from the story "The Battle that Ended the Century", by H.P. Lovecraft, illustrates perfectly this idea of an alternative subculture on the periphery of the system:

> Mr Talcum's report on the event, illustrated by the well-known artist Klarkash-Ton (who esoterically depicted the fighters as boneless fungi) was reprinted after repeated rejections by the discriminating editor of the Windy City Grab-bag – as a broadside by W. Peter Chef. This, through the efforts of Odis Adelbert Kline, was finally placed on sale in the bookshop of Smearum and Weep, three and a half copies finally being disposed of thanks to the alluring catalogue description supplied by Samuelus Philanthropus, Esq.

However, it is not only occultism, magic, religion or books banned by the Inquisition or dictatorships that are to be found in bookshop alcoves and basements, any title bearing the aura of what is secret, little known, of a book for the happy few, the immense minority, connoisseurs, initiates, can be lodged in that crypt for relics or the strong box. When published, most books are democratically available to everyone: the price is calculated according to factors in the present. As the years go by, according to the good fortune of a work (and author), its rarity or aura, its status as a classic and its power as a myth, prices can rocket and enter an aristocratic dimension, or plummet until it is worth the same as any rubbish or cast-off. A book can be hunted down as much for its magical powers as its market value, and both factors often go together. When George Steiner, for example, reminisces about his discovery of the work of Borges, he does so in these terms:

> I recall an early connoisseur in the cavernous rear of a bookstore in Lisbon showing me – this was in the early 1950s – Borges' translation of *Orlando* by Virginia Woolf, his prologue to a Buenos Aires edition of Kafka's *Metamorphosis*, his key essay on the artificial language devised by Bishop John Wilkins, published in *La Nación* in 1942, and (rarest of rare items) *Dimensions of My Hope*, a collection of short essays published in 1926 but, by Borges' wish, never reprinted. These slim objects were displayed to me with an air of fastidious condescension. And rightly. I had arrived late at the secret place.

In Paris the Alain Brieux bookshop combines antique books and prints with human skulls and nineteenth-century surgical equipment. An authentic cabinet of curiosities. The image of the antiquarian bookshop as a store of rarities oscillates between real referents and what is imagined, like all images with regard to that human impulse we call fiction. The Flourish and Blotts bookshop, in Diagon Alley, with a secret doorway behind Charing Cross Road in

London, is one of the establishments where Harry Potter and the other student magicians go to stock up on school books at the start of each year. The Livraria Lello & Irmão in Oporto was used as the location for the filming of the screen version. On the other hand, Monsieur Labisse's bookshop in "Hugo", which has similar charms, was made expressly for the film. Forty thousand books were required to that end. Alfred Hitchcock also used a Hollywood studio to re-create a bookshop, the Argonaut in San Francisco, in order to shoot a famous scene in "Vertigo". The place is renamed the Argosy in the script and portrayed in the terms we have been outlining: an emphasis on its antiquity, a twilight scene, a supply of old volumes that preserve esoteric knowledge, and above all a specialist focus on the California of the pioneers that justifies the visit of Scottie, in his search for data on "sad Charlotte" as defined by Pop Leibel, the fictional bookseller inspired by the real Robert D. Haines who befriended Hitchcock as a result of the latter's visits to the Argonaut. "She died," continues Leibel. "How?" enquires Scottie. "By her own hand," replies the bookseller, and he smiles sadly. "There are so many stories . . ." The screenplay reads: "It has gone dark inside the bookshop and the characters are reduced to silhouettes."

I have just discovered on the web that the Book City bookshop in Hollywood has closed down. It was a huge store of second-hand and bargain-basement volumes, a sort of West Coast replica of Strand, a stone's throw from the Boulevard of the Stars. They also sold screenplays. There were big cardboard boxes full of them, at $10, $5 or $1: for the price of pulp fiction, typed scripts, stapled together, scripts that were never filmed, perhaps never even read, bought by weight from the production companies that received them in excess, with black-and-white, opaque and transparent plastic covers, bound with plastic spirals, the same plastic that Andy Warhol so adored.

VIII

America (II): From North to South

The Leonardo da Vinci Bookshop in Rio de Janeiro must be the most poeticised in the world. Márcio Catunda dedicated a poem, "A Livraria", to it, in which he describes the passageway leading to its entrails in the basement of the Edifício Marquês de Herval, and those shop windows luridly lit to create artificial daylight. The manager, Milena Piraccini, photocopied it for me, and I remember talking to her about the history of an institution that the previous year – it was the end of 2003 – had existed for fifty years. We were standing next to two desks, where two huge calculators posed as fake cash registers, computers being banned, next to a complete collection of La Pléiade. Her mother, Vanna Piraccini, an Italian with a Romanian father, officially took over the business in 1965, after the death of her husband Andrei Duchade, though she had managed it from the very beginning. Vanna faced the greatest adversities in the history of the trade and overcame them: economic recessions, the long military dictatorship, and the fire that completely destroyed the shop in 1973. Her friend Carlos Drummond de Andrade wrote: "The subterranean shop/exhibits its treasures/as if defending them/from sudden famines."

Right opposite, another bookshop has existed in that underground gallery, one that was also to become a landmark: Berinjela. Founded by Daniel Chomski in 1994 – as I was told by the publisher Aníbal Cristobo, who lived in Rio at the beginning of the century, "It's a bookshop that reminds me of the one in the film 'Smoke': a meeting place for writers that can as easily lead to a recording label as a publishing house (it brought out the four issues of *Modo de usar*, perhaps the best contemporary poetry magazine in Brazil), or a quasi-clandestine den for the organisation of championships of that mysterious game, *futebotão*, or simulated football." I imagine a synergy is created between the two shops similar to the one once experienced on rue de l'Odéon. Though underground. Not anymore. I now discover while updating this book, which is eternally behind the times, that Leonardo da Vinci closed its doors in 2015. Half of that energetic embrace disappeared.

Also dedicated to the Livraria Leonardo da Vinci is a poem by Antonio Cicero, which I have a photocopy of and will translate:

> Rio seemed infinite
> to the adolescent I used to be.
> Boarding the Castelo bus alone,
> jumping off at the end of the line,
> walking fearlessly,
> to the centre of the forbidden city,
> in a crowd that didn't notice that
> I didn't belong there, and suddenly,
> anonymous amid the anonymous,
> feeling euphoric, sure I belonged there,
> and them to me, going into side streets,
> alleys, avenues, arcades,
> cinemas, bookshops: Leonardo
> da Vinci Larga Rex Central Colombo
> Marreca Íris Meio-Dia Cosmos
> Alfândega Cruzeiro Carioca
> Marrocos Passos Civilizacão
> Cavé Saara São José Rosário
> Passeio Público Ouvidor Padrão

Vitória Lavradio Cinelândia:
places I didn't know before
opening onto infinite streets
corners forever spreading
across every city that exists.

An adolescent gazing at the city, its spaces and culture. An eroti-cised, all-consuming gaze. For Juan García Madero, poetry – in the beginning – is to be found in the arts faculty of the U.N.A.M. and his room in the Lindavista suburb, but it soon shifts to certain bars and cafés and visceral-realist haunts and bookshops where he can satisfy his hunger on those lonely days when he has nobody to talk to. In the opening pages of Roberto Bolaño's *Savage Detectives*, liter-ature is sexualised: it could not be any different given his adolescent protagonists. Juan discovers a poem by Efrén Rebolledo, recites it, imagines a waitress riding him and masturbates several times. Soon after, one of the literary gatherings ends in a blowjob. While drink and sex lord it over literature by night, by day it is framed by book-shops, in the labyrinth of which he tries to find "two disappeared friends":

> Since I don't have anything to do, I've decided to go look-ing for Belano and Ulises Lima in the bookstores of Mexico City. I've discovered the antiquarian bookstores Plinio el Joven, on Venustiano Carranza. The Lizardi bookstore, on Donceles. The antiquarian bookstores Rebeca Nodier,

at Mesones and Pino Suárez. At Plinio el Joven the only shop assistant is a little old man who, after waiting obsequiously on a "scholar from the Colegio de México", soon fell asleep in a chair next to a stack of books, supremely ignoring me. I stole an anthology of Marco Manilio's *Astronómica*, with a prologue by Alfonso Reyes, and *Diary of an Unknown Writer* by a Japanese author set during the Second World War. At Lizardi I thought I saw Monsiváis. I tried to sidle up next to him to see what book he was looking at, but when I reached him, Monsiváis turned and stared straight at me, with a hint of a smile, I think, and keeping a firm grip on his book and hiding the title, he went to talk to one of the assistants. Provoked, I filched a little book by an Arab poet called Omar Ibn al-Farid, published by the university, and an anthology of young American poets put out by City Lights. By the time I left, Monsiváis was gone.

The passage comes from a sequence (December 8, 9, 10 and 11 in the first part, "Mexicans Lost in Mexico (1975)") devoted to the bookshop aspect of Mexico City. And to bibliokleptomania: a practice as old as books themselves. There are descriptions of visits to Rebeca Nodier, Sótano, Mexicana, Horacio, Orozco, Milton, El Mundo and La Batalla del Ebro bookshops, the owner of the latter being "a little old Spaniard by the name of Crispín Zamora", to whom he confesses that "he stole books because he didn't have any money". In total: two books Don Crispín gives him, and twenty-four books he steals in three days. One of them is by Lezama Lima: we never find out the title. It is inevitable that in a novel about growing up bookshops are linked to voracious desire. In *Paradiso*, one of the characters suffers a sexual dysfunction related to books and a friend plays a joke on him, in a bookshop, in fact:

148

When the bookseller came in, he asked him, "And has James Joyce's *Goethe* arrived, the one that's just been published in Geneva?" The bookseller winked at him, detecting the mocking nature of his question. "No, not yet, though we're expecting it any day now." "When it arrives, keep a copy for me," said the person talking to Foción, who did not get the joke referring to a book that had never been written. The voice was thick, coated with crispy meringue saliva, his sweaty hands and forehead revealing to boot the violence of his neuro-vegetative crises. "The same collection has a Chinese Sartre from the fourth century BC," said Foción. "Ask the bookseller to keep a copy of that too." "A Chinese Sartre who must have discovered a point of contact between *wu wei* and the nothingness of the Sartrean existentialists."

The crazy conversation about invented books continues, until the bookseller's interlocutor leaves the premises, walks up calle Obispo and goes to the hotel bedroom where he is living. Then the narrator tells us that he was suffering from "a sexual crisis that showed itself in an artificial, precipitate cultural anxiety that became pathological when he confronted the latest books in bookshops and the publication of rare books." Foción knows that and enjoys the passing lunacy in "the labyrinth", which is what he calls bookshops. Erection. Fetish. The accumulation of stocks. The accumulation of erotic experiences is like a summation of different readings: their trace is virtual, pure memory. Stealing or buying books or receiving them as presents means possessing them: for a systematic reader, the shape of his library can be read, if not as a correlative of his whole life, at least as a parallel to his development as an individual during his youth, when that ownership is decisive.

Guillermo Quijas was eighteen when his grandfather, the teacher and bookseller Ventura López, asked him to take the manuscript of a book to a designer, then to the printer, and finally collect the copies. As if those invisible bytes magically gave rise to volumes with pages, a smell and weight. However, that book did not actually come out of nothing: its existence formed part of a chain of meaning that went back as far as the 1930s when a very youthful Ventura López worked his socks off to get a grant and graduate as a rural teacher and, sometime later, as a primary-school teacher. He was sacked from his teaching job because he was the driving force behind an agricultural cooperative and had joined the Communist Party in 1949. Then with the help of some comrades in a similar situation he created a common fund that allowed them to open a bookshop-cum-stationery shop, which became a cultural centre and literacy project that in the end also published a list of books about local culture. The Maestro died in 2002 but La Proveedora Escolar (the School Supplier) still exists in Oaxaca, thanks to his grandson's vocation. The two premises he inherited and five new ones coexist with Quijas's personal project, the Almadía publishing house, an Arabic word that means "boat".

While orderliness tends to predominate in bookshops that sell new books, chaos reigns in second-hand shops: the disorderly accumulation of knowledge. The names of the bookshops themselves often suggest as much. In calle Donceles and adjacent streets we find Inframundo, El Laberinto or El Callejón de los Milagros (Miracle Alley), non-computerised shops where finding a book depends exclusively on a precarious system of classification, good fortune, inertia and, above all, the memory and intuition of the bookseller. Echoes of the grotto or cavern, of the Zarathustra bookshop described by Valle-Inclán – that Spanish-Mexican, universal writer, and exceptional brain – in *Bohemian Lights*: "Shelves of books kick up a fuss and cover the walls. Four horrific prints from a serial novel paper over the four panes of glass in the door. The cat, parrot, dog and bookseller converse in the cavern." In Caracas La Gran Pulpería del Libro (the Big Book Grocery Store) takes the reality of a subterranean bookshop to the extreme, by overflowing: books pile up on the floor as if they had spilt from the shelves that had been attempting to contain them for years. Its owner, the historian and journalist Rafael Ramón Castellanos, who founded the business in 1976 and has combined ever since work as a bookseller and writer, was asked in an interview about how the books were classified and he replied that all attempts at computerising them had failed and that everything was in "his memory and the memories of the shop assistants and his son Rómulo".

When I was having lunch one day with Ulises Milla in mid-2012 in a restaurant in Caracas it suddenly occurred to me that that was the nearest I would ever be (at least phonetically) to Ulises Lima. The history he recounted was a history of exile from Spain and Latin America, a history of the migrations that populated that territory and built a culture the route map to which Bolaño drew with jagged edges. Bookshops that transform deep, natural and overwhelming sorrow into individual memories that are human, brief and always evanescent. Benito, Leonardo and Ulises: three generations of publishers and booksellers with a surname that suggests speed, distance and translation. *Ulises Milla* – I thought in that restaurant serving meat accompanied by cream cheese and avocado – is almost a tautology. He spent fifteen years dedicated to graphic design, as a strategy to dodge the family inheritance. But he designed books. And he ended up as a publisher and bookseller.

Benito Milla was born in Villena, Alicante, in 1918, and, as the secretary of the Libertarian Youth of Catalonia, became part of the Republican exile of 1939. After a few years in Paris, where Leonardo, his first son, was born, his wife persuaded him ("my grandmother was behind all my grandfather's house moves") to move to Montevideo where he started out with a book stall in the Plaza de la Libertad and finally founded Editorial Alfa and managed several cultural magazines for sixteen years of his life, between 1951 and 1967, years of economic crisis and political conflict in Uruguay that would lead to the military dictatorship in the following decade. "My grandfather left Montevideo in 1967 to go to Caracas and take charge of the newly established Monte Ávila Editores," he told me. "Alfa continued in Montevideo in the hands of my father and in 1973 we moved to Buenos Aires taking the publishing house with us, from where we had to flee when the military came to power after the death of Perón; it wasn't until 1977 that Leonardo landed in Caracas and the Venezuelan period of Alfa began, which for administrative reasons had to be called Alfadil." His grandfather's project would have a third phase in Barcelona ("my grandmother is Catalan"), from 1980 until his death in 1987, when he was a partner in the Laia publishing house. That ended badly. Closing the circle. As if circles, which are tangible spaces, could be closed in the multiple time of parallel universes. He was the publisher of Juan Carlos Onetti,

Eduardo Galeano, Mario Benedetti and Cristina Peri Rossi (there is pride in Ulises' voice). He progressed from anarchism to a humanism whose key word – as Fernando Aínsa has reminded us – was *bridge*: between human beings and their reading, between the countries of Latin America, between both shores of the Atlantic. And between different generations of the same family: Leonardo Milla, who as a child did not eat breakfast until the first book of the day was sold, transformed Alfa Publishing into the Alfa Publishing Group in the 1980s and expanded its network of bookshops (though he was never aware that it could be called a chain) with two premises known as Ludens and three as Alexandria 332 BC (the year when Alexandra the Great defeated the Persians in Egypt and started building the city and its myth).

In 1942, while he was inventing his own language based on shorthand, which he called "*la taqui*", and in which several pieces of writing have been preserved that have yet to be decoded, Felisberto

Hernández and his wife, the painter Amalia Nieto, opened a bookshop, El Burrito Blanco (the Little White Donkey), in the garage belonging to the house of his in-laws. Naturally, it was a failure. Montevideo is a mysterious city and the capital of a mysterious country full of such anecdotes and stories. It is similar to Switzerland and Portugal in its dimensions and pace of life. During the time I spent in Argentina, I used to travel to the neighbouring country every three months to renew my tourist visa, receive the payment for my articles in *El País* and visit its bookshops, full of decatalogued Argentinian books and Uruguayan books you could only buy in Uruguay, like those published by the local branch of Alfaguara and by Trilce. With each fresh incursion I would uncover layers of a history of periodic migrations. And for that reason I wasn't surprised to find other traces in Peru, years later, on my only visit to its capital.

El Virrey (the Viceroy) in Lima has a corner with a chessboard between two armchairs. The ceiling fans turn slowly, like a gentle whisk. Everything is wood, books and wood. And the distant memory of exile. I decided to investigate the bookshop's history and with that in mind I asked the bookseller whether a summary existed somewhere. Her name was Malena. She said she would have to speak to her mother and gave me the email of Chachi Sanseviero, to whom I wrote straight away hoping for an interview. It wasn't possible, her excuse was that she had lost her voice, but with her reply she sent the text she had written for *Cuadernos Hispanoamericanos*. The Virrey in Lima opened its doors in 1973 financed by savings made in anticipation of a long exile from Uruguay. Its logo carries an image of the Inca Atahualpa holding a book in one hand and a *quipu* in the other: the means of communication of the two cultures, the imposed and the original, united in a symbol of assimilation. Apparently, the Inca leader, when he found out that Chachi's book was sold as the genuine history of the true god, threw it to the ground in order to reaffirm that the truth was on his side of the pantheon. Chachi writes of the bookseller as somebody who always defers reading and transforms books into "eternal possibilities", "because, except in a very few cases, she never finishes reading them". She leafs through them, takes them to the counter, perhaps even home, to her desk or bedside table, where she will not finish reading them either.

The family tradition took another turn or performed an unexpected pirouette in 2012 when Walter and Malena opened their own bookshop, Sur, with the idea of following in the path their father Eduardo had pioneered. I can see on the web that it is a delightful bookshop in which the straight lines of the shelves and the curves of the tables of new titles join up to ensure that books are one hundred per cent the protagonists. I sometimes think the Internet is the limbo where the bookshops I could not experience personally await me. A limbo of virtual spectres.

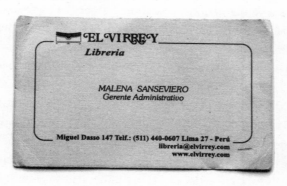

After spending the crucial years of his adolescence in Mexico City, following the opposite route to the one followed by Ernesto Guevara twenty years earlier, in 1973 Bolaño travelled overland to Chile, where he intended to support Salvador Allende's democratic revolution. He was arrested a few days after the Pinochet coup and saved from likely death thanks to the fact that one of the policemen guarding him had been a schoolfriend. He returned to Mexico also overland to complete the life experiences that would nourish his first masterpiece. He died three months before I arrived in the Chilean capital. In El Fondo de Cultura Económica bookshop I bought the Planeta editions of *The Skating Rink* and *Nazi Literature in America*. In the latter, the most extended biographies belong to "the fantastic Schiaffino brothers" (Italo and Argentino, *alias* El Grasa) and Carlos Ramírez Hoffman (*alias* El Infame). Two Argentinians and a Chilean.

Although he spent most of his life in Mexico and Spain, which, which formed the settings for much of his work, his literary allegiance was with the Southern Cone. As a Latin-Americanist he read widely work from the whole continent, as an adoptive Catalan and Spaniard he read his contemporaries, as a passionate admirer of French poetry he learned from its great masters, as a compulsive reader he devoured every title of world literature that was put before him. As a young man in Mexico he fought the figure of Octavio Paz regarding what he meant in terms of cultural politics; in his adult life he would periodically encounter enemies, literary translations from the armies against which he competed in his meetings in Blanes with fans of war games and strategy, but most of all he felt part of the tradition of the Southern Cone – if such a tradition really exists – and in his ambitious writer's mind that tradition was split in two: poetry and narrative. Chile and Argentina. Bolaño the poet felt close to Lihn and Nicanor Parra. And near and far at the same time, as regards Pablo Neruda, who is to Chilean poetry what Borges is to Argentinian narrative: they are Monsters, Fathers, Saturns devouring their children. It is strange that Juan Rulfo was not held in esteem by Mexican writers in the second half of the last century whereas Paz certainly did play that portentous, castrating role (as even Carlos Fuentes did too). I often wonder what would have happened if Rulfo had become the principal model for Spanish-American writers in our *fin de siècle* and had occupied the place history reserved for Borges. The rural, anachronistic, minimalist Rulfo, who looked to the past, who believed in History, who said no, in the place of urban, modern, precise Jorge Luis Borges, who looked to the future, who scorned history, who said yes. In "Dance Card", Bolaño tells the story of his copy of *Twenty Love Poems and a Song of Despair* and the long distance it travelled between town after town in southern Chile, and then around Spain, and recounts how at the age of eighteen he had read the great poets of Latin America and how his friends were split into supporters of Vellejo or Neruda and that he was thoroughly isolated as a supporter of Parra. In this account, Chilean poetry is organised into dancing partners, with descendants and disciples of Neruda, Huidobro, Mistral and De Rokha, and the heirs to Parra and Lihn. His alliance with Parra and Lihn is fissured by Neruda, the crevice through which the hugeness of Neruda slips, an influence no poet in the Spanish language can escape. In "Dance Card", recognition of Neruda's political inconsistency leads to a crazy excursus on Hitler, Stalin and Neruda himself and a genuinely Bolañesque passage on institutional repression and common graves, the International Brigades and the torture racks. Ultimately, Neruda remains a contradictory mystery.

When his sister gave him Neruda's book, Bolaño was reading the complete works of Manuel Puig. In terms of story-writing it was in "Sensini" (from *Telephone Calls*) where he best defined his connections with left-wing committed Argentinian literature, through the character of Antonio Di Benedetto. The theoretical essay "The Vagaries of the Literature of Doom" was where the Chilean positioned himself in respect of Argentinian literature and tackled the question of the canon with no holds barred. Bolaño repeatedly recalled his debt to Borges and Cortázar, without whom one cannot grasp the encyclopedic ambition of his work, his interest in autofiction and the short story or structure – the paths opened up by

Hopscotch, The Savage Detectives and 2666. It was in the latter in particular that he put himself forward as Borges' greatest heir, launching into severe criticism of his Argentinian contemporaries and the short cuts and roundabout routes they took to elude the centrality of Borges: those who followed Osvaldo Soriano, those who saw Roberto Arlt as the Anti-Borges, those who championed Osvaldo Lamborghini. That is to say, many writers who aren't mentioned, Ricardo Piglia and César Aira.

During the three of four days I spent in Santiago, I decided, no doubt in a rush, that Libros Prólogo was the bookshop that most interested me. I noted at the time:

> It's not as big as the University Library in Alameda (with its wall-to-wall carpets and 1970s look) or the Chilean Feria del Libro chain, nor does it have the charm of the second-hand bookshops on calle San Diego, but it is well stocked and in calle Merced, next to a cinema, theatre and café and close to the antiquarian and second-hand bookshops in calle Lastarria.

I haven't kept any other notes. I remember it as a place of resistance, a centre that nourished cultural life during the dictatorship, but I have no way of proving that or finding out. Nothing on search engines. Perhaps mine was the delirium of a traveller seduced by *Night in Chile*, the novel in which Bolaño constructs the lunatic discourse of the priest Sebastián Urrutia Lacroix, who under the pseudonym of Ibacache celebrates the savage, reactionary poetry of Ramírez Hoffman in *Distant Star*, and who in the final part of the novel remembers the lessons in political theory he gave to the Junta and the literary conversations that took place in the house of Mariana Callejas. The character is inspired by the Opus Dei priest José Miguel Ibáñez Langlois who wrote for the newspaper *El Mercurio*

under the pseudonym of Ignacio Valente, and was the author of books of philosophical and theological theory (*Marxism: Critical Vision, The Social Doctrine of the Church*), of literary criticism (*Rilke, Pound, Neruda: Three Key Contemporary Poets, Reading Parra,* and *Josemaría Escrivá, as a Writer*) and of poetry with a fondness for oxymoronic titles (*Dogmatic Poems*). He was not merely the most important literary critic during the dictatorship and the transition, he also gave seminars on Marxism to the Junta. That is, Pinochet was one of his pupils. Pinochet: the reader, the writer, the lover of bookshops. Ricardo Cuadros has written:

> Ibáñez Langlois has never acknowledged or denied his presence at the literary soirées held by Mariana Callejas in her big mansion in the wealthy district of Santiago that she ran with Michael Townley, her husband, a D.I.N.A. agent; those get-togethers were real enough and in the mansion's basement among others Carmelo Soria, a Spaniard working for the U.N., was tortured to death.

That basement in a "taken over" house is the exact opposite of what the great majority of bookshops in the world have been, still are and will ever be. There were and there are bookshops with the name of Cortázar's story in several cities (Bogotá, Lima, Palma de Mallorca . . .) because the title has been freed of its associations with the story and come to mean "space taken over by books". But the story, on the contrary, speaks about how they disappear. The narrator of "House Taken Over" regrets that no new books have arrived in the French bookshops in Buenos Aires since 1939 so he cannot continue to nourish his library with them. If the political interpretation of the story is correct and the writer is creating a metaphor for Peronism as the invader of private spaces, it is no coincidence that the first part of the house taken over includes the library. The protagonist's sister is a weaver; he is a reader. But, after the first takeover, reading is gradually erased from his life. When the house is definitively taken over and brother and sister close the door for good, they will only take with them the clothes they are wearing and a clock, but no books, the cord has been cut.

When I returned to Santiago de Chile ten years later, I felt in a state of trance, like a sleepwalker pursuing at night the threads he had left trailing on his daily treks, as if in some invisible intrigue. It was twelve noon, the blistering sun beating down, and I was walking through the Lastarria district on the verge of unconsciousness. By chance I had just found the hostel where I had lodged on my only other previous stay: perhaps it was the charge of erotic memories that had provoked my mechanical promenade, which suddenly cloaked my skin with that of someone else, the person I used to be in my early twenties. I was not surprised to find myself suddenly outside Libros Prólogo, the bookshop that had most caught my attention at that time, on those days that followed my nights in that hostel with its games, kisses and topsy-turvy sheets. Nor to see Walter Zúñiga behind the counter, as if he had been waiting for me in the same shirt, with the same wrinkles, for ten years.

"What are you reading so intently?" I asked after browsing for a few minutes.

"A biography of Fellini written by Tullo Kezich that I bought yesterday in La Feria," he replied, with the big ears of an old man who really knew how to listen. "It's odd, I've had this book here for ages, two copies, in fact, it's extraordinary that I've never sold it."

"So if you've got it, why did you buy another?"

"It was so cheap . . ."

We spoke for a while about the bookshop's other branch, which had closed down, and he confessed that the ones that really worked for him were his Karma bookshops, "specialising in fortune-telling, Tarot, New Age and martial arts". I asked him for a copy of a recently published book about a pioneering cybernetic project during the years of Salvador Allende's government—

"*Cybernetic Revolutionaries*," he interrupted as he keyed away. "Right now I'm out of stock, but I'll get you a copy in a couple of days," and he'd already picked up the telephone and was ordering it from the distributor.

A few minutes later he bade farewell with a flourish: he gave me his card. He had corrected the telephone number in black ink. It was exactly the same card I had in my bookshop archive. The same red-lettered typography. "Libros Prólogo. Literatura-Cine-Teatro". That was a very strong connection to that traveller I had been ten years earlier. Everything had changed in the city and myself except for that card. Touching that stirred me from my sleep-walking, dragged me violently from the past.

It was only natural then that I should walk fifty paces, cross the street and enter Metales Pesados and the wavelength of the present. Not an ounce of wood in the place, only aluminium shelves, the bookshop as a giant Meccano structure that welcomes books as fervently as an ironmonger's or a computer laboratory. There was Sergio Parra, in black suit and white shirt, a dandy and all sinew, sitting on a metal folding chair behind a café terrace table. I asked him for a copy of *Leñador* (*Woodcutter*) by Mike Wilson, which I had been hunting for in the Southern Cone for months. He handed it to me, hiding his gaze behind his paste glasses. I asked him about Pedro Lemebel's books and now he did finally look me in the eye.

I later discovered he had led the campaign backing Lemebel for the National Literature Prize, and that they were friends, poets and neighbours. But right then I had eyes only for the large poster of the writer and performer and the prominent display of all his books, because every bookseller deals in visibility. He recommended a couple of books I did not have, which I bought. "Metales Pesados is more of an airport than a bookshop. At any moment Mario Bellatin will walk in, or a person Mario or somebody else encouraged to drop by, friends of friends from all over the world, many leave their suitcases here, because they've already checked out of their hotels and still have a few hours to go up the hill or to the Fine Arts Museum. As I practically live here, since I work here from Monday to Sunday, I've become a kind of reference point."

The bookshop as an airport. As a place of transit: for passengers and books. A pure to-and-fro of readings. Lolita, on the other hand, far from the centre, in a corner of a residential district, preferred people to stay on. It also had a writer behind the counter: Francisco Mouat, whose passion for football had led him to devote a corner of the shop to sport. The journalist Juan Pablo Meneses accompanied me to that recently opened bookshop and showed me how Juan Villoro, Martín Caparrós, Leonardo Faccio and other friends we had in common were sparsley represented there by volumes they had devoted to the small round god. Mouat's gaze is gentle and his gestures are pleasant and welcoming, despite his intimidating height; I'm not surprised he has three full reading groups a week every Monday, Wednesday and Friday.

"A book a week is quite a pace," I say.

"We've kept that up for some time. I have readers who've been following me for years. When I opened Lolita I brought them to this new place."

Loyalty is there in the slogan: "We can't live without books." Loyalty is on the logo: a dog that belonged to the Mouat family: she looks at us, embossed on the spines of the books from the Lolita publishing house.

When on my last day in Santiago I finally visited Ulises, that space so crammed with books where the distorting mirrors that reflect the shelves and the volumes *ad infinitum* fly over and multiply you, wonderful ceiling mirrors designed by the architect Sebastian Gray, perhaps because I was in one of the most beautiful, most Borgesian of bookshops in the world, the fourth vertex of an invisible rectangle, I reflected how the other three, Libros Prólogo, Metales Pesados and Lolita, gave material form to the three tenses of every bookshop: the archival past, the transitory present and the future of communities united by desire. How, in combination they form the perfect bookshop, the bookshop I'd take to a desert island.

And I suddenly remembered a scene I had forgotten. A repeated, distant scene, a fading echo or call from a black box in the depths of the ocean, and the accident. I must be nine or ten, it's a Friday evening or Saturday morning, my mother is in the butcher's or bakery or supermarket, and I'm killing time in the neighbourhood newsagent's, Rocafonda, on the far outskirts of Barcelona. As there is no bookshop in the district, I am a true addict of kiosks, with their superhero comics and video-game magazines, of the tobacconist's Ortega, who has quite a window display of his collection of books and popular educational magazines, and of this newsagent's in the same street where the Vázquez brothers and other schoolfriends live. There are less than a hundred books at the back, behind the stands with coloured card, birthday cards and cut-outs; I have fallen in love with a manual for the perfect detective; I remember its blue cover, and I remember (and the power of the memory upset me, as I left Ulises and got into a taxi and headed to the airport) how I would read a couple of pages every week, standing up, how to get fingerprints, how to make an identikit photo, every week until Christmas or Sant Jordi finally arrived and my parents gave me the book I had so coveted. At home, after I had read it, I realised I knew it by heart.

How could I ever forget that for a large part of my childhood I had two vocations: writer and private detective. Something of the second stuck with me in my obsession for collecting stories and bookshops. Who knows whether perhaps we writers are not, above all, detectives investigating ourselves, Roberto Bolaño characters?

On the terrace of the Café Zurich in Barcelona, Natu Poblet, who runs La Clásica y Moderna bookshop in Buenos Aires, told me that in 1981, when she gave up architecture to devote herself to the family business, with two years still to run of the last dictatorship, they organised classes on their premises in literature, theatre and politics, given by people banned from the university, like David

Viñas, Abelardo Castillo, Juan José Sebreli, Liliana Heker, Enrique Pezzoni or Horacio Verbitsky. "The classes turned into literary conversations, my brother and I took along wine and whisky, lots of people came and the conversations went on till very late," she told me as she downed a glass of Jameson's; that was when the idea of harnessing a bookshop to a bar was born. It implied a 180 degree turn. Her grandfather, the Madrid bookseller, Don Emilio Poblet, founded the Poblet Brothers chain in Argentina at the beginning of the twentieth century. Her father, Francisco, opened La Clásica y Moderna in 1938 with his wife, Rosa Ferreiro, and brother and sister Natu and Paco took charge of the business after their father died in 1980. That was the year the Junta ordered the burning of a million and a half books published by the Publishing Centre of Latin America. After seven years of activity in the catacombs, with democracy re-established, they commissioned the architect Ricardo Plant to

radically transform the space that ever since has been a bar and a restaurant, as well as a bookshop and a hall for exhibitions and concerts. ("The first three years we opened twenty-four hours a day, but then we started to have problems with night-time drunks and decided to adopt a more conventional timetable.") Since then actors like José Sacristán and singers like Liza Minnelli have performed there. The piano was a present from Sandro, a habitué of La Clásica y Moderna from its frenetic heyday, and whose life story can be gleaned from the titles of some of his albums: "Beat Latino", "Sandro de América", "Sandro . . . Un ídolo", "Clásico", "Para mamá".

"I often dream of Dad's bookshop," Natu Poblet confessed as she drained her glass and we began a long stroll round night-time Barcelona. In Río de Janeiro Milena Piraccini straight away talked to me about the importance that Vanna, her mother, attached to personal contact with each of her customers, a trait of her character which could be explained by her forebears in Europe. In Caracas Ulises Milla told me about his Uruguayan family and about other booksellers from Montevideo and Caracas like Alberto Conte, who had taught him so much. Chachi Sanseviero writes:

> My teacher was Eduardo Sanseviero, a great bookseller and disciple of Don Domingo Maestro, a notable Uruguayan bookseller. Eduardo's weakness was chess, history and antique books. But he also liked poetry and had the strange gift of bringing poems into the conversation like funny stories. An unrepentant Communist, in times of despots, he enjoyed organising small conspiratorial cells. But at the end of the day, he went back to his feather duster and arranging his books.

The tradition of bookselling is one of the most secretive. Often it is a family affair: Natu, Milena, Ulises, Rómulo and Guillermo and Malena, like so many other booksellers, are in their turn the children and even grandchildren of booksellers. Almost all of them began as apprentices in the bookshops of their parents or other traffickers in printed paper. Rafael Ramón Castellanos remembers that, when he reached Caracas from the interior of Venezuela, he worked in a bookshop, Viejo y Raro (Old and Rare), that belonged to a former Argentinian ambassador: "Later on, in 1962, I created my own bookshop with the knowledge that I had acquired," the Librería de Historia that preceded the Gran Pulpería de Libros.

Isn't the figure of the bookseller rather odd? Would it not be easier to understand writer, printer, publisher, distributor, or even a literary agent? Might this oddness explain the lack of genealogies and anatomies? Hector Yánover, in *Memorias de un librero*, illuminated these paradoxes in a split second:

This is the book of a bookseller with pretensions. These are the first lines of that book. These words constitute the first on the first page. And all these words, lines and pages will make up the book. Do you, hypothetical readers, have any idea how horrific it is for a bookseller to have to write a book? A bookseller is a man who reads when he rests, and what he reads is book catalogues; when he goes for a walk, he stops in front of the windows of other bookshops; when he goes to another city, another country, he visits booksellers and publishers. Then one day this man decided to write a book about his trade. A book inside another book that will go to join the others in the windows or on the shelves of bookshops. Another book to arrange, mark, clean, replace, remove definitively. A bookseller is the being who is most aware of the futility of a book, and of its importance. That is why he is a man torn apart; a book is a commodity to buy and sell and he now constitutes that commodity. He buys and sells himself.

Yánover ran the Librería Norte in Buenos Aires and, according to Poblet, he was the city's most important bookseller in the final quarter of the last century. His daughter Débora now holds the reins of the business. He was also responsible for a renowned record collection which allowed one to hear how Cortázar and Borges, amongst others, recited their work. When the author of *The Pursuer* travelled back to his country he made the Librería Norte his centre of operations: he spent the whole of his first day in the city there and it was there that his admirers could leave letters and parcels of books for him. I do not know if those records are in a corner of the Bolaño Archive, or whether he listened to their dead voices as he did to opera and jazz. However, the bookshop that marked the life of the author of *Fictions* was the Librería de la Ciudad (the City's Bookshop), which was next to his house, on the opposite side of the calle Maipú, inside the arcade that goes by the name of Galería del Este. He visited it daily. He gave dozens of lectures there for free on matters that appealed to him and launched in its rooms the titles of the Library of Babel, the collection that he was commissioned to edit by the Milanese publisher Franco Maria Ricci and which was partly co-published by the bookshop itself. Borges and Cortázar didn't meet in a bookshop, but in a private house on Diagonal Norte, where the younger of the two turned up to discover that the Maestro had so liked his story "House Taken Over" that it was already at the printer's. They met again, years later, in Paris by which time they had both been honoured by the Académie Française. I have not been able to identify the bookshop where Cortázar bought *Opium*, by Jean Cocteau, the book that changed his work, I mean life, though I did find the interview with Hugo Guerrero Marthineitz in which the author of *Nicaragua, so violent yet so charming* tries to justify Borges' behaviour during the military dictatorship which he had backed to restore order and during which he had also defined himself as "a harmless anarchist" and as "someone revolutionised" who was "against the state and against the frontiers of states" (as his biographer, Edwin Williamson, amongst others, has pointed out). And who chose to die in Geneva. Cortázar's rhetorical gymnastics are similar to those we find in Bolaño's lines on Neruda: "He wrote some of the best stories in the world history of literature: he also wrote *A Universal History of Infamy*."

That is the model for *Nazi Literature in America*, a book written at a distance from Europe. Complexity is the most difficult thing to judge: Ibáñez Langlois defended Neruda and Parra, both fathers of Bolaño the poet, and supported the career of Raúl Zurita, whose poems written in heaven seem to have influenced to some extent the work of the infamous Ramírez Hoffman. It is not too far-fetched to read the whole of Bolaño's oeuvre as an attempt to understand his own damaged, lost, re-formed library, with as many absentees as fellow travellers, compounded by the distance that did not allow him to fully understand what was happening in Chile while at the same time affording him the critical lucidity necessary for oblique readings, a complex, contradictory library, decimated by house moves and rebuilt in European bookshops. We read in one of the articles collected in *Between Parentheses*:

As for my father, I don't remember him ever giving me a book, although occasionally we would pass a bookshop and at my request he would buy me a magazine with a long article in it on the French electric poets. All those books, including the magazines, along with many other books, were lost during my travels and moves, or else I let people borrow them and never saw them again, or I sold them or gave them away.

But there's one book I'll never forget. Not only do I remember when and where I bought it, but also the time of day, the person waiting for me outside the bookshop, what I did that night, and the happiness (completely irrational) that I felt when I had it in my hands. It was the first book I bought in Europe and I still have it. It's Borges' *Obra poética*, published by Alianza/Emecé in 1972 and long out of print. I bought it in Madrid in 1977 and, although Borges' poetry wasn't unfamiliar to me, I started to read it that night and didn't stop until eight the next morning, as if there was nothing in the world worth reading except those poems, nothing else that could change the course of the wild life that I'd lived until then, nothing else that could lead me to reflect (because Borges' poetry possesses a natural intelligence and also bravery and despair – in other words, the only things that inspire reflection and keep poetry alive).

There is no ideological questioning. There is no moral suspicion. Borges quite simply does not belong to the revolutionary tradition, though that does not reduce his value. He is less problematic than Neruda. In *Advice from a Follower of Morrison to a Fan of Joyce*, Bolaño and A.G. Porta refer insistently to the bookshops of Paris: the bookshop as a bunker for political reading (the character reads *El Viejo Topo* [*The Old Mole*] there): the bookshop as an invitation to the moral voyeur ("I have always liked bookshop windows. The surprise you get looking through the glass and finding the latest book by the biggest bastard or the most out-and-out hoodlum"), the book-shop as something beautiful in itself ("I have been in two or three of the most beautiful bookshops I have ever seen"). One of them, although he does not say which, must be the fake Shakespeare and Company. Its remake. His idea of filming *Ulysses* in Super-8 comes from that visit.

In "Vagabond in France and Belgium", one of the stories in *Last Evenings on Earth*, a character by the name of B. takes a walk round the second-hand bookshops in Paris and in one on rue du Vieux-Colombier finds "an old copy of the magazine *Luna Park*" and the name of one of its contributors, Henri Lefebvre, "suddenly lights up like a match struck in a dark room", and he buys the magazine and goes into the street, to lose himself as Lima and Belano did before him. Another name, this time of a magazine, now lights up on this page I am writing: *Berthe Trépat* was the name he and Bruno Montané chose for a mimeographed magazine they published in Barcelona in 1983. The light doesn't last long, but it is enough for us to be able to read about certain traditions of writers and booksellers, certain genetics common to the history of literature and bookshops, that is, culture, forever shifting – like a geological fault, like a quake – between the candle and the night, between the lighthouse and the night-time firmament, between the distant star and dark sorrow.

IX

Paris Without Its Myths

In 1997, the film director and writer Edgardo Cozarinsky premiered the docu-drama "Fantômes de Tanger" ("Phantoms from Tangier"), with dialogue in French and Arabic. The protagonist is a writer in crisis who reaches the shore of Africa in pursuit of some of the American spectres who have appeared in this book and the French kind who helped create the myth of the international white city. Their opposite is a boy who is looking for a way to emigrate to Spain. Literary Tangier coexists with poverty-stricken Tangier, the one that is shameful. Writing and sexual tourism interpenetrate in an uneasy relation where the boundaries are clear: customer and worker, exploiter and exploited, the one who has francs or dollars and the one aspiring to have them, with French as the *lingua franca* on both sides, in conflict despite an apparent dialogue. The traces of Foucault and Barthes fuse with those of Burroughs and Ginsberg, and converge in the brothels where young Moroccans have always prostituted themselves.

The documentary side of the film focuses on the survivors of that would-be golden era that is suddenly shown to be quite murky. "Everybody has passed this way," says Rachel Muyal in the Librairie des Colonnes, "through this bookshop." And she follows this with an anecdote I expect she has told many a time: "I saw Genet, who was drinking coffee with Choukri, when a shoeshiner came and asked whether anyone wanted their shoes polished, then Juan Goytisolo took out a 500 franc note. That must have been a couple of years before he died." Three contemporary myths in a single frame that only the bookseller seems to want to preserve intact. "I feel no nostalgia whatsoever for International Tangier, it was a wretched period," says Choukri when interviewed in the film. And Bowles badmouths Kerouac and the rest of the beats. And Juan Goytisolo told me he never met up with Genet in Tangier. And Rachel Muyal insisted years later that I had got it wrong. Cozarinsky's film is in one of my trunks from my travels; it is a V.H.S. copy you can't watch anymore.

Who knows who is right, if indeed anyone can be? All myths exist to be shattered.

I am particularly interested in the reading that the author of *For Bread Alone* gives of that gilded foreign legion. From his perspective, infected by his economic dependence on Paul Bowles who helped him write his first book and translated it into English, thus launching him on the international market, Genet was little more than an impostor, not only because his poverty was not comparable to the real poverty suffered by the Moroccans Choukri describes so graphically in his autobiographical books, but also because he did not speak a word of Spanish, which meant his tales of the underbelly of Barcelona or certain parts of Tangier could not be taken seriously. He christened Bowles the Recluse of Tangier, because he spent the last years of his life lying in bed and because, in his view, he never properly connected with the Arab culture around him. One only has to read Bowles' letters to realise that – in effect – though he physically resided in Morocco, his cultural focus was the United States, where he mentally spent more and more time as he grew old. Nonetheless, his intellect allowed him to grasp that the traffic of Anglo-Saxon writers was turning the city into a masquerade, into a fiction, and the visitors never bothered to explore Moroccan society in depth, no doubt because he himself was not interested in such a total view. In a 1958 article titled "Worlds of Tangier" he wrote: "A town, like a person, almost ceases to have a face once you know it intimately," and that requires time. At some point in the next forty years he decided a certain level of intimacy was enough. In 1948, in a letter written in the Hôtel Ville de France in Tangier, Jane said to him: "I still like Tangier, maybe because I have the feeling of being on the edge of something I will some day be part of."

Paul Bowles in Tangier begins: "How ridiculous. I think nothing is more ridiculous than that exaggerated nostalgia for the Tangier of yesterday and that longing for its past as an international zone." However, I keep wondering why Choukri really writes this book, or its twin, *Jean Genet and Tennessee Williams in Tangier*, to what extent his desire to demystify is not connected to the fact that he will only continue to be read in the West if he writes about French or Anglo-Saxon celebrities. It is not clear and never will be. The pain seeping through his words is undeniable; he is not killing his own father in vain: "He liked Morocco, not Moroccans." The Cabaret Voltaire edition of his portrait of Bowles was launched in Tangier, in mid-2012, by its translator, Rajae Boumediane El Metni, and by Juan Goytisolo: in the Librairie des Colonnes, naturally.

In her notebook of reminiscences, Muyal describes her first encounter with Choukri ("We were having dinner on that wonderful scented terrace of La Parade restaurant on a summer's night with my pretty young cousins when a young stranger tried to give us flowers. When he saw we weren't going to accept them, the boy started to take the leaves off and eat the petals"), the way she was shocked by her reading of *For Bread Alone* because she was unaware of such extreme, blatant poverty in her own city, and how he often intervened in the conversations on literature and politics in his many visits to her establishment. Tahar Ben Jelloun translated him into French, so he had two exceptional translators in the two most important languages in the world of publishing, but *For Bread Alone* soon became one of those books famously banned in its own language: "Two thousand copies were sold in a few weeks, I received from the Ministry of the Interior a note banning the sale of this book in any language." Nevertheless, fragments of his book in Arabic were published in newspapers in Lebanon and Iraq. When the narrator of Teju Cole's *Open City* (2011) asks another character to recommend him a book "in keeping with his idea of authentic fiction", the latter doesn't hesitate to jot down the title of Choukri's most famous book on a scrap of paper. He contrasts him with the more lyrical Ben Jelloun, "an Orientalist", integrated into Western circles, while Choukri "stayed in Morocco, lived with his people", never leaving "the street". In another novel published a year later and on another continent, *Street of Thieves*, Mathias Énard also has his narrator defend the Moroccan writer's magnetic qualities: "His Arabic was hard like the blows his father rained down on him, hard as hunger. A new language, a way of writing I thought was revolutionary." An American writer of Nigerian extraction, Cole hits the nail on the head when he defends the importance of Edward Said for our understanding of Oriental culture: "Difference is never accepted." What Choukri did for the whole of his life was precisely that: he defended his right to be different. Critically, nearing and distancing himself from those who gave him recognition, as always happens in life, in every kind of negotiation.

In *Never Any End to Paris*, Enrique Vila-Matas talks of Cozarinsky, whom he often came across in cinemas in the French capital: "I remember I admired him because he knew how to combine two cities, two artistic allegiances", he notes in fragment 65 in his book. He is referring to Buenos Aires, Cozarinsky's birthplace, and Paris, his adopted city; but the fact is that there is a tension between two places in all his work: between Tangier and Paris, between the West and the East, between Latin America and Europe. "I especially admired his book *Urban Voodoo*, an exile's book, a transnational book, employing a hybrid structure very innovative in those days." If Bolaño had a re-encounter with Borges in Madrid, Vila-Matas discovered the stories of Borges in the Librairie Espagnole in Paris, following in Cozarinsky's footsteps: "I was knocked out, especially by the idea – found in one of his stories – that perhaps the future did not exist."

I am also knocked out by the fact that this idea was suggested to him on premises run by Antonio Soriano, a Republican exile who nourished the hope of a future without Fascism. The Spanish diaspora sustained the cultural activity of resistance at the back of the Librairie Espagnole, as well as in Ruedo Ibérico. The project is linked, as is almost always the case in the history of a bookshop, with a previous one, the Librairie Espagnole León Sánchez Cuesta, inaugurated in 1927 in five square metres of rue Gay-Lussac, with two window displays: one devoted to Juan Ramón Jiménez and the other to young poets like Salinas and Bergamín. It was run by Juan

Vicéns de la Llave, who went so far as to consider publishing books in Spanish from Paris (the first was *Ulysses* in Dámaso Alonso's translation). In order to return to Madrid during the turbulence in Spain in 1934 he left the bookshop in the hands of a former employee, Georgette Rucar, but during the war, as the official responsible for Republican government propaganda in its Paris Embassy, he used the premises as a centre for spreading the ideas that were being crushed by Franco's army. After the Second World War it was Rucar – as related by Ana Martínez Rus in "San León Librero: las empresas culturales de Sánchez Cuesta" ("St Leon the Bookseller: the Cultural Enterprises of Sánchez Cuesta") – who made contact with Soriano, who had settled down as a bookseller in Toulouse, to suggest he took over the stocks of the old bookshop. Rather than *Bookshops*, this book could be called *Metamorphoses*.

When Vila-Matas arrived in Marguerite Duras's attic in 1974, he witnessed the last gasps of that world, if not the photographs of its autopsy. As a mature man, the author of *A Brief History of Portable Literature* revises his initiatory experience in Paris, in the Paris of his personal myths, like Hemingway, Guy Debord, Duras or Raymond Roussel, where everything evokes a splendid past that has necessarily been lost, which paradoxically never goes out of fashion. Because each generation relives a kind of Paris in its youth, which only as one grows older can be gradually demystified.

Someone had drawn a graffiti sketch of Duras in the emergency exit of La Hune, with her famous saying on the left: *"Faire d'un mot le bel amant d'une phrase."* It took me five trips to Paris to discover that of its hundreds of bookshops, perhaps the best three are Compagnie, L'Écume des Pages and La Hune. On my previous visits, apart from persisting with Shakespeare and Company, I stepped inside all those I encountered, but for some reason these three never figured on my itineraries. So, before leaving on my last trip, I asked Vila-Matas himself for advice, and once there, I sought out and found

them. I discovered the poster of Samuel Beckett (his arboreal face) against a cork background on a wall in Compagnie. And the art deco shelves in L'Écume des Pages. And that unlikely staircase and the whitest of columns in the middle of La Hune, part of the refurbishing in 1992, the work of Sylvain Dubuisson. The first is located between the Sorbonne, the Musée de Cluny and the Collège de France. The second and third are close to the Café de Flore and Les Deux Magots and open every day until midnight in Saint-Germain-des-Prés, perpetuating the old bohemian tradition of combining bookshop, wine and coffee. Although in the time separating the writing of these lines from their publication, La Hune has already disappeared (like the odd other bookshop mentioned by me).

When Max Ernst (after marrying Peggy Guggenheim and becoming a habitué of the Gotham Book Mart), Henri Michaux (after bidding farewell to literature to concentrate on his painting), or André Breton (after his American exile) returned to a Paris without the bookshops on rue de l'Odéon, they found in La Hune a new space where they could converse and browse. One need only reflect that in 1949 La Hune, the same year it moved to 170 Boulevard Saint-Germain, hosted the exhibition and auction of the books, manuscripts and furniture from Joyce's Paris flat (he died in 1941), together with part of Beach's archive on the publishing history of his masterpiece, on behalf of the writer's family. Soon after Michaux began to experiment with mescaline and the graphic work he produced led to books in the mid-1950s like *Misérable miracle* and exhibitions like "Description d'un trouble", in the Librairie-Galerie La Hune. Its founder, Bernard Gheerbrant, who died in 2010, was a key figure in intellectual life in Paris and directed the Club des Libraires de France for over a decade. Because of his importance as a publisher of texts and graphic art, his archives are preserved in the Centre Pompidou, where he curated the exhibition "James Joyce and Paris" in 1975. After a brief and failed attempt to explore other approaches, La Hune finally shut down in June 2015. The artist Sophie Calle decided she would be the last person to buy a book. The last customer, the last reader. Her performance began a period of mourning that has yet to end, and which isn't restricted to its Parisian customers but felt by all of us who passed through its doors and left ever so slightly, but quite definitely, changed.

Like most of the bookshops mentioned in this essay, these three are fetishes in themselves and places for the exhibition of fetishes. A fetishism that goes beyond the classical Marxist definition, according to which all goods are phantom fetishes, which hide their status as manufactured commodities and maintain an illusion of autonomy in relation to their producers; a fetishism promoted by the agents of capital (publishers, distributors, booksellers, every one of us) who have fun (we have fun) championing cultural production and consumption as if they were not subject to the tyranny of *interest*; a fetishism that borders on the religious and even on the sexual (in Freudian terms): the bookshop as the deconsecrated temple where idols, objects of worship are housed, like a store of erotic fetishes, of sources of pleasure. The bookshop as a partially deconsecrated church transformed into a sex shop. Because a bookshop feeds on the energy generated by objects that seduce by virtue of their accumulation, by the difficulty of defining demand, which becomes palpable when one finally locates the object that arouses, demands an urgent purchase and a possible subsequent reading (the arousal doesn't always survive, but the percentages of the price of the book, the expenditure and profits do remain behind, like ashes).

Dean MacCannell has analysed the structures of tourism and provided a basic schema: the relationship of the *tourist* with the *view* via the *marker*. Namely: the visitor, the attraction, and all that denotes it as such. The crucial element is the marker that indicates or creates the value, importance and interest of the place and transforms it into something potentially touristic. Into a fetish. The shop selling would-be antiques in Beijing was a fantastic marker. Although the value may be iconic in the first instance, in the end it becomes a discourse as well: the Eiffel Tower is first a postcard, a photograph, and then the life of its inventor, the history of its controversial construction, of other towers in the world, the topography of Paris where that surrounds it and which can be seen from the top. The most meaningful bookshops in the world highlight, with more or less subtlety, the markers that add commercial potential or transform them into tourist spots: antiquity (*founded in, the oldest bookshop in*), size (*the biggest bookshop in, so many miles of shelving, so many hundreds of thousands of books*) and the chapters in the history of literature to which they are linked (*the base for such and such a movement, visited by, the bookshop where X bought,*

visited by, founded by, as can be seen in the photograph, bookshop linked with).

Art and tourism are similar in their need for that luminous signage that draws a reader towards the work. Michelangelo's "David" would attract little attention if it were an anonymous work in the municipal museum of Addis Ababa. After publishing *The Golden Notebook* very successfully in 1962, two years later Doris Lessing sent a new novel to several publishers, under the pseudonym of an unpublished writer, and they all but one rejected it. In the case of literature, publishers first generate the markers, through the blurb on the back cover or the press release, but critics, the academy and bookshops soon create their own, which will determine the book's fortune. Sometimes authors themselves do that, consciously or unconsciously, by structuring a narrative around the conditions in which the work was produced, or the state of their lives at the time. Suicide, poverty or the context of the writing are often the kind of elements that are incorporated into the marker. That narrative, the legend, is one of the factors that allows a text to survive, to live on as a classic. The first part of *Don Quixote* supposedly written in prison and the second part a reaction against the usurping of Cervantes' characters by Avellaneda; the reading of *A Journal of the*

Plague Year as if it were not a novel; the legal procedings against the authors of *Madame Bovary* and *Les Fleurs du mal*; the broadcast reading of *The War of the Worlds* and the collective panic created by the chronicle of that apocalypse; Kafka on his deathbed ordering Max Brod to burn his work; the manuscripts of Malcolm Lowry that were burnt, that disappeared; the scandal surrounding *Tropic of Cancer* and *Lolita* and *Howl* and *For Bread Alone*. The marker is sometimes unpredictable and created years later. That is the case of novels rejected by many publishers like *One Hundred Years of Solitude* or *The Conspiracy of Fools*. Of course, it was not used as a selling point when they were – finally – published, but when they were a success it was recovered as part of the mythical narrative: their *predestination*.

The stories behind several books published in Paris like *Ulysses*, *The Naked Lunch* or *Hopscotch* have clearly been fetishised and now constitute commonplaces in the history of contemporary culture. For the beat generation, which felt it was heir to symbolism and the French avant-garde, *Ulysses* was the obvious reference point for their idea of a rupture. Written in the heady days in Tangier, shaped by Ginsberg and Kerouac, completed in France, *The Naked Lunch* was submitted to Maurice Girodias, the Olympia Press editor on the Left Bank, who did not understand that rubbish and declined to publish it, but eighteen months later when the publication of a few fragments had begun to build the novel's reputation, a reputation for outrageous obscenity, a marker, Girodias' interest in the manuscript was rekindled. By that time, the success of *Lolita* had made him a rich man, and Burroughs' novel, the writing of which was by now but a hazy memory for the author, helped him become even wealthier. He fitted within a fine French tradition: that of the dealer in scandalous books, often banned for being pornographic or obscene, which were published in Switzerland and entered France thanks to the inevitable bribes at the frontier, and which in

the twentieth century were published in Paris and even reached the United States through a motley array of picaresque subterfuges.

Kerouac wrote about *On the Road*: "*Ulysses*, which was thought to be a difficult read, is today thought of as a classic and everybody understands it." We find the same idea in Cortázar, for whom this tradition is central and who linked himself to Paris, not only in the way he contextualised the first part of his novel, but also through a partial rewriting of Breton's *Nadja*. In a letter to his publisher, Francisco Porrúa, he cites the same reference point as a paradigm of difficulty, rupture, resistance and distinction for his contemporaries: "I reckon this must always happen; I'm not familiar with the contemporary reviews of *Ulysses*, but I expect they went something like this: 'Mr Joyce writes poorly, because he doesn't write in the language of the tribe.'" Like *The Naked Lunch*, *Hopscotch* has a structure that functions on the basis of fragments, collage, chance, and has a politically revolutionary intent: the destruction of the bourgeois ordering of discourse, the exploding of literary conventions that are so similar to social conventions. That is why in his letters to his publisher the writer tries to spell out the marker, the discourse that should guide the reading of the book. We have to make an effort to imagine the difficulties of a publishing relationship carried out through epistolary means, the delays, misunderstandings, lost letters (for example, the envelope with the mock-up of the novel Cortázar put together that went missing):

> I would prefer it if this book was not highlighted as "a novel". That would rather cheat the reader. I know only too well that it is a novel and that its intrinsic value resides in its appearance as a novel. But I wrote it as an anti-novel and Morelli takes it upon himself to say that and spells it out very clearly in the passages I quoted to you previously. As a last resort, I think one should emphasise what we might call the axiological sides to the book: the persistent, exasperated denunciation of the inauthenticity of human lives [. . .] the irony, the derisory tone, the self leg-pulling whenever the writer or characters descend into philosophical "seriousness". After *On Heroes and Tombs*, you must understand that the least one can do for Argentina is to denounce at the top of one's voice the ontological "seriousness" of the creeps our writers aspire to be.

Hopscotch immediately struck a chord with his youthful contemporaries. The Paris he delineates revives the classic image of the bohemian city; the proliferation of topographical details transforms it into a possible guide for cultural tourists, which has been underlined by editions that incorporate a map or a list of the writer's favourite cafés; its encyclopedic dimension (literature, painting, cinema, music, philosophy . . .) means a reading can never be exhaustive. A classic work is one that always offers a new reading. A classic is a writer who never goes out of fashion. And Paris was precisely where fashion as we understand it today was born, so that it is hardly surprising that at least until the 1960s, and thanks to a continuous stream of artists from all over the world, it was able to sustain a seductive horizon of expectations for certain readers in respect of certain works, a fetishist aura. Pascale Casanova writes:

> Gertrude Stein neatly summed up the question of the localisation of modernity in a single sentence: "Paris," she writes in *Paris-France* (1940), "was where the twentieth century was." As site of the literary present and capital of modernity, Paris to some extent owed its position to the fact that it was where fashion – the outstanding expression of modernity – was created. In the famous *Paris Guide* of 1867, Victor Hugo insisted on the authority of the City of Light, not only in political and intellectual matters, but also in the domain of taste and elegance, which is to say of fashion and everything modern.

The logic that partially explains the relationship between Greek and Roman culture in antiquity, when revision, continuity, imitation, importing and usurping were the ways in which the empire could secure cultural hegemony, in which the original myths were re-formulated (from Zeus to Jupiter) and the epic rewritten (from Homer's *Iliad* and *Odyssey* to Virgil's *Aeneid*) could be our model for understanding the relationship between the United States and France in the contemporary era. Although London is also of cultural importance in the nineteenth century, Paris establishes itself – as we have seen – as the international centre of literature and the visual arts. In the 1920s and 1930s, celebrities like Hemingway, Stein, Beach, Dos Passos, Bowles or Scott Fitzgerald found in Paris the feeling of being at the heart of bohemia. For a whole generation of American intellectuals – the names selected are a tiny fraction of all those who travelled to Paris and took their ideas from there like so many souvenirs – France was a model for cultural *grandeur* and an adopted heritage. If Hemingway was right and the French capital was "a moveable feast", it is hardly surprising that he could leave in the 1930s, when the Nazis came to power in Germany and the Second World War finally broke out. Picasso stayed in Paris where he created the marketing system for contemporary art; Beach also stayed on and Hemingway returned as a soldier of liberation. But the majority of the French avant-garde and American novelists met up again or for the first time in New York, together with artists, gallery owners, historians, journalists, architects, designers, film directors and booksellers. The same city where, after big exhibitions like the Van Gogh or Picasso, the Museum of Modern Art began to create from that subsoil its own narrative for contemporary art, first raising the standard of abstract expressionism and then pop art with Andy Warhol and the Factory leading the way. The 1950s and 1960s are fascinating because the American writers who are most in step with the times continue to visit Paris. But their approach is different. When Kerouac or Ginsberg travel to France they do so – reversing the route taken by Bowles – stopping off at Tangier, as if one city was not more important than the other. Kerouac's mother tongue was French, Ferlinghetti translates surrealists like Jacques Prévert. Later on other U.S. writers with strong links to the fiction-alised bookshop like Paul Auster – Mallarmé's translator – will travel to Paris but the key literary reference points for the later generations are American, not European. Paris has been transformed into a Library of Universal Literature, while San Francisco, Los Angeles, Chicago or New York are continually launching bookshops destined to be some of the most important cultural centres of the twentieth century. Whether for good or for evil, and not on the soil of the United States, whether as ambassador or intruder, one such is the second Shakespeare and Company.

In the documentary "Portrait of a Bookstore as an Old Man", somebody says that George Whitman was the most American person he had ever known, because he was completely pragmatic and penny-pinching: the tasks in the bookshop had to be carried out by young lovers of literature, who did not receive a wage in return, but a bed, a meal and – though he does not say this – wonderful experiences: working and living in Shakespeare and Company, in the heart of Paris. Whitman simply created the dream of every young American reader: the bookshop responded to a stereotype – like Flourish and Blotts in *Harry Potter* – and was a tourist attraction with a very powerful marker, as important for a student of literature as the Eiffel Tower or the "Mona Lisa", with the extra bonus that you could *live* there; like the map in the edition of *Hopscotch*, it allowed you to create a literary space, to transform it into a home or hotel. "Living the dream"could have been its slogan. And it did so via a conceptual and commercial operation that went back to Sylvia Beach's original Shakespeare and Company, which can be seen from two perspectives: after-life or legacy on the one hand; appropriation, or even usurping, on the other. Whitman said in an interview:

"She never found out anything about our intentions. We waited until she died, because if I'd have asked her and she'd said no, I couldn't have taken over the name after she died. All the same I think she would have said yes." Clearly if he chose not to call his business Maison des Amis des Livres, it was because he was Anglo-Saxon and saw the commercial potential of a name that guaranteed a stream of tourist pilgrims. And because of his insecurity.

The film depicts an unstable, despotic bookseller, as prone to handing out wounding insults as to being poetically maudlin, using his guests as volunteers in a labour camp whose working conditions he never properly spells out. Despite the bookshop's handsome income and the 5 million euro estimated value of its building, he was a frugal, bohemian bookseller who spent no money on clothes or food, and had no social or emotional life outside his picturesque kingdom. We will never know whether he burnt his hair off with two candles in front of the camera because he was suffering from senile dementia or to save on the cost of a barber. And he called

his daughter who now owns the business Sylvia Beach Whitman.

To be fair, his portrait should be balanced with the chronicle *Time Was Soft There. A Paris Sojourn at Shakespeare & Co.* by Jeremy Mercer. Whitman appears in its pages as an unstable old man, but also as very generous, affectionate and dreamy, ready to share his essential books and personal memories of Paris with anyone who sleeps in his beds. Memories of Lawrence Durrell drunk at night after spending all day writing *The Alexandria Quartet*; of Anaïs Nin, who may have been the bookseller's lover; of Henry Miller, the beat generation and Samuel Beckett, who naturally only ever paid silent visits; of all the books and magazines sent on their way by his bookshop; of Margaux Hemingway, whom he guided through Paris in search of her grandfather's city.

What was and is Shakespeare and Company? we wonder, after seeing the film and reading the book. A socialist utopia or a business run by a miser? A tourist icon or a really important bookshop? Was its owner a genius or a madman? I do not think answers exist to these questions and, if they do, they won't be black or white, but a range of greys. It is quite clear that L'Écume des Pages and La Hune are not mythical bookshops in the sense that Shakespeare and Company is, and are not internationally renowned, and that forces us to ask yet again: what is the stuff that myths are made of? And, more particularly, how can we demythologise them?

I too am guilty of contributing to these processes of mythologising (mystifying). All journeys and all readings are partial: when I finally visit Le Divan, the origins of which go back to the 1920s in Saint-Germain-des-Prés, resurrected by Gallimard in 1947 and lodged in the 15th Arrondissement since 1969, and research its history; when I discover Tschann, founded in Montparnasse in 1929 by two friends of the leading lights in the artistic life of that once bohemian, now chic district, the Tschanns, whose daughter Marie Madeleine was a decisive supporter of Beckett's work in France,

I will at last be able to repay the persistence of translator Xavier Nueno, who I hope will introduce me to the present person in charge, Fernando Barros, who emphasises in interviews that he is equally conscious of the past and the future of the bookshop; when – finally – my reading or travels or friends take me to other neighbourhoods and new bookshops, my topography of Paris will change and with it my discourse. In the meantime, I accept the limitations of this impossible, future encyclopedia, which is as chiaroscuro as they all are and which I am perpetually writing.

X

Book Chains

From 1981 Shakespeare and Company also becomes a chain of *independent* bookshops, with four branches in New York and all near university campuses. Although many universities have their own bookshop that sells manuals, reference books and above all textbooks, T-shirts, tracksuits, mugs, posters, maps, postcards and other tourist items linked to the university experience, Barnes & Noble has colonised this market with more than 600 college bookshops in the United States, in addition to 700 plus branches in cities, each with its own Starbucks (it remains to be seen how this figure will be affected by the announcement in 2013 that a third of their premises would be closed down over the next ten years). Although the first bookshop with that name opened in 1917, the Barnes family has had interests in the printing industry from the 1870s. A hundred years later it became the first bookshop to advertise on television. And in the present century the main threat to the survival of small independent bookshops. Which is quite paradoxical, because many businesses that start with a single shop tend to multiply and become links within the same brand or chain. Many well-established chains also began as single, independent bookshops. Long before it owned dozens of branches throughout Mexico, Ghandi was a bookshop to the south of the capital, opened in 1971 by Mauricio Achar. The biggest chains in Brazil originated as projects started by immigrants: Joaquim Inácio da Fonseca Saraiva, from the Trás-os-Montes region of Portugal, opened the first Saraiva in 1914, although at the time it was called Livraria Acadêmica; the first Nobel was founded in 1943 by the Italian Claudio Milano (in 1922 his grandson adopted a leasing system and branches quickly multiplied); the Livraria Cultura was the idea of a German-Jewish immigrant, Eva Herz, and arose from the idea of the book-lending service she started from the front room of her house in 1950; it did not become a bookshop until 1969. The three empires were born in the same city, São Paulo, and spread throughout the country. Family Christian Stores now have almost 300 branches and in 2012 they donated more than a million Bibles to be distributed by missionaries across the world, but the Zondervan brothers began with remainders from de-catalogued stock on a farm in the 1930s. Their growth was down to the success of their cheap editions of out-of-copyright religious works, such as a number of English translations of the Bible.

Thanks to the fact that Holland was a haven for Calvinists and to the absence of religious and political censorship, it became one of the great world book centres in the sixteenth and seventeenth centuries. The Elzevir family was pre-eminent among its printers, and between 1622 and 1652 published authentic pocket-book classics annotated by academics. Martyn Lyons reminds us that the 1636 edition of Virgil's complete works was such a success it had to be reprinted fifteen times. Pocket-sized classics were known as "Elzevir editions", regardless of whether the Elzevirs were the publishers. Despite their success, this kind of publication was aimed at the literate elite. One has to remember that the *Encyclopédie*, a genuine best-seller that sold almost 25,000 copies, was mainly purchased by the nobility and clergy, the social classes whose pillars it was undermining. Ordinary people read mostly slim chapbooks, booklets full of drawings, or the *bibliothèque bleue* bound with the blue paper from packets of sugar that were distributed by itinerant sellers, known as *colporteurs* in French, *Jahrmarksttrödlers* in German and *leggendaio* in Italy. The lives of saints, nonsense stories, farces, parodies, drinking and rabble-rousing songs, myths and legends, tales of chivalry, harvest calendars, horoscopes, gaming rules, recipe books and even abbreviated versions of universal classics were the real best-sellers before the explosion of the romantic and realist novel in the nineteenth century and its spread in the form of mass-produced serial fiction.

The book as a money-making success began with Walter Scott and was consolidated by Charles Dickens and William Thackeray. The volume of sales of books by Scott was so high in Europe that from 1822 his novels appeared simultaneously in English and French and in 1824 a parody of his fictions, *Walladmor*, where Scott himself figured as a character, was published in Germany because, as we know, there is no better guarantee of success than imitation or parody. The Lévy brothers launched a collection of works that cost

1 franc in Paris in the middle of the century. Michel and Calmann had become wealthy by commercialising opera libretti and plays and opened one of the great nineteenth-century bookshops on the Boulevard des Italiens, where there was a bargain section. Apart from investing in the bookshop, they also poured money into railways, insurance companies and public services in the colonies. In the same period Baedeker and Murray popularised travel guides that could now be bought like so many other kinds of book from infinite outlets: grocery stores, kiosks, itinerant sellers, independent bookshops and chains. In *Reading and Riding* Eileen S. DeMarco has studied the network of Hachette bookshops in French railway stations, a project that lasted almost a century, from early in 1826 to the outbreak of the First World War in 1914, with the launching of the first premises in Paris in 1853 en route. Trains rapidly became the principal vehicle for books: their trucks transported paper, printing presses, spare parts, the workforce, writers, finished books from one city to another and, above all, readers. The chain based its efficiency, for the first time in history, on the contracting of female shop assistants, *femmes bibliothécaires*, given that the initiative was called Bibliothèque des Chemins de Fer. In the letter Louis Hachette sent to the owners of the main railway companies in France to persuade them of the viability of his proposal he emphasised its pedagogic nature, since the light, portable books would have an educational aspect as well as providing entertainment for the journey. By July 1853 forty-three branches had opened their doors and offered close on 500 titles. The following year they set up the daily press that over time would become their main source of income. And three years later they incorporated part of the output of other publishing companies, thus maintaining a monopoly on sales in stations. This was extended to the Métro network at the end of the century.

*

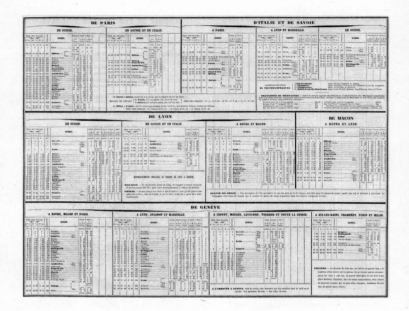

The A. H. Wheeler bookshop chain had a monopoly on book sales in stations in India until 2004. Like that of Hachette – which is now a transnational publishing group that shifts 250 million books a year – its railway history is fascinating reading. The first branch opened its doors in 1877 in the station of Allahabad, after Émile Moreau and his partner T. K. Banerjee borrowed the name from someone who probably never stepped on Asian soil, Arthur Henry Wheeler, who owned a bookshop chain in London. An agreement with the Indian government gave them a monopoly on the distribution of books and newspapers, with an evident social and educational intent: for over a century it was the main way culture reached the most remote parts of the country, where A. H. Wheeler was often the only bookshop for many miles around. With independence on the horizon, in 1937 Moreau transferred his share in the ownership to his Indian friend and partner, whose family has run it ever since. The company entered the present century with some

600 sales points in almost 300 stations, but it lost the monopoly in 2004 in a nationalistic political move made by Lalu Prasad Yaday, the Minister for Railways, against the British resonances in the Indian company's name. However, the decision was revoked six years later: the bookshop chain is too emblematic of the landscape for it not to be treated as part of the country's cultural heritage.

As Shekhar Krishnan explains in the article in the *Indian Express*, my source for this information, "See you in Wheeler's" is a common expression in Mumbai. The name is so deeply rooted in the country's daily life. It is common to meet friends or acqaintances in its bookshops and kiosks to buy a newspaper before boarding the train and sharing the journey home, and conversations about politics and literature have been organised for decades in those sales points where people stand and drink their cups of tea.

Rudyard Kipling was born in Mumbai and his fate was linked to the name of "Wheeler", shared by the editor of the *Civil and Military Gazette*, the first daily newspaper that the future writer worked for at the age of seventeen. He spent two thirds of the day at the paper's office, even in hellish summer temperatures: sweat and ink transformed his suit into the coat of "a Dalmatian dog" in the words of one of his companions. His train journeys to cover imperial events in Hindu and Muslim territories, with stays of six months that anticipated his famous trips to Japan or South Africa supplied him with anecdotes and atmosphere for the first stories he published in 1888 in "The Railway Library", the paperback series published by A. H. Wheeler who thus became his first publishers. Over time memory would cloak those colonial experiences within the dreamlike, mythical exoticism of novels like *Kim* or *The Jungle Book*.

Both the Hachette and Moreau and Banerjee networks of bookshops followed British models; in 1848 five years before the first French outlet, a similar one already existed in London's Euston

Station, the property of WHSmith, probably the first large book chain ever. The company benefited from the railway boom to such an extent that the son of the founder was able to use its success as a springboard for an illustrious political career. In parallel his bookshop was being cloned across the country as big train stations also spread with their concourses large enough to accommodate bootblacks and florists; and there was a progressive refinement of railway travel, which was soon to offer the same luxuries and advantages as ocean liners and hotels. At the end of the eighteenth century and beginning of the nineteenth – as Frédéric Barbier explains in his *Histoire du livre* – London bookshops had already opened up to the street through their shop windows, posters, signs and even announcers or billboard men who invited passers-by to go in. In fact, the book was now assuming its natural role as a commodity: the list of the remaining titles in the same series or from the same publishers was advertised in the last pages of the book; front pages took on a uniform design to reinforce the identity of a list and innovative illustrations were incorporated; the price began to be printed on the book as a ploy to hook readers or as a publicity device. La Bibliothèque des Chemins de Fer sold books at prices ranging between 0.75 and 2.50 francs. The average price of a book in France fell from 6.65 in 1840 to 3.45 francs in 1870. Series at 1 franc were created, because the consumption of printed media was multiplying as was the number of sales points, and those where you could borrow. And mobile libraries and bookshops that like trains connected up with the nervous heart of the Industrial Revolution. And professional readers: in the nineteenth century there were people who made a living from reading the news out loud or reciting passages from Shakespeare with a flourish. The anachronistic, histrionic Bruce Chatwin did this as a child in Stratford-upon-Avon.

Mobility is the great invention of the nineteenth century. The train changes perceptions of space and time; it not only speeds up human life, but transforms the idea of a network, a network structure, into something that can be explored in its entirety in a few days, even though it is so vast. A whole system reduced to body size. Travellers, who only knew how to read silently, after a period of adaptation, now learn to do so in movement. Not only that: they can also look up from the page, thread together the fragments they have read and imagined with the fragments of life they see through the window (thus preparing for the arrival of the cinema). Lifts appear and allow cities to grow vertically after too many centuries of horizontal expansion. The heavy furniture of the aristocracy and haute bourgeoisie slims down into light items that allow for house moves. "The street lords it over the room," as Renato Ortiz translates this into spatial terms. The swiftest, most massive migrations in the history of humanity take place. The Universal Exhibitions of Paris and London, fruits of industrial growth and imperial expansion, are responses to the need to make that supremacy public on the world stage. They are megaphones, monstrous shop windows for the Myth of Progress. Fashion is born, develops at a vertiginous pace that requires mass production, the new consumer society, based on the requirement that everything, absolutely everything must have a sell-by date. Fashion and lightness also shape books: paperbacks, cheap miniatures, discounted titles, bargain boxes, trestles where second-hand books are displayed. All that happens in England and France, in London and Paris, the same contexts where the modern bookshop is created and, alongside, the bookshop chains.

The first Hudson News, with its offering of newspapers and trade books as we know it today, opened in La Guardia Airport in 1987 after a previous attempt in Newark. It now has 600 sales points in the United States. It belonged to the Hudson Group until it was acquired by Dufry in 2008, a Swiss group specialising in duty-free shops. Until his death in 2012 Robert Benjamin Chen was the visible head of the firm that over decades had principally focused on the distribution of newspapers and magazines. According to his obituary in the *New York Times* he received a court sentence in 1981 for bribing the newspaper distributors' union in return for favourable terms. The Hudson Group opened hundreds of bookshops and kiosks in airports, train stations and coach terminals throughout the world and also ran adjacent fast-food restaurants. Because if the world speeds up in the nineteenth century, the United States is responsible for a second big spurt after the two World Wars. And independent bookshops and book chains – if that polarisation is entirely valid and is not challenged in part by an infinite number of intermediate states – develop their structure in the twentieth century, and from the 1950s begin to incorporate the big changes in the consumption of space and time brought by mass culture in North America. The shopping centre that initially imitates a European model (the arcade) is established in city centres, and progressively becomes a suburban phenomenon. And the theme park melds into the fast-food restaurant: in the same year that Disneyland is launched, the first McDonald's franchise is opened, and, with the motel, both connected through the U.S. roadway network, an imperial complex that is duplicated by the air routes, the twentieth-century equivalent of the nineteenth-century European rail networks.

Bookshops in the second half of the twentieth century possess the agglutinating character of shopping malls, where the display of books, kindergarten, children's playground, entertainment palaces, restaurants and, gradually, videos, C.D.s, D.V.D.s, video games and souvenirs cohabit or are neighbours. This vibrant, rather bookish North American model for urban living is copied in large measure by other countries like Japan, India, China or Brazil, and by extension everywhere else. The old empires have no choice but to adapt to that hegemonic tendency in terms of a massive leisure offering that ensures the indiscriminate sale of cultural consumer items. Thus, WHSmith and the Coles supermarkets will merge to create Chapters. And Fnac, born in 1954 as a kind of literary club with a socialist ethos, will end up selling televisions and owning some eighty branches in France and more than sixty in the rest of the world. All chains have something in common: what they have on offer is dominated by American cultural products.

THE CIRCULATING LIBRARY.

In his *Atlas of the European Novel 1800–1900*, Franco Moretti has drawn maps of the influence wielded by writers like Scott, Dickens, Dumas, Hugo, Stendhal or Balzac, and of the viral spread on the Old Continent of sub-genres like the sentimental, nautical, religious, Oriental or silver-fork novel (which were sometimes only read in certain regions). This allows him to analyse the logic of the novel form during the nineteenth century as a rendering of two predominant models:

> Different forms, different Europes. Each genre has its geography – its geometry almost: *but they are all figures without a centre.* See here how strange novelistic geography is – and doubly strange. Because, first, the European novel closes European literature to all external influences, it strengthens and perhaps even establishes its *Europeanness.* But then this most European of forms proceeds to deprive most of Europe of its creative autonomy: two cities, London and Paris, rule the entire continent for over a century, publishing half (if not more) of all European novels. It's a ruthless, unprecedented *centralisation* of European literature. Centralisation: the centre, the well-known fact; but seen for what it really is: not a given but a process. And a very unlikely process: the exception, not the rule, of European literature.[. . .]With the novel, then, a *common literary market* arises in Europe. One market: because of centralisation. And a very uneven market: also because of centralisation. Because in the crucial hundred years between 1750 and 1850 the consequence of centralisation is that in most European countries the majority of novels are, quite simply, *foreign books.* Hungarian, Danish, Italian, Greek readers familiarise themselves with the new form through French and English novels, *models to be imitated.*

If we were to apply Moretti's analytical method to the stock of Barnes & Noble, Borders, Chapters, Amazon or Fnac, as he does to nineteenth-century circulating libraries and *cabinets de lecture*, beyond the corresponding percentage of local titles, we would find that the global consumption of fiction is above all the consumption of products from North America or inspired by them. The same strategy that England and France pursued with the novel form in the nineteenth century was adopted by the United States, which in Hollywood films and later in television series created a model of audio-visual fiction that was *worthy of being imitated* – just as London and Paris imposed their idea of the bookshop – a way of shaping the space for the experience of family life (with the television at its centre), the experience of watching films (in multi-screen cinemas) and the experience of reading (fusing bookshop, souvenir shop and Starbucks-style cafeteria).

Consequently the big North American book chains are the epitome of that way of conceiving the distribution and sale of culture that we call bookshop chains and constantly mark out with the adjective "big". Because the small chain, the half-dozen of book-shops with the same owner and the same brand, may still be capital-ised locally, a feature of independent businesses, while the big chains are nearly always transnational conglomerates, where the book-seller has ceased to be simply that, because he has lost that direct – artisan – relationship with books and customers. The bookseller is a shop assistant or executive director or buyer or personnel manager. Bookshop chains, subject to shareholders and boards of manage-ment, trigger series of events that are typical of large enterprises: Waterstones was created in 1982 by Tim Waterstone after he was fired by WHSmith, which in its turn bought it in 1999, only to sell it years later to the company that had already purchased its main rival, Dillon's, the branches of which were transformed into Waterstones. Under its new management Waterstones in Cardiff cancelled a reading by Patrick Jones the poet, after the Christian Voices Association threatened to boycott the event because the book was "blasphemous" and "obscene".

When I visited London early in 2016 I had the opportunity to interview James Daunt, the managing director of its 300 branches as well as owner of the eight branches of his Daunt chain. When we met in the cafeteria in the Piccadilly Waterstones, I was surprised that the first thing he did was ask me what I wanted to drink, go to the bar, ask for a coffee and serve me with a broad smile. The 52-year-old James Daunt struck me as being tall and elegant with a friendly, extremely soothing manner yet one that contrasted with his sharp, incisive eyes. He was appointed in 2011 by the Russian multimillionaire Alexander Mamut, who had just bought the practically bankrupt chain from the H.M.V. Group for 67 million euros. In other words, I interviewed the man who set about saving Waterstones.

"How did things look when you were put in charge of Waterstones in 2011?"

"The chain was bankrupt. Kindle had made big inroads and the market had been reduced by a quarter. What did I do? My first thought was that I must motivate the booksellers, but unfortunately before I could do that I had to sack a third of my staff. My idea was to change Waterstones into a company where I myself would feel comfortable working. It wouldn't be easy, if you think how fixed retail prices are a thing of the past and Amazon can sell books up to 40 per cent cheaper than you can. Consequently the bookseller must make up for the price difference with his humanity, commitment and enjoyment of the synergy existing between the reader, the book and himself. Amazon cannot offer that kind of synergy."

"What were the main changes you introduced, apart from the cutback in staff?"

"Changing a bookshop is a slow process. Hatchards was a

historic, very important bookshop, but it was going downhill, and it took three years to reinvigorate it within the Waterstones framework. We are also managing to do that with other shops in the chain: our takings increased from £9 to £13 million last year. The first thing I did was to put my trust wholeheartedly in our booksellers and give them the independence to decide which books they wanted to sell and which they didn't. To that end I was forced to make Waterstones the only chain that didn't allow publishing houses to purchase window or table display space. Previously Waterstones had earned £27 million from selling display space. But it means being pressurised by the publisher and your bookseller isn't free to select books, he isn't the curator of his own bookshop: the job ceases to be stimulating. The purchase of display space creates bookshops that are all the same. The other big change I introduced was in the area of returns. We've gone from 27 to 3 per cent and my aim is nil."

"The whole system is based on the delivery of new stock and regular returns. You must have a hard time negotiating that with publishers . . ."

"They hated these measures. You have to be courageous if you want to change the publishing world. I met with them and asked them the following: 'Have you got a better idea, because if we don't make changes this business is done for.' They gradually came round. If you are a great publisher, building an important list, you can survive with us; but if you are only interested in novelty, mediocre books you can sell using gimmicks, you will sink."

"What's your relationship with your customers, your readers?"

"The challenge we face is satisfying the most intellectual customer without frightening off the least intellectual. I want taxi drivers to feel at home in all my bookshops. They are people who read a lot, whether it's newspapers or books, and I want them to come into my shops and find what they want to read. I'm not being disingenuous, I know that Waterstones is a middle-class bookshop and my customers in Daunt's have cachet. Each bookshop must get to know its clientele and not attempt to compete with the supermarkets or other establishments that sell books."

"What is a Waterstones bookseller like? A Daunt's one?"

"I hope they will end up being similar. A good bookseller must be friendly, interested in culture and able to communicate that interest, be committed to books and what's more energetic (we mustn't forget it is physical work, too). We want young, well-read staff who choose us because they realise we value a spirit of curiosity and a passion for books. That's why we're changing the design of the space. Whenever I go to Spain I visit La Central, one of my models, like Feltrinelli in Italy."

"You can see that in the warm, welcoming wood on the first floor that recalls La Central in Callao, Madrid. It's clear the same designer is behind these projects: the Argentinian Miguel Sal—"

'Indeed! I would have dinner with Miguel whenever he came to London. He was an intelligent, amusing and provocative man . . . What's more he was an excellent customer, he always ended up buying books like a madman. His recent unexpected death was a great shock."

"What do you think about Amazon's great new idea, opening bookshops that exist physically?"

"I have just returned from Seattle. The bookshop is amazing. The books aren't placed on their side but face up, showing the front cover. There are only 5,000 and they are arranged according to a mathematical pattern; there is no hierarchy of taste, no possible sense that you are discovering anything. They have deconstructed the idea of a bookshop: it would be ridiculous under any other name, but as it is Amazon it's brilliant. Because one should never forget that WHSmith isn't a bookshop and Amazon certainly is."

"Who better to go to war against Amazon than an Amazon?" asked Jan Hoffman in a report on McNally Jackson Books published in the *New York Times*. The warrior would be Sarah McNally, who installed the Espresso Book Machine in an emblematic corner of a bookshop famous for its generosity towards Latin American writers (managed by Javier Molea), for its many activities and its stock of geographically organised books – a machine able to print and bind in a matter of minutes any of the 7 million titles in the bookstore-cloud that depends on the tangible Manhattan bookshop.

In a scenario engineered physically by Barnes & Noble and virtually by Amazon, after the closure of hundreds of Borders bookshops, the American Booksellers Association launched the Book Sense and IndieBound campaigns, the keystones of which are a literary prize and a list of the most sold books that only takes into account those purchased in independent bookshops (unlike the *New York Times*, which tots up the sales in kiosks, chains, drug-stores and gift shops, as well as the numbers from the publishers themselves, thus often doubling the figures for the same book). In 2010 André Schiffrin commented on that situation in *Words and Money*:

> New York, which in the post-war years had some 333 book-stores, now has barely thirty, including the chains. A par-allel development had taken place in Britain, where the Waterstones chain, which had driven many of the in-dependents out of business by its use of huge discounts, was itself bought up by WHSmith. Long known for its commercialism and political caution, WHSmith soon changed its new purchase into a chain focusing on dis-counted paperbacks.

*

In his book the publisher uses various labels to differentiate quality bookshops from bookshop chains: "bookstores with a cultural function", "intellectual bookstores", "landmark bookstores", and refers to the protectionist strategies pursued by the French government to guarantee their survival. Years later Hollande's government introduced others. Unlike the Video Club, though never scaling the heights of the Library, the Bookshop wears a halo of prestige, a traditional importance comparable to the Theatre or the Cinema, as a space that must be conserved and developed through state support. This consciousness does not exist in the United States, but it wouldn't be at all surprising if the void left by Borders, rather than being filled by other chains, was occupied locally by new establishments with intellectual ambitions, and offering a personal touch, aspiring to become centres of culture and future landmarks. Places intensely active on social media, with good web pages, and able to offer printing on demand or nearby printing facilities. Small shops that serve coffee and home-made cakes or offer writing workshops, like those sophisticated wine bars that provide wine-tasting courses. Bookshops where the dust is not dusted by anonymous cleaning agencies, but by the booksellers themselves, wanting to remember the precise spot for each of those rare, minority, hand-crafted, out-of-fashion volumes that don't belong in the big book chains and which only booksellers from the family of Beach, Monnier, Yánover, Steloff, Sanseviero, Ferlinghetti, Milla, Montroni or McNally will know how to place on shelves or tables for new books, and thus give them visibility.

XI

Books and Bookshops at the End of the World

What was the first thing I did when I arrived in Sydney? I looked for a bookshop and bought a paperback edition of Chatwin's *The Songlines*, the Spanish translation of which I had read some time ago, and of *Austerlitz* by Sebald, which had just been published in English. The next day I visited Gleebooks and got one of the first stamps on my invisible passport, which at the time (mid-2002) had what you might call a *transcendent* significance for me; I made pilgrimages to cemeteries, cafés, museums, the temples of modern culture I still worshipped. As you will have guessed by this point, I embraced my status as a cultural tourist or meta-traveller some time ago and stopped believing in invisible passports. Nonetheless, I think the metaphor is quite apt and, in the case of bookshop-lovers, could serve to camouflage a fetishist and above all consumerist drive, a vice that at times seems too much like Diogenes syndrome. I returned from that trip to Australia with twenty books in my rucksack, some of which I discarded in my various house moves before I read, leafed through, or even opened them.

As I was saying: the next day I went to Gleebooks, though I bought the two key books for that trip in an ordinary bookshop. One must distinguish between the world's great bookshops and emergency bookshops. The latter supply our most urgent reads, the ones that cannot wait, bring light relief on a flight or train journey, allow us to buy a last-minute present, and give us – on the same day it has been released – the book we've been waiting for. Without these emergency bookshops, the others would not exist, would have no meaning. A city must have a range of book outlets: from the kiosk to the main bookshop, there is a whole gamut of modest and middling bookshops, of book chains, best-seller sections in supermarkets, second-hand bookshops, bookshops specialising in film, comics, crime fiction, university textbooks, the media, photography or travel.

I ventured to 49 Glebe Point Road, that colonial-style house with its Uralite porch supported by metal columns, because my guidebook singled it out as the finest Australian bookshop, one that had several times won the prize as the best in the country. It was July 2002 and this book just one project among many. My notes from that visit, anchored in time, contrast with the bookshop's web page, constantly being updated. "Founded in 1975", I now read in my old handwriting. "Wooden shelves", I read:

> An appearance of chaos (there are even books on the floor). The back opens onto a rough-and-ready yard with a few trees. A large amount of Australian, Anglo-Saxon and

translated literature. They sell Moleskine notebooks. A mural with the front covers of books signed by their authors. A delightful attic, carpeted like the floor beneath, with lots of natural light, fans and wooden beams, an exposed roof. An edition of Carey's novel on the Kellys, imitating old paper and typography. An up-to-date magazine stand. Literary events are held in the attic. I leaf through a novel about a nineteenth-century prison shot through with absurd humour.

Peter Carey's *True History of the Kelly Gang* was published in Enrique de Hériz's Spanish translation a few months before my trip. In yet another display of his ability to ventriloquise, the Australian writer takes on Ned Kelly in the first person: the orphan, horse-thief, pioneer, reformer, outlaw and policeman. Oedipus and Robin Hood reincarnated at the end of the world. Namely, an interpretation of European myths in a country that, to invent itself as a nation, turned its back on a complex, ancient local culture while simultaneously trying to exterminate or assimilate the indigenous population. Like all Australian bookshops, the layout of Gleebooks demonstrates the unhealed scar that runs across the island continent like a trail of gunpowder: sections called "Aboriginal Studies" and "Australian Studies", because two Australias are thrusting themselves on a single map and each defends its own boundaries.

There are no more bookshops in my archive from that trip to Australia: none of those I visited in Brisbane, Cairns, Darwin or Perth seemed particularly seductive. I found the main titles for my research on Spanish migration to the other end of the planet in museum shops. Ten years later I visited Melbourne and had the chance to get to know its two main bookshops, which *did* seem memorable: Reader's Feast Bookshop, in whose armchairs I discovered contemporary Aboriginal literature through Tara June Winch, and Hill of Content, without doubt my favourite, as much because of its books as its context. The whole city is articulated through its café cult, so bookshops seem like an appendix to a ritual whose rhythms are totally in step with those of reading. Pellegrini's is an old cafeteria and Italian restaurant, a real Melbourne institution, less than a hundred metres from Hill of Content, and Madame Brussels a sophisticated spot on the third floor of the building opposite. Between vintage antique (the owner speaks dialect to her assistant in the kitchen) and retro modern (only the crockery in Madame Brussels is really old) is where I began to read *Under the Sun*, Chatwin's letters, and *Travels*, the anthology of Bowles' travel writing, both recently published and still not to be seen in my bookshops in Barcelona, yet displayed in the window of one of these bookshops at the end of the world.

Cappuccinos served in Melbourne and the insistence on teatime, the excellent wines and beach huts, pavement cafés and restored arcades can all be seen as a tug-of-war between a Mediterranean, European, and international, if you will, style of life and a degree of resistance to abandoning the British colonial past, the Commonwealth heritage. Just like South Africa: the same cappuccinos, teatime, fine wines, colourful beach huts, the pavement café culture now shared by the majority of countries across the world, the same arcades (and, basically, identical restoration). In the most picturesque in Cape Town, the Long Street Arcade, bookshop and café rub shoulderers with antiquarian bazaars and shops selling militaria, a mixture you find in all city arcades in what was once the British Empire.

What was the first thing I did when I landed in Johannesburg in September 2011? Naturally, I asked after the best bookshop. I could not visit it until my last day when on my way to the airport I asked the taxi driver to stop and give me sufficient time to get to know it. It was Boekehuis specialising in literature in Afrikaans, the only bookshop I know that occupies a whole villa, surrounded by gardens and protected by a high wall and a watchtower. A hundred years old, the colonial-style building used to be the residence of the daughter of Bram Fischer, a leading anti-apartheid activist. The fireplaces have been blocked but it retains a homely atmosphere, the cafeteria is a kind of oasis and the carpets in the children's section welcome storytellers of a weekend. Now that I possess the library that I need and can store books on my tablet, when travelling I only buy those titles that can be really useful to me, the books I cannot easily find in my city and really want to read. So I bought nothing in Boekehuis. Nor in the Book Lounge, the best bookshop in Cape Town.

I had André Brink's *Praying Mantis* in my suitcase. Set in the country's murky dawn, the novel is a rewriting of the true story of the trouble-making Cupido Cockroach, who became a fervent missionary and experienced in his own black flesh the conflicts that were to plague South Africa's future. Both *True History of the Kelly Gang* and several books by J. M. Coetzee employ the same strategy: a manuscript found and rewritten, a dialogue with material from the past. The re-imaginings of the country's troubled beginnings is there in Coetzee's own beginnings as a novelist: the first part of *Dusklands*, "The Vietnam Project", starts with: "My name is Eugene Dawn. I cannot help that. Here goes," and the second part, "The narrative of Jacobus Coetzee", in which J. M. Coetzee figures as translator: "Five years ago Adam Wijnand, a bastard, no shame in that, packed up and trekked to Korana country." *Disgrace* could be translated into Spanish as *Vergüenza, Shame*. Just before my trip to South Africa I had read *Estética de laboratorio*, by Reinaldo Laddaga, one of the few good book-length essays, like *The World Republic of Letters* or *Atlas of the European Novel*, in which the author does not focus on one language or a concrete geographical area but tries to draw a *mappa mundi*: literature cannot be understood if one retains an anachronistic faith in frontiers. Unlike Laddaga's previous books, where he wrote about Latin American literature, this new title situates the spectre of present-day literature on a wavelength similar to mine (Sebald, César Aira, Sergio Chejfec, Joan Didion, Mario Levrero, Mario Bellatin), alongside other areas of contemporary artistic creation, like music or the visual arts. One chapter analyses an aspect of *Disgrace* that had escaped me though I had read it several times. In the course of the novel, David, the protagonist, tries to write an opera, the story of Byron in Italy, and the fiction concludes with a desolate image: the character tuning his daughter's old banjo, wondering whether the throat of a dying dog could bring the woeful tone the work requires, sitting on an old chair, under a beach parasol, with jet black, incomprehensible Africa extending as far as his eyes can see, and which does not speak

English and is not familiar with the myths and languages of Old Europe. Laddaga argues that this creative endeavour that obsesses David throughout the novel contains the seed of all Coetzee's later books: pages written from meagre materials, like jottings, diaries, interviews and letters, without the prestige of "the literary", failed essays, attempts to fine-tune a music that refuses to be sublime, where the writer's alter egos appear on the scene and reiterate their inability to elaborate a perfect, rounded story in the twenty-first century.

So similar to Hill of Content or Eterna Cadencia that they could be sisters, the Book Lounge is a charming bookshop with large wooden tables and sofas and a basement with rugs that makes you want to stay on and live there. Its aesthetic is completely classical and therefore familiar, but when I walked around, I confronted an enigma. As I looked at the books, shelf by shelf, I kept finding empty spaces. The first was Paulo Coelho: his novels and self-help books were not there and a small card noted their absence. The second was Gabriel García Márquez. The third, Coetzee. In each case, the same little card with the same message: "Ask for his books at the counter." What could Coelho, García Márquez and Coetzee have in common? The bookseller was chatting to a friend and I was too shy to interrupt, so I killed time taking photographs of the shop and browsing. Finally she was free and I asked her to solve the riddle. And she did: they are the three most stolen-from writers. The only ones people steal from. So we keep their books here, she said, pointing to big piles behind her. I asked her for Coetzee's. There was not one I did not already have at home, but I leafed through his Nobel Speech again, beautifully cloth-bound by Penguin, which I purchased in the Seminary Co-op years ago. I scoured the edition of *Disgrace* that Penguin Classics had just published with notes and intended for university students for a reference to the aesthetic of precariousness, to the opera that David is writing as the seed of Coetzee's future fiction, or to its poor execution on an out-of-tune banjo in a place only inhabited by dogs. All in vain.

Summertime is the book where Laddaga's intuitions most strike a note. His analysis goes as far as *Diary of a Bad Year*, but it is in Coetzee's later masterpiece to date where he might have reached a splendid epiphany. A harsh, fictionalised memoir, it is a novel without a centre, without a climax. And yet I remember with peculiar intensity the night John spends with his cousin in a truck, a powerful scene like a whirlwind within a maelstrom despite an apparent indolence, the veneer of non-action. That is the precise moment the reader feels he is at the end of the world. It is a powerful sensation: like crossing Australia or South Africa or the United States or the north of Mexico or Argentina, and suddenly halting after hours journeying through monotonous landscape, stopping at a service station or a village, suddenly being in the middle of nowhere, feeling dizzy at a frontier post where you gaze at the horizon and anticipate the barbarians who never in fact appear, an anguish that prompts the inevitable question: what the devil am I doing here?

In Patagonia I followed the traces of Chatwin like nowhere else on the planet. My copy of the Muchnik edition of his first work thickened out over those few weeks until it became a folder: ridges caused by pencil underlinings were joined by bus tickets, postcards, tourist leaflets, like the ones for the Harberton Ranch or Milodón's Cave. There were two moments when I felt nearest to the author of *Anatomy of Restlessness*: when I interviewed the grandson of Hermann Eberhard ("In the morning I walked with Eberhard in driving rain. He wore a fur-lined greatcoat and glared fiercely at the storm from under a Cossack cap") in Punta Arenas, who told me of the strange visit by writer and biographer Nicholas Shakespeare, who, at one point in the interview, became obsessed with buying his old fridge, since he collected them, and kept returning to the subject of domestic electrical goods until it became the only topic of conversation, and when I walked around Puerto Consuelo to the legendary cave and ended up being chased by a pack of dogs. I had to jump over fences, because the path ran across private property, until finally, by the time I was feeling scared to death, a rough, unkempt guy stepped out of a rusty mobile home that had been converted into a permanent abode and calmed those hellish dogs down. Chatwin, creator of myths: you could not possibly have done everything you describe in your book and yet what an intense feeling of truth radiates from everything you wrote.

What was the first thing I did when I arrived in Ushuaia in the spring of 2003? I visited the Prison Museum and in its souvenir shop bought *Uttermost Part of the Earth* by E. Lucas Bridges, the story of his life at the end of the world, among the Yahgans (indigenous people), the Onawas (nomad hunters) and his family of British immigrants (owners of the Harberton Ranch, the first on Tierra del Fuego). It is one of the best travel books I have read and the antithesis of Chatwin's story. Bridges pits unity against the latter's fragmentation; and against his superficiality – inevitable given the speed of most memorable journeys – a depth seldom seen in the Restless Tradition. Its author studied the language of the aboriginals, befriended them, established a bridge between both cultures that *In Patagonia* does not even surface as a possibility between Hispanic and Anglo-Saxon cultures. Bridges' truth is superior to Chatwin's. Strange but true: literary truth comes in degrees and honesty, unverifiable though it is because with time, facts become ever more elusive, can have a profound effect. A traveller can often see what the native is unable to appreciate, but it is not the same to be a tourist at the end of the world as to have lived there.

I imagine that what I felt on my fleeting stays in Tierra del Fuego, the Cape of Good Hope or Western Australia, that *frisson* of the remote and the finite, must have been similar to what Roman travellers and medieval pilgrims experienced when they contemplated the different ends of the earth with Celtic resonances where Western Europe hurls itself into the sea. After reaching Santiago de Compostela, a university city with an annual bookselling and book-pawning fair which dates back to 1495, the pilgrims would continue for three or four days until they came to Finistère, where on the beach they would burn clothes they had worn over months of wandering before beginning their slow trek home, on foot, as always. If all religions share some things, it is the need for the book, the idea that walking brings one nearer to the gods and the conviction that

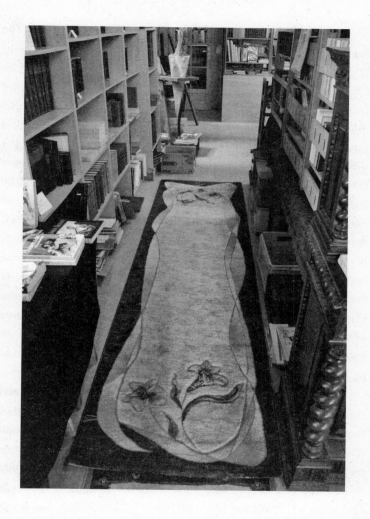

the world will come to an end. For the ancients that certainty was
expressed in physical terms: at a certain point, once a particular
frontier had been reached, it was impossible to go any further. We
have mapped the most remote corner of the globe and eliminated
the mystery of space: all that remains for us to do is to register the
end of time.

It has been our fate to witness the demise of the paper book, though it is proving so slow perhaps it will never happen at all. Yet in Bécherel in Britanny, birthplace of the fictional material shaped by Chrétien de Troyes that was so worthy of imitation, a few miles from the French *département* of Finistère, in a single afternoon I visited with François Monti the translator seventeen bookshops and art galleries linked by ink and calligraphy. Bécherel forms part of a spider's web of small bookselling towns that may seem anachronistic, but are very striking. Hay-on-Wye was the first, founded by Richard Booth in 1962; today it has thirty-five bookshops. Small bookselling towns exist in Scotland, Belgium, Luxembourg, Germany, Finland, France and Spain. Before 1989 there was not a single bookshop in Bécherel. Its old textile glory had been reduced to street names: rue de la Chanvrerie (Hemp Street), Rue de la Filanderie (Weaving Street). The imposing merchants' residences speak of the fifteenth, sixteenth and seventeenth centuries, when this area exported the best Britanny linen. The bed and breakfast where we stayed had a distaff and a bookcase full of books. I have never seen so many bookshops with wall-to-wall carpeting.

The houses are old, but the shops selling old books are new and their lack of order is carefully contrived: a retro scenario within vintage architecture. With its two floors and a conservatory adorned with metal sculptures next to the presbytery garden, the Librairie du Donjon is one of the most beautiful I have ever visited. Nonetheless, I find it hard to forget that I am in the midst of a tourist operation. That Bécherel is a book theme park. An old dynamic has been turned upside down: libraries, in total economic crisis, with their collections of games and videos, are more vigorous than ever, yet bookshops are being transformed into museums as part of a strategy for survival.

Or are disappearing: I have just discovered on the web that Boekehuis shut down in 2012.

Some bookshops, remote if one measures their distance from Barcelona, are to be found at the end of the world. But every single one inhabits a world that perhaps is very, very slowly moving towards its end.

XII

The Show Must Go On

In Venice too I felt that one of the worlds we call a *world* was coming to an end. It was the beginning of December and high tide was daily transforming the Piazza San Marco into a pond with duplicated columns, into a lagoon crossed by wellington-booted tourists, into a shipwreck of metal tables with long legs that liquid reflection changed into metallic herons' legs. It was an opportune moment to pay a visit to Acqua Alta, the place Luigi Frizzo has transformed into one of the world's most photogenic bookshops, with a long gondola stuffed with second-hand volumes in the middle of the central aisle, and a side room that floods several times a year. Planks allowed me to photograph the floor the tide had invaded, part of a city that is adrift, and the stairs Frizzo had built with books gave me access to a beautiful view over the canal. Acqua Alta is not just a bookshop: it is a postcard shop; it is a community of cats; it is a store with boats and baths full of magazines and books; it is a place where you can converse with friendly Venetians who come daily to meet tourists; it is – in the end, above all – a tourist attraction. A notice on the door welcomes you in English to the "most beautiful bookshop in the world". When you leave, your memory full of photos, you purchase a bookmark, a calendar, a postcard, at most a history of the city or a collection of travel pieces written by distinguished visitors, and that is how you pay for your entrance to the museum.

Many beautiful traditional bookshops have not joined the tourist circuit or have managed to ignore its siren song. London's John

Sandoe Books, for example, has everything an amateur photographer could desire: its façade unites three eighteenth-century buildings in a single picturesque image with dark wooden windows that reflect the clouds, and inside on three floors 30,000 volumes are piled on tables or placed on movable shelves, and stairs up and down connect the poetry or children's basement with the other rooms, full of ideal corners to be captured by your camera's megapixels. But the gorgeous body has a soul I realised when I was about to leave, having leafed through several books without plumping for any. As is my wont, I asked at the till if they had anything on the shop's history. Then Johnny de Falbe – who, I later read, has been working there since 1986 and is also a novelist – began to perform magic. As if it were bait on a hook, he first regaled me with a delightful little book, *The Sandoe Bag*. A miscellany to celebrate fifty years. While I was glancing through that, a pamphlet on display behind his back caught my eye: "The Protocols of Used Bookstores" by David Mason, which I bought for £5. We talked about the author, a Canadian bookseller, and suddenly de Falbe disappeared – as any self-respecting magician must at some stage – only to reappear with *The Pope's Book Binder*, Mason's memoirs, recently imported from Ontario. Before becoming one of North America's great booksellers, he lived in the Beat Hotel, with Burroughs typing furiously in the next-door room, and sought refuge more than once in Whitman's Shakespeare and Company. On his return to Canada he could feel his vocation as a bookseller germinating deep down. I willingly bought this book that I didn't know I wanted for £25. On the other hand, I left Acqua Alta without buying a thing.

There are two photos of the original Shakespeare and Company in the cafeteria in the Laie bookshop on Barcelona's calle Pau Claris: one of the façade and one of the interior, with Joyce talking to his publishers around a table. To the right you can see dozens of writers' portraits on the wall, above a defunct fireplace. It is a miniature gallery, a résumé of the history of literature, an altar to idolatry. Monnier says of La Maison des Amis des Livres: "This bookshop hardly had the look of a shop, and that wasn't on purpose; we were far from suspecting that people would congratulate us so much in the future for what seemed to us precariously makeshift." Sylvia Beach purchased the sofas for her bookshop in the flea market, where later Whitman presumably bought his (perhaps they were the same ones!). Steloff transported her few pieces of furniture and the handful of books with which she stocked her bookshop for the first time on a horse-drawn cart. When such an apparently careless aspect lasts for decades, it becomes a stylistic feature and therefore partly a marker. The essence of tourism is that echo from the past, and a classic bookshop, with its veneer of antiquity, must engineer a degree of disorder, an accumulation of strata linked to what cliché identifies with the Great Tradition of Knowledge: an apparent chaos that gradually reveals its orderliness. In the entrance to Acqua Alta you also find locally made products and as you walk through the different rooms, despite the dust and variegated displays, you start to decipher a system of classification that no bookshop can escape.

Similarly, the original Bertrand, Lello, the Librería de Ávila, City Lights, the Librairie des Colonnes or Shakespeare and Company have been transformed into museums of themselves and the fragment of the cultural history they represent, and always have more photographs of writers – as representative icons of the printed word – than of philosophers or historians. That is why people talk, quite unjustly, of *literary bookshops*. With the exception of the ones in Lisbon and Paris, they are also museums of a single bookshop, without branches or clones. The transformation of City Lights into a tourist attraction is practically happening in real time, within the framework of a culture obsessed by distinction and the hectic pace of myth-making that goes with pop culture. The first Shakespeare and Company was part of the American Express circuit and a

tourist-laden coach would stop for a few minutes on rue de l'Odéon so photographs could be taken of the place where Joyce published his famous novel, where Hemingway and the glamorous Fitzgeralds used to hang out. All these shops and others that imitate the bohemian image, the historical importance appear on the lists that have proliferated over recent years in newspapers and on web pages of the world's most beautiful bookshops. It is the case with Another Country in Berlin, a reading club and second-hand bookshop for titles in English. Autorenbuchhandlung, with its refined taste in poetry collections and literary café, and the neighbouring Bücherbogen, five parallel silos dedicated to books on contemporary art and cinema, both in Savignyplatz and under the railway lines: they are the city's best, most beautiful bookshops. The Writers' Bookshop gives material form to a classical ideal of the contemporary bookshop. Book Loans, a *spectacular* ideal: its interior design is fully synchronised with the content of the volumes that comprise its stock. Another Country, on the other hand, simply tries to replicate on a small scale the dusty second-hand bookshop doubling as a hostel that gave Whitman such a good return, with a fridge full of beer and American students, hung-over or night-owls, reading as they slump on the sofas. Their presence on the lists is the result of two factors: they can be located (and recognised) in English (and the journalists compiling these lists tend to be Anglo-Saxon) and can be summed up by a single image (which is *picturesque* and responds to what we recognise in the paintings, prints and photographs that circulate globally and tend to be repeated, that is, perpetuated through the basic mechanism that regulates tourism and culture: imitation.)

These lists are often headed by a bookshop I have yet to visit, the Boekhandel Selexyz Dominicanen in Maastricht, whose shelves and tables of latest books are housed in a *spectacular* Gothic structure, a *genuine* Dominican church that was converted in 2007 by architects Merkx and Girod into a shrine to what our era understands as *culture*. They used three metal floors with stairs that ascend with the columns towards the top, fully exploiting the height of the nave: upwards to the place of light and the old God. Irony places a table in the form of a cross at the end of the nave, in the empty altar space, as if the ritual of communion were solely about reading (consumption moves to the nearby cafeteria). Four years later the same architects refashioned the original façade with a rust-coloured door that looks like a triptych when open and a box or wardrobe when closed. No doubt it is a masterpiece in architectural and interior design terms, but it is not so clear that it is a fantastic bookshop. It shuts at 6.00 p.m. and stocks are exclusively in Dutch. Yet that does not matter: style is more important than content in the global circulation of the image. What is picturesque is more vital than the language that leads to reading. The split between the community of readers that allows the bookshop to exist and the tourists who come regularly to photograph it constitutes an essential feature of a bookshop in the twenty-first century. Previously the bookshop became a tourist attraction when its historical importance and picturesque condition hit the radar; over recent years architectural originality, almost always linked to excess, the grandiose and appeal to the media, has perhaps become a more influential marker than the two traditional ones.

I hope the reader will forgive my abuse of italics at the beginning of the previous paragraph: I wanted to emphasise three concepts: spectacle, authenticity and culture. If in the twentieth century the building of opera houses, theatres, concert halls, cultural complexes and libraries followed the model of the contemporary cathedral, this same tendency has only appeared with any force in the domain of bookshops in the present century. The first – now second in most lists, after losing first place when Selexyz was inaugurated – was the Ateneo Grand Splendid that in 2000 reshaped the interior of a cinema-cum-theatre on Avenida Santa Fe in Buenos Aires dating back to 1919, preserving its dome painted in oils, its balconies, boxes and rails and stage with its dark red curtain. The lighting is dazzling, three circular levels of bulbs create the impression that one is at once inside a monument and in the midst of a spectacle in full swing. An uninterrupted spectacle, where the lead role doesn't fall to customers or booksellers, but to their surroundings. Part of the Yenny chain, the bookshop does not possess particularly remarkable stocks, but guarantees a tourist experience as much for occasional visitors as for locals and keen readers. It offers the experience of being in a unique place, even though what is on offer is identical to what you find in the chain's others branches. While Fnac can clone itself in the interior of any historical building, converting Nantes Palace of the Stock Exchange into a space identical to the underground area in Barcelona's Arenas Shopping Centre, which on the outside still appears to be – respectively – a neo-classical building and a bullring, the Ateneo Grand Splendid displays the uniqueness that is most valued in the symbolic marketplaces of virtual tourism (the image) or of physical tourism (the visit).

I am quite sure that Eterna Cadencia, at one end of Palermo in the same city of Buenos Aires, is a better bookshop, and probably even more beautiful than the Ateneo Grand Splendid. Wooden floors, stately armchairs and tables, excellent stocks set out on shelving that covers the walls, a delightful café on a refurbished patio where all manner of literary events are held, a list published under the same name, and lamps that transport you to Hollywood bookshops. Clásica y Moderna, like the bookshop with that name on Avenida Callao, like Guadalquivir just along the street that specialises in Spanish publishing houses, follows a similar style to the one Eterna Cadencia has re-created in the twenty-first century. We find in all three the same sober style and traditional attention to detail of some of the great bookshops that sprang up in the 1980s and 1990s, like Laie, Robinson Crusoe 389 or Autorenbuchhandlung. And in others that have opened their doors in the last ten years like the Book Lounge: lots has been written about taste; our era is characterised by the tremendous range.

One can see the project of La Central in Barcelona as a possible migration of the main tendencies from the last quarter of the twentieth century to those of the twenty-first, always with the proviso that we must not forget the importance of *uniqueness*. The first premises were opened on calle Mallorca in 1996 with a design similar to those I have just mentioned, intimate and human (in step with the reader's body). Conversely, the second, La Central del Raval, inaugurated in 2003, synchronises with Selexyz and Ateneo Grand Splendid in its transformation of an eighteenth-century Chapel of Mercy into a bookish zone, respecting the original architecture and, consequently, the monumental proportions and high ceilings that dwarf humans. However, it has a monastic sobriety, a sense of measure that has disappeared in what might be seen as the third phase of an unpremeditated project: La Central de Callao, in Madrid, inaugurated in 2012, completely refurbished a mansion from the beginning of the twentieth century, preserving its wooden staircase, brick walls, wood and ceramic ceilings, hydraulic-tiled floor and even its painted chapel, and adding, apart from shelves and thousands of books, a restaurant, bar and permanent exhibition of all kinds of objects directly or indirectly linked to reading, such as notebooks, lamps, bags or mugs. Although the ceilings of each of the three floors are relatively low, the extremely high interior patio, with its monumental alphabet soup, brings it in line with one of the main tendencies in our century: a grandeur that allows bookshops to compete with the other cultural icons of contemporary architecture.

After it opened, one of its owners, Antonio Ramírez, who embodies the tradition of the nomadic bookseller (the path his life has followed recalls Bolaño's: Colombian by origin, he started in the trade in Mexico City, perfected his training in Paris's La Hune and Barcelona's Laie before starting his own business), published an article (together with Marta Ramoneda and Maribel Guirao) entitled "Imagining the Bookshop of the Future" where he declared:

> Perhaps it is only possible if we locate ourselves in the dimension that cannot be replaced: the cultural density that the material nature of the paper book implies, or rather think of the bookshop as the real space for effective encounters between flesh-and-blood people and material objects endowed with a unique appearance, a unique weight and form, at a precise moment in time.

And he goes on to list the features of that future space that must already be partially present. Ramírez speaks of an architecture for pleasure and the emotion that abolishes all barriers between reader and book, and helpfully sketches in a hierarchy of what is on offer, where the bookseller acts as choreographer, meteorologist, hyper-reader or mediator and has to hand the emotional and practical elements that will stimulate the reader's memory and channel his choices – purchases – in the direction that can bring him most pleasure. His emphasis on the bookshop as a summation of concrete physical experiences is of a piece with the architecture and interior design we find in a place like La Central de Callao; where the spectacular enters into dialogue with our inner selves, the latest fashion complements stocks, the physical feel of paper or card comes into contact with appetites whetted in the bar or restaurant. Unlike other great bookshops of our time, it is plumb in the centre of the city, in a place where crowds walk by, and competes directly with Fnac or El Corte Inglés, aware that – unlike them and their lack of architectural singularity – it can become a tourist attraction if its grandiose tone and picturesque ambience are incorporated into the world circuit of images.

The division of bookshop chains into those that respect the peculiar characteristics of the space that welcomes them and those that impose a single design on all their branches becomes quite problematic in two Mexican instances: the bookshops that belong to the Fondo de Cultura Económica and the El Pendúlo group. The former is a Latin American chain, with spectacular southern premises like the Centro Cultural Gabriel García Márquez in Bogotá, inaugurated in 2008 and spanning 1,200 square metres, or the Centro Cultural Belle Époque in Mexico City that is two years younger and a few metres smaller. While the former and the complex it is part of were created from zero by Rogelio Salmona in the middle of the Colombian capital's historic centre, the Librería Rosario Castellanos is part of the reshaping of the Lido, an emblematic cinema from the 1940s, carried out by Teodoro González de León. It is a dazzlingly white cathedral-like nave where the arrangement of bookshelves and sofas brings to mind a Pharaoh's hieroglyph. The bookshop's ceiling was designed by Jan Hendrix the Dutch artist and represents ancient scripts using vegetation. Naturally, it has a café inside, though it occupies a tiny space.

Conversely, the first El Pendúlo bookshop opened its doors in La Condesa district in the 1990s as a clear fusion of bookshop and café, which would be accompanied by the hybrid combination of concert hall and literary academy in line with cultural centres proliferating at the time throughout the Western world, and anticipating the main response bookshops would give to the digital threat: one word symbolises the mix: *cafebrería*. The bookshop as a rendezvous point, as a place for business meetings, private classes, events, in a subtly Mexican ambience (tablecloths and plants). Over time they have opened six premises that maintain a unique style adapted to the features of each new space. In Polanco, for example, the restaurant, bookshop and bar are almost entirely equal in terms of square metres occupied, but the bookcases are instrumental in creating the unifying thread, the overall *tone*, in forging harmony between the different sections with their diverse cultural products: music, cinema, television series, art books . . . In Colonia de Roma the wall at the back of the bookshop is called on to provide the interconnecting function, transformed as it is into a hyperbolic bookcase crammed with books bordering the stairs to the first floor and terrace, evoking Patrick Blanc's vertical gardens. In El Pendúlo del Sur there is a huge purple panel that plays on its echo of contemporary art. In Santa Fe we find, in its stead, murals that recall pre-

Columbian art and Miró. There is a common corporate image that flirts with individual design features that are memorable and cool. Clearly the grand bookshop is an important development, interacting with installations and other features of contemporary design and art that can be seen in those vast places: particularly walls and above all ceilings. In addition to those in Buenos Aires, Maastricht, Madrid or Mexico City, the same kind of projects have sprung up in our century in the United States, Portugal, Italy, Belgium and China.

The Last Bookstore occupies the former premises of a bank in downtown Los Angeles and has preserved the original giant columns: the counter is made entirely of books and overlooked by a sculpture of a large fish that has also been made from hundreds of books. The old industrial premises in Lisbon's Alcántara district,

home to Ler Devagar, have preserved – intact and rusty – the printing press from the old days and have at the back a vast wall packed with books that is continuously flown past by a bicycle with wings that open and shut as if applauding in slow motion. The applause is for a project that is without parallel in the bookselling world. Having had two former shops, one in the Barrio Alto and the other in an old weapons factory, Ler Devagar is now the most widely stocked bookshop in Portugal. It is a limited company with forty shareholders who receive no return on their investment, and enjoy no hope of one, because they have purchased all the books in the main premises and those in other parts of the country. It is a huge library that sells books and encourages one to read slowly. It is also a first-rate cultural centre, where things are always happening. I can't think of a better definition of an ideal bookshop. The white platforms that make up the ceiling in Bookàbar, the bookshop and café in Rome's Palazzo delle Esposizioni, have been set on an incline and punctured as if they were supremacist sculptures. An installation of books hanging on threads from the ceiling dominates the view of Cook & Book in Brussels. In the case of Beijing's Bookworm a giant orange awning fights the *horror vacui*. Because it is all about humanising the space, reducing the dizziness provoked by all those square metres between the walls, about camouflaging the height of ceilings that are on a factory rather than human scale.

The majority of these twenty-first-century bookshops have one or two cafeterias, if not a restaurant, harmoniously inscribed in a varied whole where books provide an Ariadne's thread. Décor, furniture, a children's section disguised as a games room, or the interplay between different colours and textures respond to an interior design of the emotions, the aim of which is to prolong a customer's stay in the bookshop transforming it into an experience that draws on all the senses and on human relationships. I think that minimalism is more than a stylistic resource: it can be read as a statement of intent. A hierarchy is established on three levels. At the top is the architecture, almost always propelled by straight lines in a space so huge it ends up imposing itself on everything that exists there but doesn't fill it, to the tiniest letter. At an intermediate level the stairs, picture windows, shop windows, murals, sculptures, period furniture and lights are the protagonists whose function is to try to reduce the intensity of a space that was usually conceived for a different kind of social function and has now been recycled and refurbished. At the bottom comes the display of the small, minimal books, the raison d'être of the whole structure, which can never be as important as they were in the twentieth century when bookshops were made to measure, to fit our hands and eyes, because of the magnificence, the lighting, the art-gallery or vintage-store status of their new abode.

In this way, the bookshop becomes a possible metaphor for the Internet: as on the web, texts occupy a significant but small, limited space in comparison to what is invaded by the visual, and above all by what is so indefinite and empty. As in cyberspace, where things are always happening, and are mostly invisible, a visitor to these multi-spaced bookshops is conscious that stories are being told in the area of children's books, that a poet-singer is performing in the

cafeteria, that the new-books table or window display has been changed that morning, that a book launch will begin in a moment, that there is a new dessert menu in the restaurant or literary workshops are about to finish their first session. As in the virtual world, we are witnessing new forms of socialising, social networks, but the bookish variety clings to personal contact, to the fulfilment of the senses, the only thing the Internet cannot offer us. 10 Corso Como makes its intentions very clear via the "slow shopping" tag at the heart of its spectacular bookshop project. The longer you linger mentally or physically in the atmosphere of the shop, the more you buy and consume. Although the Italian chain has premises in Seoul and Tokyo, only the *original* in Milan adds a bookshop to its fusion of hotel, café-restaurant, garden, art gallery, and clothes and design shop. If the centre of gravity is still occupied by a cinema in the Trasnocho Cultural complex in Caracas, opened in 2001, a cinema around which are grouped gastronomic, artistic or bookish spaces (the El Buscón bookshop), it is testament to a twentieth-century trend, which in any case never caught on; multi-screen cinemas are usually on the top floor and bookshops are simply just another shop with no particular uniqueness or prestige. In 10 Corso Como the nucleus comprises the restaurant and the hotel, around which we find a couple of cultural outposts that legitimise the cultural activities of the complex as a whole. 10 Corso Como's bookshop only has this generic name: Book and Design Shop, because it has no meaning beyond its glamorous context. In an era when gastronomy is now recognised as an art, culture has broadened its boundaries and these can be traced in tourist experiences that encompass every form of cultural consumption. Something similar has been happening from the inception of modernity: when Goethe travelled through Italy his visits to bookshops formed part of the *spatial continuum* that shaped every journey alongside churches, ruins, the houses of learned men, restaurants and hotels. Travel and bookshops have always stimulated a love of the marketplace.

Intellectual pleasure fuses with voluptuous delight. Today's bookshops are learning more than ever from the success of shops in contemporary art museums where catalogues are only part of what is on offer, and usually not even the most significant items, there alongside jewellery, clothes and, generally, industrial design pieces. Objects become a focus of attraction that is strengthened by a minimalist context highlighting the unique facets of every item. As in my encounter with that teapot in Beijing we often find the same T-shirt or cup in another shop, at a lower price, but then it does not enjoy the prestigious aura lent by the Pompidou Centre or the Museum of Modern Art. So it is not *exactly* the same object. If it were only a few metres away, within the framework of the exhibition, we would not be able to touch it, but we can do so in the shop. We can touch everything in a bookshop, and that is not the case in a museum or the most important libraries. And buy. The profit margins on arty presents are much higher than on books. New bookshops are very clear about how tactile experience adds value to their offerings: premises cannot simply justify their existence as the physical space for electronic sales, they must offer everything that web pages can't provide.

And that necessarily involves luxury. Because a visit to a bookshop distinguished by its history, architecture, interior design or publishing stock spotlights us as subjects who like luxury, members of a different community to the one that consumes culture in shopping centres and the big chains. Paul Otlet, in his *Traité de Documentation* (1934), already writes: "Comfort competes with luxury and beauty in sales rooms. A refined atmosphere, comfortable lounges, fresh flowers. Some bookshops like Brentano's, Scribner's or Macmillan are real palaces." Megalomaniac bookshops have existed at the very least from the eighteenth-century Temple of the Muses. Policy in eighteenth-century salons was regulated precisely by refinement, by an aristocratically refined taste. With the advent of democracy, the dream of the troubadours is multiplied exponentially: whether readers belong to the communities of greatest excellence of their era depends on their culture, education, artistic insights and not on their acquisitive power or blood. Nevertheless, it is true that if one wants to be able to evaluate and interpret the architecture, design or stock of spectacular bookshops it is a costly educational process and not everyone can afford the trips that allow one to explore the places that enjoy a high-profile presence in tourist guides. And, as in all tourist scenarios, different levels of awareness, intellectual insight and class fictions coexist: as many as the brains and gazes browsing there at a particular moment.

In *A Life of Books*, Joyce Thorpe Nicholson and Daniel Wrixon Thorpe make it very clear that Australian booksellers in the 1970s were aware that it was crucial for their premises to connect with what the authors called "a trendy appearance". They mention Angus & Robertson in Sydney, whose owners decided to paint each floor a different colour when they moved to new premises; the Angus & Robertson, in Western Australia, that upped and went to a period hotel and tavern and started a campaign based on the coupling of "books and beer", and the Abbey's Henry Lawson's Bookshop, in the basement of the Hilton Hotel in Sydney, with its black wood bookcases and impressive offer of "any book published in Australia". There are many other precedents for the spectacular bookshop waiting to be disinterred in libraries, newspaper collections and personal reminiscences. Two nineteenth-century stations that were converted into bookshops still exist: Barter Books opened its doors in 1991 in Alnwick, Northumberland, and four years later Walked a Crooked Mile Books did so in Philadelphia.

The revamping of hotels, railway stations, cinemas, palaces, banks, printers', art galleries or museums as bookshops is a constant over recent decades and has accelerated in the twenty-first century. In a new historic context, in which recycling has taken on a new

meaning, in which culture has been digitalised and, above all, in which the existence of all that is real is – simultaneously – physical and virtual, these cathedrals to the written word acquire a deeply capitalist, religious-cum-apocalyptic significance that also reveals unprecedented artistic ambition. The impact of the spectacular is decisive on both fronts. Via El Pendúlo's web page you can make virtual visits to each of its *cafebrerías*. Google Images and other platforms are awash with photographs of the world's most beautiful, most interesting, most spectacular bookshops. For the first time in the history of culture these bookshops achieve access straight away to the international tourist circuit, markers gather pace and generate immediate contagion – at a stick and paste rate – on web pages, social media, blogs and microblogs and create a desire to visit, get to know, travel and photograph without any recourse to History or the participation of famous writers or acclaimed books. The photograph of a church, railway station or theatre transformed into a bookshop: that image is more compelling in the new logic of tourism than the 100,000 books in the picture or their 10 billion words.

XIII

Everyday Bookshops

J. R. R. Tolkien's first poem, "Goblin Feet", was published in a poetry collection by Oxford's Blackwell's Bookshop that cancelled his debt in exchange for the advance on his rights, and because he had been a regular customer in that establishment founded in 1879 by Benjamin Henry Blackwell, which was later transformed into a publishing concern by his son Basil, the first member of the family to go to university and the publisher of the author of *The Lord of the Rings*. As the business grew and became a chain, each branch attracted its parishioners, its usual suspects, its congregation, people who chose Blackwell's in Edinburgh, Liverpool or Belfast as their everyday bookshop.

If you hunt around the main premises in Oxford, it is still possible to imagine how the few square metres where the business was created gradually increased until several houses were transformed into a single monster of a house. As you enter, to the left, a nineteenth-century fireplace and wooden beams are the archaeological traces of the original establishment. If you ask, you can visit the reconstructed founders' office next to the fireplace on the floor above, where pipes, spectacles and letter-openers are laid out on the table as if they had been left there only a few hours before, and not a whole century. The successive owners of Blackwell's bought up all the flats in the building as business expanded. The most recent, definitive extension is a huge basement at the back that occupies the space under Trinity College Gardens. It has its own name: the

Norrington Room. It is an Olympic swimming pool of shelves and books. In the 1960s and 1970s, during the frequent power cuts, it relied on kerosene lamps that ensured people could still read, whatever the obstacle. I imagine those readers as if marooned in a post-nuclear bunker. From above, despite the rectangular shape, it looks like a giant brain. This is what it is: the brain of a collective intelligence, which its eighty employees are for the most part; what Oxford University is, expanding exponentially and intellectually, just like its best bookshop.

The last time I was in Berlin, before I went to photograph the decomposing remnants of the Karl Marx bookshop, quite by chance, I bumped into César Aira. We went to the nearest cafeteria and chatted for a while about the latest literary titles out in Argentina. "We would meet almost daily," he said halfway into the conversation, "in the International Argentina, Francisco Garamona's bookshop, Raúl Escari, Fernando Laguna, Ezequiel Alemián, Pablo Katchadjian, Sergio Bizzio and other friends." Dominated by a sofa and a small table for your glass of wine, the site of the Mansalva publishing house is probably the only bookshop in the world where you can buy most of Aira's books, even in translation, although naturally there will always be ten or twenty that not even Garamona can supply. One of those places where ways belonging to another era have become established. Like the Ballena Blanca, Alejandro Padrón's place in Mérida, Venezuela, where university teachers like Diómedes Cordero and writers like Ednodio Quintero meet daily to talk about the country's great poets, about Japanese literature or political issues in Spain or Argentina, while they prepare the next edition of the famous *Bienal de Literatura Mariano Picón Salas*, which was to inspire the exploits of Aira and an army of Carlos Fuentes clones in *The Literary Conference*. Because literature is polemical, and is about the future and about books to imagine.

"In the afternoon our bookshop seemed more like a club where scientists, literati and artists met up, talked, to find relief from the prosaic nature of daily life," wrote Mikhail Osorgin on the subject of the legendary cooperative in Moscow, The Writers' Bookshop. Although conversations about literature are as old as Western culture, it is, of course, in the seventeenth and eighteenth centuries that they would become institutionalised as literary *conversazione*. It should be no surprise then that this coincided with the moment when bookshop and café began to fuse into a single organism, as Adrian Johns has observed in *The Nature of the Book*. Apprentices were part of the family and the boundaries between private space and public business were not at all obvious, so that the presence of armchairs, seats and sofas, where one could enjoy reading while drinking, was often due to the fact that they belonged to the bookshop owner's house. Since then many booksellers have developed salons and literary conversations that double as debates about culture and sessions for buying and selling: "The foremost example of 'amphibious mortal' was surely Jacob Tonson. Among aristocrats he looked like a bookseller; among booksellers he appeared an aristocrat." The confusion between private and public life parallels the confusion between bookshop and library. Samuel Pepys in his diaries writes of bookshops where "seats were available so customers could read for as long as they wished". And booksellers themselves in the eighteenth century were the driving force behind lending libraries that were much more democratic than literary societies and the only way in which artisans' apprentices, students or women could have access to literature without incurring the huge expense of the cost of a book. One could even say that, despite appearances, bookshops have never really been sure about their real boundaries.

On my travels I have converted many into havens, fleeting homes far from the home I did not actually possess, and found refuge in their ambiguous nature. I remember my daily visits to the basement of Leonardo da Vinci during my stay in Rio de Janeiro, to the Seminary Co-op when I lived in Chicago and to the Book Bazaar in Istanbul for as long as my foolish haggling lasted trying to secure that Turkish travellers' book, to the Ross bookshop in Rosario on every one of my sojourns in that city with a river without shores, even though it was in the nearby premises of El Ateneo that I found the complete works of Edgardo Cozarinsky, and, in its café, where I read *Rinconete y Cortadillo* and *El licenciado Vidriera*. Since re-establishing myself in Barcelona, whenever I escape to Madrid, as well as visiting La Central in the Reina Sofía art museum, I try to have a coffee in Tipos Infames, a bar and gallery in step with the latest trends in international bookshops; I go to say hello to Lola Larumbe who manages Rafael Alberti in such a charming, professional manner, a bookshop designed by the poet and painter in 1975, where water seems to swirl over the basement; I visit Antonio Machado, in the basement of the Circle of Fine Arts, with its delightful selection of books from small Spanish bookshops and by whose cash register over the years I have discovered the main studies of bookshops that I have used for this essay. I go to Naples twice a year and am duty-bound to visit Feltrinelli's in the Central Station and the Librería Colonnese, on via San Pietro a Majella, surrounded by churches, artisans making Nativity cribs, remains of ancient walls and altars dedicated to San Diego Maradona.

There is no doubt that a bookshop is much more hospitable when, as a result of repeated visits or coincidence, you strike up a friendship with one of the booksellers. When I lived in Buenos Aires and Rosario and had to leave the country every three months, I used it as an opportunity to explore parts of Uruguay by sea, land and river. Every one of my journeys ended in La Lupa, the bookshop where one of its owners, Gustavo Guarino, gave me leads into Uruguayan literature on every visit: only by travelling to the place where things happen do you find access to what resists visibility on the Internet. One of the pleasures that awaits me in Palma de Mallorca is La Biblioteca de Babel, where I can lose myself in its essay and fiction sections, and Literanta, where critic and cultural activist Marina P. De Cabo stands behind the counter; it was she who discovered me when we became interested in the work of Cristóbal Serra. For years I visited La Central de Raval in Barcelona on Fridays, knowing that César Solís would be there to recommend the latest titles from Latin America, or supply me with the latest book by Sebald or on Sebald to be published in one of the main European languages. Ever since he moved to Madrid, I now go to Damià Gallardo, in the Centre for Contemporary Culture's Laie bookshop, who solves my problems as a reader. Because every good bookseller must be something of a doctor, chemist or psychologist. Or barman. Francisco, Alejandro, Gustavo, Marina, César and Damià form part of my own bookseller tradition, the restless tradition of habits you take up again as soon as you arrive in distant cities where you once lived for a while.

Austerlitz, the hero of W. G. Sebald's novel of that name, experiences the most decisive moment of his life in a second-hand bookshop near the British Museum, one that is owned by a beautiful woman whose name is a pure haven of rest: Penelope Peacefull. While she is solving a crossword puzzle and he absent-mindedly flicking through architectural prints, two women are talking on the radio about "the summer of 1939, when they were children and had been sent to England on special transport". Austerlitz's mind and body are invaded by a kind of trance: ". . . and I stood there as still as if on no account must I let a single syllable emerging from that rather scratchy radio escape me." Because those words allow him at a stroke to recover his own childhood, his own journey and arrival in England escaping from a Europe in flames, his own exile: years his memory had erased completely. In a bookshop he suddenly remembers who he is, from which Ithaca he has come.

Childhood and especially adolescence are periods when you fall in love with bookshops. I spent so many Saturday afternoons browsing among the shelves of Rogés Llibres, the ground floor of the Garden City of Mataró that had been converted into a second-hand bookshop, that I am quite unable to shape them chronologically or date them. I am sure those sessions only took place at the weekend and in the holidays, because during the school term I went in the opposite direction towards the city centre. On my way I would go into the Caixa Laietana Library, where I read all the Astérix, Obélix and Tintin comics and took out all the *Alfred Hitchcock and the Three Investigators* and Sherlock Holmes novels, and on my way home at dinnertime I would pop into Robafaves, which I discovered much later was a cooperative and one of the most important bookshops in Catalonia, where a book was launched nearly every evening, and I'd listen as if in church or class to those words that, although they were there between mouth and microphone, objects as tangible as the books surrounding me, sounded remote, an incomprehensible babble, completely disconnected from my firm desire to be a writer.

When I was fourteen or fifteen I accompanied my father on his visits to homes in another neighbourhood in Mataró, next to the Central Park, the velodrome and municipal swimming pool, where as a child I saw peacocks, races and cyclists and my own body diving into the water as if I was not scared of all those litres of blue chloride. After an eight-hour day at the telephone company my father worked as an agent for the Readers' Circle. First he would distribute the new catalogues and then we picked up the cards with the orders from the subscribers and processed them and a few weeks later when all the books had arrived at our house, my mother helped us organise them by street and finally we took them to their new owners and collected payment. Some customers forced us to go back two, three or even four times, because they never had the 950 or 2,115 pesetas their order cost. Conversely, others bought five, seven or nine books every two months and always had the 10,300 or 12,500 pesetas ready because they were expecting us and so much wanted to start reading. I suppose it was in one of those family flats or flats belonging to old ladies or single men, complete strangers, that I first saw well-stocked private libraries and decided that, one day, when I was a writer, I would have one too. The first aspiration was too abstract to be more than pie in the sky; the second, on the other hand, assumed a tangible form that, like girls' bodies, was pure desire.

In *Auto da Fé* Elias Canetti writes that a child is at the mercy of the wares of any old tradesman dealing in books, as soon as they can read and walk. He concludes that young children should be brought up in private libraries. He is probably right because I cannot recall a single book I bought in Rogés Llibres or in Robafaves that changed my life: the great reads in my life came later (or simply: late), when I had moved away from Mataró. Nonetheless, Robafaves is the most important bookshop in my life because there I was introduced to something I had glimpsed in those private houses: a life in which books played an intimate part. In 2666, Amalfitano muses that a book probably came to him via Laie or La Central. I could say the same about most of my library, a third, perhaps, to which one should add the "restless" titles bought in Altaïr and the comics purchased in Arkham. The other two thirds come from my travels and what publishers' publicity departments send me. I have sent dozens of boxes from Rosario, Buenos Aires and Chicago: libraries and the nomadic spirit are always wedded in my mind. My own experience of cities is shaped by the intersection between strolling and bookshops, so most of my usual itineraries cling to certain shops as my personal hubs or stops. Streets, bookshops, squares and cafés represent the routes of modernity and settings for two essential acts: conversation and reading. While literary writing, which until a few decades ago was still taking place at café tables, has been retreating into private space, or at best to libraries, talks and readings, premeditated or chance encounters, and the diary, novel or magazine, it continued to be articulated in the social sphere of metropolitan life. Blogs and social media allow you to exchange data and ideas in the cosmopolis, but your body continues to tread a local, domestic topography.

As we read in "The Journey of Álvaro Rousselot", one of the stories in *The Insufferable Gaucho*, Bolaño thought that the bookshops of Buenos Aires and their contents had lives of their own. In other words, it is not only the movement of readers' bodies that threads together the different bookshops in a city, books themselves shift and wander, open lines of escape and create itineraries. That was the idea that inspired the Barcelona theatre director Marc Caellas when he decided to adapt Robert Walser's *The Walk* into a walk around the Argentinian capital. Its pages were suddenly incarnated by an actor, a stroller, who wanders round the various emblematic spaces in the modern city as happens in the story. Of course, one is the bookshop:

> As now an extremely splendid, abundant bookshop came pleasantly under my eye, and I felt the impulse and desire to bestow upon it a short and fleeting visit, I didn't hesitate to step in, with an obvious good grace, while I permitted myself, of course, to consider that in me appeared far rather an inspector, or bookkeeper, a collector of information, and a sensitive connoisseur, than a favourite and welcome, wealthy book buyer and good client. In courteous, thoughly circumspect tones, and choosing understandably only the finest turns of speech, I enquired after the latest and best in the field of belles-lettres. [. . .] "Certainly," said the bookseller. He vanished out of eyeshot like an arrow, to return the next instant to his anxious and interested client, bearing indeed the most bought and read book of enduring value in his hand. This delicious fruit of the spirit he carried carefully and solemnly, as if carrying a relic charged with sanctifying magic. His face was enraptured; his manner radiated the deepest awe; and with that smile on his lips that only believers and those who are

inspired to the deepest core can smile, he laid before me in the most winning way that which he had brought.

I considered the book, and asked, "Could you swear that this is the most widely distributed book of the year?"

"Without a doubt!"

"Could you insist that this is the book one has to have read?"

"Unconditionally."

"Is this book also definitely good?"

"What an utterly superfluous and inadmissible question."

"Thank you very much," I said cold-bloodedly, left the book that had been most absolutely widely distributed, because it had unconditionally to have been read, where it was, and softly withdrew, without wasting another word.

"Uncultivated and ignorant man," the bookseller shouted after me, for he was most justifiably and deeply vexed.

The walker created by the Swiss Walser, in some bookshop in Boedo speaking with an Argentinian accent, making fun of conventions, of literature tied to sales figures, of the absurdity of the world of culture, being directed by a Catalan. Marginal centres and central margins, abolished frontiers, translations, changes of city, quantum leaps, transcultural interactions: welcome to any bookshop.

The same relationship between periphery and centre that I experienced quite unawares when I visited Rogés Llibres and Robafaves, as if they were mazes, second-hand and antique bookshops and shops for the latest titles, can also be established between bookshops in the centre of Barcelona and those on the city's fringes. Gigamesh was the first shop I entered in Barcelona and I soon started to explore others selling comics, science fiction and heroic fantasy that surrounded it and still do, like a plague of aliens proliferating over time in the vicinity of the Paseo de San Juan. The area of that impossible centre occupied by Laie, Documenta, Altaïr, Alibri and La Central, and so many others, is small and walkable. Until the end of 2015 you only had to cross El Born, a district without bookshops, to reach La Negra y Criminal that Paco Camarasa ran for almost fifteen years in a backstreet of Barceloneta. Now both districts are orphaned. Bookshops imitate the neighbourhoods that welcome them: this place could only exist among those fishermen's houses, and in Gràcia a mere fifteen minutes' walk from the Arco de Triunfo, Taifa and Pequod are unimaginable without the context of a locality, a context of nearness. Camarasa and José Batlló, the Alma Mater of Taifa (now run by his heirs, Jordi Duarte and Roberto García) are two of the key individuals in Barcelona's world of books that finds its originating myth in the pages Cervantes devoted to it in *Don Quixote* and has always negotiated the city's literary bilingualism. Taifa has been the pre-eminent bookshop north of the Diagonal since 1993, as La Negra y Criminal is south of the Ronda Litoral. Batlló is a poet, publisher and legend. He is famous for his culture, for being a great friend to his friends and for his skirmishes with customers he is capable of scolding depending on the titles they buy. Those he has sold most over the last twenty years are *Hopscotch* and *City of Prodigies*. Second-hand books are in cell-like spaces at the back, as if to remind us that it is normal for novels and essays to cease to circulate, for publishers to shut down, for us to be forgotten. Similarly Pequod, the belly of the whale that, as they say, was born yesterday, sells both new and second-hand books, because we live in hybrid times. Despite its small surface space, this bookshop transforms itself into a gallery for micro-exhibitions, an area for conversations about Italian literature and an aperitif bar at the weekends, and spreads itself around social media, because nothing new exists solely in the world of what we can touch.

In a second circle – orbit within an orbit – other Barcelona bookshops have vied for recognition over the last few years. I am thinking, for example, of +Bernat, the bookshop and restaurant on calle Buenos Aires, next to the Plaza Francesc Macià, that is managed by Montse Serrano and defines itself as a "cultural store", the favourite haunt of Enrique Vila-Matas since he switched neighbourhoods. Or of Llibreria Calders in calle Parlament in the Sant Antoni district with its piano and agenda forever in flames. Or of Nollegiu, in Poblenou, that Xavi Vidal has turned into an important cultural centre. Fortunately, they are not the only bookshops that have been generating urban interest far from the city centre. Because, although hubs where bookshops are concentrated have heritage value, like the popular Port'Alba that Massima Gatta has called "the Charing Cross Road of Naples", or Amsterdam's elegant Het Spui and adjacent streets, a democratic city is a network of public and private libraries and small and large bookshops: a dialogue between readers who live in multiple centres and various peripheries.

My strolls often lead me to calle Llibreteria, the ancient Decumanus in Roman Barcino, where you now find the Papirvm artisan shop and La Central in the Museum of the History of the City, one of those places – like the bookshop in the basement of the College of Architects – where Barcelona archives its own memory. The brotherhood of Sant Jeroni dels Llibreters was founded in 1553. If St Lorenzo, one of the Church's first treasurers, is held to be the patron of librarians because of his work classifying documents, the austere St Jerome, one of the Church's first ghost-writers (he wrote Pope Damaso I's letters) is held to be the patron of translators and booksellers. St Lorenzo, the man who some legends identify as the mysterious individual who hid the Holy Grail to protect it against the wave of violence that also ended his own life, died a martyr grilled to death on the outskirts of Rome: on August 10 every year the reliquary that contains his head is exhibited in the Vatican, so it can be venerated, I am not sure whether solely by librarians. St Jerome, on the other hand, after a period as an outstanding translator, went to Bethlehem in self-exile, lived in a cave and devoted his time to attacking in his writings the vices of Europe textually and beating himself with a stone in acts of penitence. He usually appears in the iconography with the Vulgate, the Bible that he translated into Latin from Hebrew – though he was an expert in ancient Greek, too – open on his desk, a skull as a symbol of *vanitas* and that stone which rumour-mongers say he used as a kind of translation diction-ary that had yet to be written: he beat himself and God revealed to him *ipso facto* the Latin equivalents of the Hebrew original.

Your city enters its bookshops through their windows and customers' footsteps, a hybrid space that is neither wholly private nor wholly public. The city walks in and out of its bookshops, because one cannot be understood without the other, so the pave-ments outside Pequod or La Negra y Criminal are always crammed with people on a Saturday afternoon or Sunday morning drinking wine and eating steamed mussels, and books on Barcelona find their way into every city bookshop, which is the space where they naturally belong. And when they start to get dog-eared, the novels, essays, biographies and books of poetry that citizens have man-handled and owned return to the city's stalls, to the Mercado de San Antonio, to the second-hand bookshops or that arcade with books and a Uralite roof that was at the back of Los Encantes where passers-by turned out to be collectors, antiquarians and rag-and-bone men.

If the metropolis vamps up its bookish dimension on Sundays in the Mercado de San Antonio or on the days Los Encantes is open, there is one day in the year when the city reproduces in its every corner that sensation Don Quixote took away with him: the city breathes the printed word. The Spanish Day of the Book was the brainwave of a Valencian, Vicente Clavel, who had established him-self in Barcelona as the youthful owner of the Cervantes publishing house. From the Chamber of Books and with the support of the Catalan Labour Minister, Eduard Aunós, he gained recognition for his project through a royal decree in 1926 in the middle of the Primo de Rivera dictatorship. Although the idea was to encourage Spanish book culture at all levels of the administration, so that every library and city would participate in one way or another in the festivities, from the very first it became polarised between mass celebrations in Barcelona and institutional, academic events in Madrid. Guillermo Díaz Plaja wrote these words in an article after Clavel's death:

> Almost half a century later the decree remains in place, with a single important change – the decree of September 7, 1930 – which switched the date of October 7 that was originally agreed – two days before the certified baptism of Cervantes – to April 23, the day of his death. This historically exact date meant that the Day of the Book in Barcelona coincided with the day of St George, the patron saint of Catalonia. When Don Gustavo Gili pointed that out, Clavel immediately retorted, "It doesn't matter. The roses for St George will flower for ever. The only risk we run is that Cervantes will be forgotten." The years gone by have shown that it was to be a happy marriage of both commemorations in the legendary Barcelona festival. The city of the Counts is without a doubt the vanguard of the Peninsula in terms of the breadth and popularity of the Day of the Book.

The year 1930 was when publishers began to launch new books in Catalan on the Dia de Sant Jordi and the general public responded with enthusiasm, while Madrid took the first steps to organise its

Book Fair on another date and the rest of the country also gradually forgot Cervantes' Day. The Civil War paralysed the publishing industry and Francoism banned Catalan and eliminated the Book Chambers by replacing them with the National Spanish Book Institute. The Day of the Book did not start to become important again in Catalonia until the 1950s. In 1963 the opening address was given by Manuel Fraga Iribarne, the Minister for Information and Tourism, who defended the need to promote literature in the Catalan language. The front page of *La Vanguardia Española* on April 23, 1977 (15 pesetas), together with a photograph of a street packed with people, reproduced in Catalan the following lines by Josep Maria de Sagarra:

> The rose has given him joy and pain
> and who can say how dearly he loves it;
> bringing more blood to his veins
> to defeat all the dragons in the world.

Thanks to an initiative taken by the First Latin American Congress of Book Associations and Chambers, from 1964 April 23 became the Day of the Book in every country where Spanish and Portuguese was spoken and from 1966 it has been International Book and Authors' Rights Day. Perhaps because not only Cervantes and Shakespeare died on that day but also other internationally known writers like the Inca Garcilaso de la Vega, Eugenio Noel, Jules Barbey d'Aurevilly and Teresa de la Parra.

I love to visit my favourite bookshops on the days prior to Sant Jordi: I buy all my books then and during *la diada* I simply like to stroll and observe, "like a better sort of tramp, a vagabond and pickpocket, or idler and vagrant", as Walser says. Like all self-respecting writers and publishers, I use these walks to check whether my books are there or not and to put them in the proper place on the shelves of my everyday bookshops. And in those where they are absent. Even in the book section in El Corte Inglés. Even on the second floor in Fnac, in the middle of the city, where I imagine many of the young sales assistants, with their B.A.s, M.A.s or Ph.D.s in literature would have been great booksellers in another – no doubt better – world, or perhaps already are in this one, which although in crisis is the only one we have.

EPILOGUE

Virtual Bookshops

Over the first few months of 2013 I watched how a bookshop that was almost a hundred years old became a McDonald's. Of course, it is an obvious metaphor, but that doesn't make it any less shocking. I am quite sure that the Catalònia, the bookshop that opened its doors on the edges of Plaza de Cataluña in 1924, was not the first to be transformed into a fast-food restaurant, but it is the only time I have personally witnessed such a metamorphosis. For three years I walked past the glass door in the morning and some-times went in to take a look, buy a book, make an enquiry until sud-denly the shutters stayed shut and someone stuck up a precarious notice, barely a page long, which read:

> After over eighty-eight years of being open and eighty-two years of activity at Ronda San Pere 3. After surviving a civil war, a devastating fire, a property dispute, the Llibreria Catalònia will close its doors for good.
>
> The severe crisis in the book trade has generated a slump in the sales of books over the last four years that has made it impossible for us to continue in these circum-stances and conditions.
>
> It has been very sad, difficult and painful to take this irrevocable decision. We have tried to find every possible solution, perhaps too late in the day, but either they didn't exist or we couldn't find them.

Nor could we have prolonged this situation, because we wanted to ensure that the business closed in an orderly way and met all its obligations. If we had continued any longer, the end would have been much worse.

As we make this decision public we would also like to remember all those who have worked throughout the years in the Llibreria Catalònia and the enterprises that depended on it, especially the Selecta publishing house, and also all our customers – some over decades and generations – and our authors, publishers and distributors. Jointly they have allowed the Llibreria Catalònia to make an important contribution to the culture of Catalonia and Barcelona.

Now and in the future, in all the forms that the dissemination of culture will take, there are and will be individuals, associations, collectives and enterprises ensuring the survival of literature and written culture in general. Unfortunately, the Llibreria Catalònia will not be part of that future.

Miquel Colomer, Director, Barcelona, January 6, 2013

Day after day I was witness to the disappearance of books, to empty shelves, to dust, that dust that is the great enemy of books, books that were no longer there, only ghosts, memories, books that were gradually being forgotten until one Wednesday they did not even have shelves where they could be, because the premises were emptied, filled with workers who yanked out the bookcases and the brackets and the place was all noise and drilling, a din that shocked me for weeks, because I had been used to the silence and cleanliness it had emanated for years; when I walked past that same door, I was met with clouds of dust, carts loaded with rubble, with debris, the gradual transformation of the promise of reading, the business

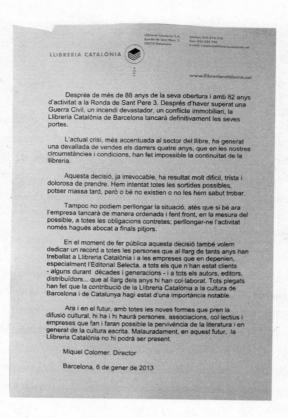

Després de més de 88 anys de la seva obertura i amb 82 anys d'activitat a la Ronda de Sant Pere 3. Després d'haver superat una Guerra Civil, un incendi devastador, un conflicte immobiliari, la Llibreria Catalònia de Barcelona tancarà definitivament les seves portes.

L'actual crisi, més accentuada al sector del llibre, ha generat una devallada de vendes els darrers quatre anys, que en les nostres circumstàncies i condicions, han fet impossible la continuïtat de la llibreria.

Aquesta decisió, ja irrevocable, ha resultat molt difícil, trista i dolorosa de prendre. Hem intentat totes les sortides possibles, potser massa tard, però o bé no existien o no les hem sabut trobar.

Tampoc no podíem perllongar la situació, atès que si bé ara l'empresa tancarà de manera ordenada i fent front, en la mesura del possible, a totes les obligacions contretes; perllongar-ne l'activitat només hagués abocat a finals pitjors.

En el moment de fer pública aquesta decisió també volem dedicar un record a totes les persones que al llarg de tants anys han treballat a Llibreria Catalònia i a les empreses que en depenien, especialment l'Editorial Selecta, a tots els que n'han estat clients - alguns durant dècades i generacions - i a tots els autors, editors, distribuïdors... que al llarg dels anys hi han col·laborat. Tots plegats han fet que la contribució de la Llibreria Catalònia a la cultura de Barcelona i de Catalunya hagi estat d'una importància notable.

Ara i en el futur, amb totes les noves formes que pren la difusió cultural, hi ha i hi haurà persones, associacions, col·lectius i empreses que fan i faran possible la pervivència de la literatura i en general de la cultura escrita. Malauradament, en aquest futur, la Llibreria Catalònia no hi podrà ser present.

Miquel Colomer, Director

Barcelona, 6 de gener de 2013

of reading into the digestion of proteins and sugar, the fast-food business.

I have nothing against fast food. I like McDonald's. Indeed, I am interested in McDonald's: I search one out on most of my trips, in order to try the local specialities, because there is always a breakfast or a fajita or a hamburger or a sweet that is the McDonald's version of one of the favourite dishes of the locals. However, that didn't make this supplantation any less painful. For months every morning I watched the destruction of a small world, occupying that same space like an ambassador from another world, and in the afternoons I read about reading and finished writing this book.

There is a traditional, multicoloured bookshop in Turin called La Bussola. All bookshops are compasses: when you study them they offer you interpretations of the contemporary world that are more finely tuned than those provided by other icons or spaces. If I had to choose another bookshop to explain partially – complete explanations do not exist – the schism within the book trade in our era it would be Pandora's in Istanbul. It has two well-stocked premises, one opposite the other: one sells exclusively books in Turkish; the other, titles in English. The prices in one are in Turkish lira; those in the other in dollars. Pandora makes a symbolic reality explicit: all bookshops live between two worlds, the local and the one imposed by the United States, traditional business (of a local sort) and the one in huge shopping centres (chains), the physical and the virtual. This metaphor is not as obvious as the one afforded by an old bookshop, a classic, vintage bookshop, a bookshop that was founded by Josep López, Manuel Borràs and Josep Maria Cruzet, survived the wintry bunker of a dictatorship and systematic harassment by a real estate company, after fierce political and moral resistance yielded to the cold, implacable, abstract rules of economics, shut down its premises, a few metres away from the Apple Store, two hundred metres from Fnac, opposite El Corte Inglés, and was transformed into a McDonald's. In effect, the Pandora metaphor is more oblique but more hopeful, because it leads to survival rather than closure. All bookshops are divided into at least two worlds and are forced to consider other possible worlds, and I write that without a scrap of naivety.

Green Apple Books – as Dave Eggers recalls in his chapter in the anthology *My Bookstore* – is lodged in a building that has survived two earthquakes, those that brought turmoil to San Francisco in 1906 and 1989; perhaps that is why one experiences between its shelves the feeling that "if a bookshop is as unorthodox and strange as books are, as writers are, as language is, it will all seem right and good and you will buy things there." I bought there a short bilingual book, published by a Hong Kong poetry festival, the English title of which is *Bookstore in a Dream*. Four lines about the bookshop as a quantum fiction really caught my attention: its multiplication through space, its mental realm, its existence in parallel universes on the Internet, a compulsive survivor of all earthquakes. If Danilo Kiš's narrator dreams of an impossible library that contains the infinite *Encyclopedia of the Dead*, Lo Chih Cheng dreams of a bookshop that cannot be mapped out. A bookshop, like any other, that is soothingly physical and horribly virtual. Virtual because digital, or mental, or because it has ceased to exist. A bookshop that is born, like Lolita in Santiago de Chile, like Bartleby and Company in Berlin or Valencia, like Librería de la Plata in marginal Sabadell. Like Dòria Llibres, which has filled the space left by Robafaves in another small Catalan city, my Mataró: at what point do projects become completely real? Bookshops of the memory, gradually invaded by fiction.

Like the one run by the wise Catalan in *One Hundred Years of Solitude*, who came to Macondo during the Banana Company boom, opened his business and began to treat the classics and his customers as if they were members of his own family. Aureliano Buendía's arrival in that den of knowledge is described by Gabriel García Márquez in terms of an epiphany:

> He went to the bookstore of the wise Catalonian and found four ranting boys in a heated argument about the methods used to kill cockroaches in the Middle Ages. The old bookseller, knowing about Aureliano's love for books that had been read only by the Venerable Bede, urged him with a certain fatherly malice to get into the discussion, and without even taking a breath, he explained that the cockroach, the oldest winged insect on the face of the earth, had already been the victim of slippers in the Old Testament, but that since the species was definitely resistant to any and all methods of extermination, from tomato slices with borax to flour and sugar, and with its one thousand six hundred and three varieties had resisted the most ancient, tenacious, and pitiless persecution that mankind had unleashed against any living thing since the beginning, including man himself, to such an extent that just as an instinct for reproduction was attributed to humankind, so there must have been another one more definite and pressing, which was the instinct to kill cockroaches, and if the latter had succeeded in escaping human ferocity it was because they had taken refuge in the shadows, where they became invulnerable, because of man's congenital fear of the dark, but on the other hand they became susceptible to the glow of noon, so that by the Middle Ages already, and in present times, and *per omnia secula seculorum*, the only effective method for killing cockroaches was the glare of the sun. The encyclopedic coincidence was the beginning of a great friendship. Aureliano continued getting together

in the afternoon with the four arguers, whose names were Álvaro, Germán, Alfonso and Gabriel, the first and last friends that he ever had in his life. For a man like him, holed up in written reality, those stormy sessions that began in the bookstore at 6.00 p.m. and ended at dawn in the brothels were a revelation.

That wise Catalan was in fact Ramon Vinyes, the bookseller and cultural activist in Barranquilla, founder of the *Voces* magazine (1917–20), first Spanish immigrant, then Spaniard in exile, teacher, dramatist and storyteller. His bookshop, R. Viñas & Co, a pre-eminent cultural centre, was burnt down in 1923 and is still remembered today in Barranquilla as one of the mythical bookshops of the Colombian Caribbean. When he went into exile in Latin America as a Republican intellectual after crossing France, he took up teaching and journalism and became the master of a whole young generation known as "the Barranquilla Group" (Alfonso Fuenmayor, Álvaro Cepeda Samudio, Germán Vargas, Alejandro Obregón, Orlando Rivera "Figurita", Julio Mario Santo Domingo and García Márquez). On one of my strangest mornings ever, I gave a taxi driver at the Barranquilla bus station the following address: calle San Blas, between Progreso and 20 de Julio. Librería Mundo. As we drove on, he told me that the names had changed, he did some consulting and discovered that I was referring to calle 35 between Carrera 41 and 43. We headed there. The Librería Mundo run by Jorge Rondón Hederich was where the legendary group of intellectuals met, the spiritual heir of R. Viñas & Co. that had been reduced to ashes twenty years earlier. When I got there, I discovered that it too no longer existed. It was obvious, but neither Juan Gabriel Vásquez (who had given me the information) nor I had thought to check it. The bookshop should have been there, but it wasn't, because for quite some time it had only existed in books:

> In any case, the axis of our lives was the Librería Mundo at twelve noon and six in the evening, on the busiest block of calle San Blas. Germán Vargas, an intimate friend of the owner, Don Jorge Rondón, was the one who convinced him to open the store that soon became the meeting place for journalists, young writers and politicians. Rondón lacked business experience, but he soon learned, and with an enthusiasm and a generosity that turned him into an unforgettable Maecenas. Germán, Álvaro and Alfonso were his advisers in ordering books, above all the new books coming from Buenos Aires, where publishers had begun the translation, publication and mass distribution of new literature from all over the world following the Second World War. Thanks to them we could read in a

timely way books that otherwise would not have come to the city. The publishers themselves encouraged their patrons and made it possible for Barranquilla to again become the centre of reading it had been years earlier, until Don Ramon's historic bookshop ceased to exist. It was not too long after my arrival when I joined the brotherhood that waited for the travelling salesmen from the Argentinian publishers as if they were envoys from heaven. Thanks to them we were early admirers of Jorge Luis Borges, Julio Cortázar, Felisberto Hernández, and the English and North American novelists who were well translated by Victoria Ocampo's crew. Arturo Barea's *The Making of a Rebel* was the first hopeful message from a remote Spain silenced by two wars.

That is García Márquez writing about those two bookshops, the one he didn't know and the one he visited, both melded into one in the virtual reality of his masterpiece. I have been unable to find photographs of R. Vinyes & Co. or Mundo on the web and I now realise that this book has found its rhythm in searches inside material books and on the non-material screen, a syntax of toing and froing as continuous and discontinuous as life itself; how Montaigne would enjoy the ability of search engines to generate associations, links, fertile byways and analogies. How his heir Alfonso Reyes would also have learned from them, about whom the narrator of the first part of *The Savage Detectives* says: "Reyes could be my little home. Reading only him and those he liked one could be incredibly happy." *In Books and Bookshops in Antiquity* the erudite Mexican noted:

Parchment was cheaper and more resistant than papyrus, but the book trade did not adopt it as a matter of course.

[. . .] Ancient producers of books preferred this light, elegant material, and there was a degree of aversion towards the weight and coarseness of parchment. Galen, the great doctor from the second century AD, was of the opinion that, for reasons of hygiene, shiny parchment hurt and tired the eyes more than smooth opaque papyrus that did not reflect the light. Ulpianus the jurist (died AD 229) examined as a legal problem the issue of whether codices made of vellum or parchment should be considered as books in library bequests, something that did not even have to be debated in the case of papyrus items.

Almost two millennia later, the slow transition from reading paper to reading onscreen gives these arguments a contemporary twist. We now wonder if the screen and the light it radiates do more damage to the eyes than electronic ink, which does not allow us to read in the dark. Or whether after someone's death it is right for their heirs to inherit, through books, vinyl records, C.D.s and hard discs, the songs and texts their parents bought for themselves. Or whether television and video games harm the imagination of children or adolescents, because they stimulate their reflexes but damage the activity of their brains and are so violent. As Roger Chartier has studied in *Inscription and Erasure, Written Culture and Literature from the Eleventh to the Eighteenth Century*, it is in Golden Age Castile that the danger fiction represents for the reader is first formally expressed, with *Don Quixote* arousing the greatest social fear: "In the eighteenth century, the discourse is medicalised and constructs a pathology of excessive reading that is thought to be an individual sickness or collective epidemic." In this period the reader's sickness is related both to the arousal of the imagination and the immobilising of the body: the threat is as mental as it is physiological. Following this thread, Chartier analyses the eighteenth-century debate over traditional reading that was called *intensive*, and modern reading that was said to be *extensive*:

> According to this dichotomy, suggested by Rolf Engelsing, the *intensive* reader was confronted by a restricted range of texts that were read and reread, memorised and recited, listened to and learnt by heart, transmitted from generation to generation. Such a way of reading was heavily impregnated with sacred purpose, and subjected the reader to the authority of the text. The *extensive* reader, who appears in the second half of the eighteenth century, is very different and reads countless new, ephemeral printed works and devours them eagerly and quickly. His glance is distanced and critical. In this way, a communitarian, respectful relationship is replaced by irreverent, self-assured reading.

Our way of reading, inextricably linked to screens and keyboards, must be about the spread, books having been produced at an ever-increasing rate, of more and more audio-visual information and knowledge platforms, of that *broadening out* with all its political implications. The loss of the ability to concentrate on a single text brings the gain of a glimmer of light, critical, ironic distance, the ability to relate and interpret simultaneous phenomena. Consequently, it brings an emancipation from authorities that restrict the range of reading, the deconsecration of an activity that by this stage in evolution should be almost *natural*: reading is like walking, like breathing, something we do without even having to think.

Whilst the apocalyptically minded revamped worn-out arguments from worlds that no longer existed, rather than accepting perpetual change as the immutable engine of History, Fnac bookshops filled up on video games and television series and prestigious

bookshops began to sell commentaries about video games and television series, as well as eReaders and eBooks. Because the moment a style ceases to be a fashion or trend and becomes mainstream, it will probably undergo a process of sophistication and end up on bookshop and library shelves and in museum rooms. As a cultural product. As a work of art. As a commodity. Scorn of emerging and mainstream styles is fairly common in the world of culture that is a field – as they all are – dominated by fashion, the ego and the economy. Most of the bookshops I have mentioned in this essay, on the international circuit where I have slotted myself in as tourist and traveller, nurture a class fiction to which more and more millions now have access – fortunately – but it is still for a minority. We represent the broadening out of the *chosen people* that Goethe met in the Italian bookshop. A class fiction that is eminently economic – as they all are – even though it wears a veneer of an education that is more or less refined. We should not deceive ourselves: bookshops are cultural centres, myths, spaces for conversations and debate, friendships and even amorous encounters, due in part to their pseudo-romantic paraphernalia that is often championed by readers who love their craftsmanship, and even by intellectuals, publishers and writers who know they form part of the history of culture, but above all bookshops are businesses. And their owners, often charismatic booksellers, are also bosses, responsible for paying the wages of their employees and ensuring their labour rights are respected, managers, overseers, negotiators skilled in the ins and outs of labour legislation. One of the most inspiring and sincere pieces of those gathered together in *Rue de l'Odéon* is in fact the one that links freedom to the purchase of a book:

> For us the business has a deep and very moving meaning. In our view a shop is a real magic chamber: when a passer-by crosses the threshold of a door that anyone can open, enters this impersonal place, one might say that nothing changes the expression on his face or his tone of voice: with a feeling of total freedom he is carrying out an act he believes has no unexpected consequences.

But which in fact is defined by those consequences: James Boswell will meet Samuel Johnson in Tom Davies's bookshop on Russell Street; Joyce will find a publisher for *Ulysses*; Ferlinghetti will decide to open his own bookshop in San Francisco; Josep Pla as a child will enter the Canet bookshop in Figueras and seal his pact with literature; William Faulkner will work in one as a bookseller; Vargas Llosa will buy *Madame Bovary* in a bookshop in the Quartier Latin in Paris a long time after seeing the film in Lima; Jane Bowles will meet her best friend in Tangier; Jorge Camacho will buy *Singing from the Well* in a bookshop in Havana and become Reinaldo Arenas's main champion in France; a psychiatrist will advise a juvenile delinquent by the name of Liminov to go to Bookshop 41 in a Russian provincial city and that will make a writer of him; François Truffaut will find a novel by Henri-Pierre Roché entitled *Jules et Jim* among second-hand books in Delamaine in Paris; one night in 1976 Bolaño will read the "First Infra-realist Manifesto" in Ghandi Bookshop in Mexico

City; Cortázar will discover Cocteau's work; Vila-Matas will find Borges. Perhaps it was only once that the fact somebody did not enter a bookshop had positive outcomes: one day in 1923 Akira Kurosawa headed off to Tokyo's famous Maruzen bookshop, renowned because of its building constructed by Riki Sano in 1909 and for its importing of international titles for the Japanese cultural elite. He was planning to buy a book for his sister, but he found that the shop was shut and left; two hours later an earthquake destroyed the building and the whole district was consumed by flames. Literature is magic and exchange and for centuries has been sustained, like money, by paper and that is why it has fallen victim to so many fires. Bookshops are businesses on two simultaneous, inseparable levels: the economic and the symbolic, the sale of copies and the creation and destruction of reputations, the reaffirmation of dominant taste or the invention of a new one, stocks and credits. Bookshops have always been the canon's witches' Sabbath and hence key points in cultural geopolitics. The places where culture becomes more physical and thus more open to manipulation. The spaces where, from district to district, town to town, city to city, it is decided what reading matter people will have access to, what is going to be distributed and thus open to the possibility of being consumed, thrown away, recycled, copied, plagiarised, parodied, admired, adapted or translated. That is where their degree of *influence* is mainly decided. It was not for nothing that the first title Diderot gave to his *Letter on the Book Trade* was: "A political and historical letter written to a magistrate about the Bookshop, its present and ancient status, its rules, its privileges, its tacit limits, the censors, itinerant sellers, the crossing of bridges and other matters related to the control of literature."

The Internet is changing that democracy – or dictatorship, depending on how you look at it – of distribution and selection. I often buy from Amazon or other web pages titles published in cities

I have visited I was unable to buy when I was there. Last year, on my return from Mexico City, where I *exhausted* a dozen bookshops looking for an essay by Luis Felipe Fabre published by a small Mexican publishing house, I decided to look on the Casa del Libro page and there it was and cheaper than in its place of origin. If Google is the Search Engine and Barnes & Noble the Book Chain, it hardly needs to be said that Amazon is the supreme Virtual Bookshop. Though that is not very precise: even if it was born in 1994 as a bookshop with the name of Cadabra.com and soon after switched to Amazon in order to shoot up the alphabetical pecking order that ruled the Internet before Google, the truth is that for some time it has been a big department store where books are as important as cameras, toys, shoes, computers or bicycles, although the brand bases its power to pull in customers on emblematic devices like Kindle, a *reader* or electronic book that creates customer loyalty to the purchase of books on Amazon. Indeed, in 1997 Barnes & Noble took it to court over its deceitful advertising (that tautology): the slogan "The world's greatest bookstore" was not true because it was a *book broker* and not a *bookstore*. Now it deals in anything that is on offer, except for eReaders that are not Kindles.

We are innate searchers of the physical world – my hunt for the non-existent bookshop in Barranquilla is only one example from a thousand – and cannot stop being that in the virtual world as well: the history of the electronic book is as gripping as a thriller. It began in the 1940s, gathered speed in the 1960s with hypertext forms of publishing and found a format in the 1970s thanks to Michael S. Hart and a description ("electronic book") thanks to Professor Andries Van Damme, of Brown University, in the middle of the 1980s. When Sony launched its book reader in 1992 with the Data Discman C.D., it did so with the tag "The library of the future". Kim Blagg got the first I.S.B.N. for an electronic book in 1998. These are the data, the possible chronologies, the clues that when combined create the feeling that we are caught between two worlds, as were Cervantes' contemporaries in the seventeenth century, Stefan Zweig's at the beginning of the twentieth or the inhabitants of Eastern Europe the end of the 1980s. In a slow apocalypse in which bookshops are at once oracles and privileged observatories, battlefields and twilight horizons in an irrevocable process of mutation. As Alessandro Baricco says in *The Barbarians*:

It is a mutation. Something that concerns everyone, without exception. Even the engineers, up there on the wall's turrets are already starting to take on the physical features of the very nomads they, in theory, are fighting against and they have nomadic coins in their pockets, as well as dust from the steppes on their starched collars. It's a mutation. Not some minor change or inexplicable degeneration, or mysterious disease, but a mutation undergone for the sake of survival. The collective choice of a different, salutary habitat. Do we have even the vaguest sense of what could have generated it? I can certainly think of a number of decisive technological innovations, the ones that have compressed space and time, squeezing the world. But these probably would not have been enough had they not coincided with an event that threw open the whole social scene: the collapse of the barriers that until now had kept a good part of humanity far from the routines of desire and consumption.

The word *desire* reappears yet again in this book, that chemical energy that draws us to certain bodies and objects, vehicles towards manifold knowledge. In the post-1991 world, with neo-liberalism strengthened by the fall of the Soviet Union, and increasingly digital and digitalised, that desire has been assuming material form in the consumption of the pixel, that smallest unit of information with which we make sense of our writing, photographs, conversations, videos and maps that explain the routes where we sweat, drive, fly or read. That is why bookshops have web pages: in order to sell us pixelated books, and so we also consume images, stories, the latest novelties and gimmicks. All this is substantial, not mere accident: our brains are changing, the way we communicate and relate is changing: we are the same but very different. As Baricco explains, in recent decades what we understand by experience and even the tissue of our existence has changed. The consequences of this mutation are as follows: "Surface rather than depth, speed rather than reflection, sequences rather than analysis, surfing rather than penetration, communication rather than expression, multitasking rather than specialisation, pleasure rather than effort."

An exhaustive dismantling of the machinery of nineteenth-century bourgeois thought, a final destruction of the last debris of the shipwreck of the divine in everyday life. The political victory of irony over the sacred. It is much more difficult for the few gods of old that survived two World Wars on paper to continue to harass us from the dull glow of the screen.

Cultures cannot exist without memory, but need forgetfulness too. While the Library insists on remembering everything, the Bookshop selects, discards, adapts to the present thanks to a necessary forgetfulness. The future is built on obsolescence; we have to discard past beliefs that are false or have become obsolete, fictions and discourses that do not shed the faintest light. As Peter Burke has written: "Discarding knowledge in this way may be desirable or even necessary, at least to an extent, but we should not forget the losses as well as the gains." That is why once the inevitable process of selecting and discarding has taken place, one should "study what has been dispensed with over the centuries, the intellectual refuse", where humanity might have got it wrong, where what was most valuable might have been cast into oblivion, among data and beliefs that did deserve to disappear. After so many centuries of long-term survival, books, because of electronic sourcing, are entering into the logic of inbuilt obsolescence, of a sell-by date. That will bring an even more profound change to our relationship with the texts we are going to be able to translate, alter and *personalise* to an unimaginable degree. It is the crossroads on the journey that began with humanism when philology questioned useless, hackneyed authorities and Bibles began to be turned into our languages via rational criteria and not according to the say-so of superstition.

If there are so many of us who keep collecting futile stamps on our foolish passports to the bookshops of the world it is because we find there the remains of cultural gods that have replaced the religious sort. From Romantic times to the present, like archaeological ruins, like some cafés and so many libraries, or cinemas and museums of contemporary art, bookshops have been and still are ritual spaces, often marked out by tourism and other institutions as ways to understand the history of culture, erotic topographies, and stimulating contexts to find material to nourish our place in the world. If with the death of Jakob Mendel or the hypertext of Borges those physical places we can cling to became more fragile and less transcendent, with the Internet they are much more virtual than our imagination might suggest. They compel us to create new mental tools, to read more critically and more politically than ever, to imagine and connect as never before, analysing and surfing, going deeper and more rapidly, transforming the privilege of unheard-of access to Information into new forms of Knowledge.

I devote many of my Sunday afternoons to surfing the web in search of bookshops that still do not exist for me, though they are out there, waiting for me. For years I have been a reader-viewer of emblematic places I have yet to visit. Very recently chance enabled me to get to know two of them: in Coral Gables, whose name had always evoked Juan Ramón Jiménez, twenty-four hours of unexpected stopover allowed me to go to Books & Books, a very beautiful Miami bookshop housed in a Mediterranean-style building from the 1920s. One weekend in Buenos Aires when I had nothing planned, I decided to take the ferry and visit Montevideo to discover finally in person an even more beautiful, equally well-stocked bookshop, Más Puro Verso, with its art deco architecture from the same era and glass display cabinet at the top of its imperial stairs. Just as I coveted those spaces, I have spent years collecting leads to others in books, magazines, web pages or videos. For instance Tropismes in a nineteenth-century arcade in Brussels; Les Bals des Ardents in Lyons with that grand door made from books and Oriental carpets that invite one to read on the floor; Bordeaux's Mollat, which has just turned every book-lover's dream into a reality, the chance to spend a night in a bookshop, and whose website is always bubbling with ideas and activities, a wholly family tradition transformed into 2,500 metres of printed culture overflowing from the very same house where no less a figure than the traveller-philosopher Montesquieu lived, wrote and read at the beginning of the eighteenth century; Candide, its architecture as light as bamboo, in Bangkok, run by the writer, publisher and activist Duangruethai Esanasatang; Athenaeum Boekhandel in Amsterdam, which Cees Nooteboom emphatically recommended to me for its classical aesthetics and, above all, for its importance as a cultural centre and writers' residence; Pendleburys, a country house devoured by a Welsh forest; Swipe Books in Toronto, because an antique bicycle hangs from its ceiling and a chessboard sits between its two readers' armchairs; Ram Advani

Booksellers, the mythical shop in Lucknow, although now I will not be able to meet Ram Advani, who died at the end of 2015 at the age of ninety-four, and whose memory is perpetuated by his daughter-in-law, Anuradha Roy; and Atomic Books, the favourite bookshop of Santiago García the scriptwriter and comics critic who in an email told me that it is one of the best in the U.S.A. for a reader of graphic novels, though they also sell literature, countercultural fanzines and even toys and punk records: "What's more, you can meet John Waters picking up his mail." I have no information about the history or importance of others, photographs have simply captivated me, because everything I have about them is in languages like Japanese, which I do not understand: Orion Papyrus, in Tokyo, with its parquet floors, its lights worthy of Mondrian and that blend of wood and metal in shelves full of art and design books, or Shibuya Publishing & Booksellers in the same city, with bookshelves in every imaginable geometric shape.

And if I ever return to Guatemala City, I will fight against my nostalgia for El Pensativo that has disappeared and will *religiously* repair to Sophos. I expect I will jot down notes on them all when I pay them a visit like someone who is paying off their debts, in a notebook similar to the one I used on that far-off trip, because I have now given up on my iPad's Moleskine app and do not like my mobile phone doubling as a camera and a notebook. You just see: what matters in the end is the will to remember.

In "Covert Joy", a story by Clarice Lispector, we meet a girl who was "fat, short, freckled and had reddish, excessively frizzy hair" but who had "what any child devourer of stories would wish for: a father who owned a bookshop". Many years ago I started to peel off the sticker with the price and barcode on any book I bought and stick them on the inside of the back cover next to the anti-theft chip. It was my way of maintaining an almost fatherly link. The last wish of writer David Markson, who died in New York in June 2012, was for his library in its entirety to be sold to Strand and thus spread around all those many, many libraries of innumerable anonymous readers. For 1 dollar, or 20, or 50, his books went there, were reintegrated into the market where they once belonged, to await their fate and fortune. Markson could have bequeathed his library to a university, where it would have accumulated dust and been visited by the few specialising in his work, but he opted for the opposite move: to share it around, break it up and subject it to the risk of totally unexpected future readings. When the news broke, dozens of the followers of the author of *This is Not a Novel* rushed to the Manhattan bookshop to locate his annotated, underlined books. A virtual group was set up. Scanned pages started to be published on the Internet. In his copy of *Bartleby the Scrivener* Markson underlined every appearance of the phrase "I would prefer not to"; in *White Noise*, he alternated "astonishing, astonishing, astonishing" with "boring, boring, boring"; in a biography of Pasternak he wrote in the margin: "It is a fact that Isaak Babel was executed in the basement of a Moscow prison. A very strong possibility that the manuscript of an unpublished novel is still around in Stalin's archives." One could turn all the marginal comments in Markson's library into one of his fragmentary novels where notes on reading, poetic impressions and reflections follow on as if it were a zapping session. It would be an impossible novel because nobody is ever going to find all the books that made up his library: many of them were bought or are being bought by people who do not know who Markson was. That gesture forms part of his legacy. A final, definitive gesture combining death, inheritance, paternity and a single one of the infinite bookshops that sum up all the rest, a unique story dedicated to world literature.

Ideas only exist in things.
David Markson, *The Loneliness of the Reader*

WEBOGRAPHY

American Booksellers Association: http://www.bookweb.org
Bloc de Llibreries: http://www.delibrerias.blogspot.com.es
Book Forum: http://www.bookforum.com
Book Mania: http://www.bookmania.me
Bookseller and Publisher: http://www.booksellerandpublisher.com.au/
Bookshop Blog: http://www.bookshopblog.com
Books Live: http://www.bookslive.co.z
Bookstore Guide: http://www.bookstoreguide.org
Book Patrol: http://www.bookpatrol.net
Courrier du Marroc: http://www.courrierdumarroc.com
Día del Libro: http://www.diadellibro.eu
Diari d'un llibre vell: http://www.llibrevell.cat
El Bibliómano: hhtp//www.bibliographos.net
El Llibreter: http://www.llibreter.blogspot.com.es/
El Pececillo de Plata: http://www.elpececillodeplata.wordpress.com/
Gapers Block: http://www.gapersblock.com
José Luis Checa Cremades. Bibliofilia y encuadernación: http://www.
    checacremades.blogspot.com.es
Histoire du Livre: http://www.histoire-du-livre.blogspot.com.es
Kipling: http://www.kipling.org.uk
Le Bibliomane Moderne: http://www.le-bibliomane.blogspot.com.es
Libbys Book Blog: http://www:libbysbooksblog.blogspot.com.es
Library Thing: http://www.librarything.com
Libreriamo: http://www.libreriamo.it
Paul Bowles Official Site: http://www.paulbowles.org
Rafael Ramón Castellanos Villegas: http://www.rrcastellanos.blogspot.
    com.es
Reading David Markson: http://www.readingmarksonreading.tumblr.
    com
Rare Books Collection de Princeton: http://www.blogs.princeton.edu/
    rarebooks/
Reality Studio. A Williams S. Burroughs Community. http://www.reali-
    tystudio.org
Rue des Livres: http://www.rue-des-livres.com
The Bookshop Guide: http://www.inprint.co.uk/thebookguide/shops/
    index.php

The Bookseller: http://www.thebookseller.com
The China Beat: http://www.thechinabeat.org
The Haunted Library: http://www.teensleuth.com/hauntedlibrary
The Ticknor Society Blog: www.ticknor.org/blog/

FILMOGRAPHY

"Before Sunrise" (1995), Richard Linklater.
"Before Sunset" (2004), Richard Linklater.
"Chelsea Girls" (1966), Andy Warhol and Paul Morrisey.
"Fun in Acapulco" (1963), Richard Thorpe.
"Funny Face" (1957), Stanley Donen.
"Hugo" (2011), Martin Scorsese.
"Julie & Julia" (2009), Nora Ephron.
"Fantômes de Tanger" (1997), Edgardo Cozarinsky.
"The Life of Others" (2006), Florian Henckel von Donnersmarck.
"Lord Jim" (1965), Richard Brooks.
"Notting Hill" (1999), Roger Mitchell.
"9 1/2 Weeks" (1986), Adrian Lyne.
"Portrait of a Bookstore as an Old Man" (2005), Benjamin Sutherland
    and Gonzague Pichelin.
"Remember Me" (2010), Allen Coulter.
"Reservoir Dogs" (1992), Quentin Tarantino.
"Short Circuit" (1986), John Badham.
"Short Circuit 2" (1988), Kenneth Johnson.
"The West Wing" (1999–2006), NBC.
"Vertigo" (1958), Alfred Hitchcock.
"You've Got Mail" (1998), Nora Ephron.

BIBLIOGRAPHY AND ACKNOWLEDGEMENTS

The author and publisher acknowledge the following sources of copyright material where noted below and are grateful for the permissions granted. Every effort has been made to identify the sources of all the material used. If any errors or omissions are brought to our notice, we will be happy to include the appropriate acknowledgements on reprinting.

Aínsa, Fernando, *Del canon a la periferia: Encuentros y transgresiones en la Literatura uruguaya*, Trilce, Montevideo, 2002.

Barbier, Frédéric, *Histoire du livre*, Armand Colin, Paris, 2006.

Baricco, Alessandro, *The Barbarians: An Essay on the Mutation of Culture*, translated by Stephen Sartarelli, Rizzoli Ex Libris, New York, 2006. © 2006 by Alessandro Baricco, English translation © 2013 by Stephen Sartarelli. Reproduced by permission of Rizzoli/Ex Libris.

Barthes, Roland, *Empire of Signs*, translated by Richard Howard, Jonathan Cape, London, 1983.

Battles, Matthew, *Library: An Unquiet History*, W. W. Norton and Company, New York, 2003.

Bausili, Mercè and Emili Gasch, *Llibreries de Barcelona: Una guia per a lectors curiosos*, Columna, Barcelona, 2008.

Beach, Sylvia, *Shakespeare and Company* Lincoln and London, Nebraska UP, 1980. Copyright © 1959 by Sylvia Beach and renewed 1987 by Frederic Beach Dennis. Used by permission of Houghton Mifflin Harcourt Publishing Company. All rights reserved.

—*The Letters of Sylvia Beach*, edited by Keri Walsh, Columbia University Press, New York, Lincoln, NE, 2010.

Becerra, Juan José, *La interpretación de un libro*, Avinyonet del Penedés, Candaya, 2012.

Bechdel, Alison, *Are You My Mother? A Comic Drama*, Houghton Mifflin Harcourt, New York, 2012.

Benjamin, Walter, *The Arcades Project*, edited by Rolf Tiedemann, translated by Howard Eiland and Kevin McLaughlin, Belknap Press, New York, 2002. Copyright © 1999 by the President and Fellows of Harvard College.

—*One Way Street and Other Writings*, translated by Amit Chaudhuri, Penguin Books, London, 2009.

Bolaño, Roberto, *2666*, translated by Natasha Wimmer, Picador, London, 2009

—*Between Parentheses (1998–2003)*, translated by Natasha Wimmer, Picador, London 2012. © 2004 by the Heirs of Roberto Bolaño. English translation copyright © 2011 by Natasha Wimmer. Reproduced by permission of Pan Macmillan via PLSclear.

—*Consejos de un discipulo de Morrison a un fanatico de Joyce*, by Roberto

Bolaño and Antoni Garcia Porta. Copyright © 1984, Roberto Bolaño y Antoni García Porta.

—"Dance Card", *Last Evenings on Earth*, translated by Chris Andrews, Vintage, London, 2007. Copyright © 1997, 2001, Roberto Bolaño. English translation © Chris Andrews, 2007.

—*The Insufferable Gaucho*, translated by Chris Andrews, Picador, London, 2014

—*The Savage Detectives*, translated by Natasha Wimmer, Picador, London, 2008. Copyright © 1998, Roberto Bolaño. English translation © Natasha Wimmer 2007, reproduced with permission from Farrar, Straus & Giroux.

—"Vagabond in France and Belgium", *Last Evenings on Earth*, translated by Chris Andrews, Vintage, 2007

Borges, Luis Jorge "Funes the Memorious" and "The Library of Babel", *Ficciones*, translated by Anthony Kerrigan, Grove Atlantic, New York, 1962. Copyright © María Kodama 1998. English translation copyright © 1962 by Grove Press Inc. Used by permission of Grove/Atlantic, Inc. Any third party use of this material outside of this publication is prohibited.

Bourdieu, Pierre, *Distinction: A Social Critique of the Judgement of Taste*, translated by Richard Nice, Routledge, 1984. © 1984, 2010, the President and Fellows of Harvard College and Routledge. Reproduced by permission of Taylor & Francis Books Ltd.

Bowles, Jane, *Out in the World: Selected Letters (1935–70)*, edited by Millicent Dillon, Black Sparrow Press, Santa Barbara, 1986. Copyright © 1985 by Rodrigo Rey Rosa.

Bowles, Paul, *In Touch: The Letters of Paul Bowles*, edited by Jeffrey Miller. Farrar, Straus, Giroux, New York, 1994.

—*Without Stopping*, Putnam, New York, 1972.

—*Travels: Collected Writings, 1950–93*, Sort of Books, London, 2010.. Copyright © 2010 by Rodrigo Rey Rosa.

Bradbury, Ray, *Fahrenheit 451*, Rupert Hart-Davis Ltd., London 1954.

Bridges, Lucas E., *Uttermost Part of the Earth*, Dutton Books, New York, 1949.

Burke, Peter, *A Social History of Knowledge II: From the Encyclopaedia to Wikipedia*, Polity Press, Cambridge, 2012. Copyright © Peter Burke 2012.

Campaña, Mario, *Baudelaire: Juego sin triunfos*, Debate Barcelona, 2006.

Campbell, James, *This Is The Beat Generation New York – San Francisco – Paris*, Secker & Warburg, London, 1999.

Canetti, Elias, *Auto da Fé*, translated from the German by C. V. Wedgwood, The Harvill Press, London, 2005.

—*The Voices of Marrakesh*, translated by J. A. Underwood, Marion Boyars Publishers, London, 1967.

Carey, Peter, *The True History of the Kelly Gang*, Faber & Faber, London, 2001.

Carpentier, Alejo, *Los pasos recobrados: Ensayos de teoría y crítica literaria*, Biblioteca Ayacucho, Caracas, 2003.

Casalegno Giovanni (Ed.), *Storie di Libri: Amati, misteriosi, maledetti*, Einaudi Editore, Turin, 2011.

Casanova, Pascale, *The World Republic of Letters*, translated by M. B. DeBevoise. Harvard University Press, Cambridge, MA, 2004.

Cavallo, Guglielmo, Roger Chartier and Lydia G. Cochrane, *A History of Reading in the West*, University of Massachusetts Press, Amherst, 2003.

Certeau, Michel de, *Le Lieu de l'Autre: histoire réligieuse et mystique*, Editions du Seuil, Paris, 2005.

Chartier, Roger, *Inscription and Erasure, Written Culture and Literature from the Eleventh to the Eighteenth Century*, Pennsylvania University Press, Philadelphia, PA, 2007.

Chatwin Bruce, *In Patagonia*, Vintage, London, 1998.

—*Under the Sun: The Letters*, edited by Elizabeth Chatwin and Nicholas Shakespeare, Jonathan Cape, London, 2010.

Chih Cheng, Lo, *Bookstore in a Dream*, The Chinese University Press, Hong Kong, 2011.

Choukri, Mohamed, *Paul Bowles in Tangier*, translated by Gretchen Head and John Garret, Telegram, San Francisco, 2008.

Clemente San Román, Yolanda, "Los catálogos de librería de las sociedades Anisson-Posuel y Arnaud-Borde conservados en la Biblioteca Histórica de la Universidad Complutense", *Revista General de Información y Documentación*, vol. 20, 2010.

Cobo Borda, Juan Gustavo, "Libreros colombianos, desde el constitucionalista don Miguel Antonio Caro hasta Karl Buchholz" (http://www.ciudadviva.gov.co/portal/node/32)

Coetzee, J.M., *Disgrace*, Vintage, London, 2000.

—*Dusklands*, Secker and Warburg, London, 1982. Reprinted by permission of The Random House Group Ltd.

Cole, Teju, *Open City*, Faber & Faber, London, 2011.

Cortázar, Julio, "House Taken Over", *Blow Up and Other Stories*,

—*Cartas: 1937–1963*, edited by Aurora Bernádez, Alfaguara, Madrid, 2000. Reproduced with permission from Editorial Alfaguara.

—*Hopscotch*, translated by Gregory Rabassa, Panther, 2014.

Cuadros, Ricardo, "Lo siniestro en el aire" (http://www.ricardo-cuadros.com/html/lo_siniestro.htm).

Dahl, Svend, *A History of the Book*, The Scarecrow Press, New Jersey, 1968.

Debord, Guy, *Commentaries on the Society of the Spectacle*, Verso, London, 1990.

DeMarco, Eileen S., *Reading and Riding: Hachette's Railroad Bookstore Network in Nineteenth Century France*, Associated University Press, Cranbury, 2006.

Diderot, Denis, *Letter on the Book Trade*, translated by Arthur Goldhammer, Daedalus, vol. 131 no. 2: pp 48–56.

Didi-Huberman, Georges, *Confronting Images: Questioning the Ends of a Certain History of Art*, translated by John Goodman, Penn State University Press, 2005.

—*Atlas: How to Carry the World on One's Back*, TF Editores/Museo Nacional Reina Sofia, Madrid, 2010.

Domingos, Manuela D., Bertrand, *Uma livraria antes do Terremoto*, Biblioteca Nacional, Lisbon, 2002.

Donoso, José, *Diarios, ensayos, crónicas: La cocina de la escritura*, edited by Patricia Rubio, Ril Editores, Santiago de Chile, 2008.

Edwards, Jorge, *Persona non grata: A memoir of disenchantment with the Cuban Revolution*, translated by Andrew Hurley, The Paragon Press, New York, 1993.

Eliot, Simon, Andrew Nash and Ian Wilson, *Literary Cultures and the Material Book*, The British Library Publishing Division, London, 2007.

Énard, Mathieu, *Street of Thieves*, translated by Charlotte Mandell, Fitzcarraldo Editions, London, 2015. Copyright © Mathias Énard, 2012. Translation copyright © Charlotte Mandell, 2014. Reproduced by permission of Fitzcarraldo Editions.

Fernández, Benito J., *Eduardo Haro Ibars: los pasos del caído*, Editorial Anagrama, Barcelona, 2005.

Fernández, Eduardo, *Soldados de cerca de un tal Salamina. Grandezas y miserias en la Galaxia Librería*, Comanegra, Barcelona, 2008.

Fernández del Castillo, Francisco, editor, *Libros y libreros en el siglo XVI*, Fondo de Cultura Económica, Mexico City, 1982.

Foucault, Michel, *The Order of Things: An Archaelology of the Human Sciences*, translated by E. Frost, Routledge, 2001.

García Márquez, Gabriel, *One Hundred Years of Solitude*, translated by Gregory Rabassa, Penguin Books, London, 1972. Reprinted by permission of Agencia Literaria Carmen Balcells.

—*Living to Tell the Tale*, translated by Edith Grossman, Penguin Classics, London, 2003.

Gil, Manuel and Joaquín Rodríguez, *El paradigma digital y sostenible del libro*, Madrid, Trama, 2011.

Goethe, J.W. von, *Italian Journey*, translated by W. H. Auden and Elizabeth Mayer, Penguin Classics, London, 1970. English translation Copyright © 1962 by W. H. Auden, renewed. Reprinted by permission of Curtis Brown, Ltd.

Goffman, Ken, *Counterculture Through the Ages: From Abraham to Acid House*, Villard Books, New York, 2004.

Goytisolo, Juan, *Count Julian*, translated by Helen Lane, Serpent's Tail, 1989.

—*A Cock-Eyed Comedy*, translated by Peter Bush, Serpent's Tail, 2002. Reproduced by permission from Serpent's Tail.

—*Forbidden Territory* and *In Realms of Strife*, translated by Peter Bush, Verso, 2003. Reproduced by permissions from Verso Books.

Guerrero Marthineitz, Hugo, "La vuelta a Julio Cortázar en 80 preguntas", from *Julio Cortázar: Confieso que he vivido y otras entrevistas*, Antonio Crespo, editor, Buenos Aires, LC Editor, 1995.

Hanff, Helene, *84, Charing Cross Road*, Avon Books, New York, 1970.

Hemingway, Ernest, *A Moveable Feast*, Vintage, London, 2000.

Hoffman, Jan, "Her Life Is a Real Page-Turner", New York Times, October 12, 2011.

Jenkins, Henry, *Convergence Culture: Where Old and New Media Collide*, New York University Press, New York, 2006.

Johns, Adrian, *The Nature of the Book: Print and Knowledge in the Making*, Chicago University Press, Chicago, 1998.

Kiš, Danilo, *A Tomb for Boris Davidovitch*, translated by Duška Miki-Mitchell, Penguin Classics, London, 1980.

—*The Encyclopedia of the Dead*, translated by Michael Henry Heim, Faber & Faber, London, 1989.

Krishnan, Shekar, "Wheels within wheels", Indian Express, June 17, 1997.

Kubizek, August, *The Young Hitler I Knew*, translated by Lionel Leventhal, Greenhill Books, London, 2006.

Labarre, Albert, *Histoire du livre*, Presses universitaires de France, Paris, 2001.

Laddaga, Reinaldo, *Estética de laboratorio*, Adriana Hidalgo Editora, Buenos Aires, 2010.

Lernout, Geert and Wim Van Mierlo, *The Reception of James Joyce in Europe Vol.1: Germany, Northern and East Central Europe*, Thoemmes Continuum, London, 2004.

Link, Daniel, "Flaubert & Baudelaire", *Perfil*, Buenos Aires, August 28, 2011.

Lispector, Clarice, "Covert Joy", *The Collected Short Stories*, translated by Katrina Dodson, Penguin Modern Classics, 2015. Copyright ©1951, 1955, 1960, 1978, 2010, 2015 by the Heirs of Clarice Lispector, translation copyright © 2015 by Katrina Dodson. Reprinted by permission of New Directions Publishing Corp. and Penguin Books Ltd.

Loeb Schloss, Carol, *Lucia Joyce: To Dance in the Wake*, Farrar Straus Giroux, New York, 2004.

Lovecraft, H. P., "The Battle that Ended the Century", *The Complete Fiction Collection, Vol. III*, Ulwencreutz Media, 2012.

Lyons, Martyn, *Books: A Living History*, J. Paul Getty Museum, Los Angeles, 2011.

Llanas, Manuel, *El libro y la edición en Cataluña: apuntes y esbozos*, Gremi d'Editors de Catalunya, Barcelona, 2004.

MacCannell, Dean, *The Tourist: A New Theory of the Leisure Class*, Shocken Books, New York, 1976.

MacNiven, Ian S., editor, *The Durrell-Miller Letters 1935–1980*, Faber & Faber, 2003. Letter from Henry Miller to Lawrence Durrell copyright © The Beneficeries of the Estate of Henry Miller 2007. Reproduced with permission of Curtis Brown Ltd., London, on behalf of the Beneficeries of the Estate of Henry Miller

Mallarmé, Stéphane, "The Book: a Spiritual Instrument", translated by Bradford Cook, *Selected Poetry and Prose*, edited by Mary Ann Caws, New Directions, New York, 1982.

Manguel, Alberto, *A History of Reading*, Harper Collins, London, 1996. © Alberto Manguel, c/o Schavelzon Graham Agencia Literaria

—*The Library at Night*, Yale University Press, London, 2008.

Manzoni, Cecilia, "Ficción de futuro y lucha por el canon en la narrativa de Roberto Bolaño", *Jornadas Homenaje Roberto Bolaño (1953–2003)*, ed. Ramón Férriz González, *Simposio internacional*, ICCI Casa Am.rica Catalunya, Barcelona, 2005.

Marchamalo, Jesús, *Cortázar y los libros*, Fórcola Ediciones, Madrid, 2011.

Markson, David, *Reader's Block*, Dalkey Archive, Champaign, IL, 1996.

Martí Monterde, Antoni, *Poética del Café: Un espacio de la modernidad literaria europea*, Anagrama, Barcelona, 2007.

Martínez López, María Esther, *Jane Bowles y su obra narrativa: ambigüedad moral y búsqueda de una respuesta existencial*, Ediciones de la Universidad de Castilla-La Mancha, Cuenca, 1998.

Martínez Rus, Ana, *"San León Librero": las empresas culturales de Sánchez Cuesta*, Gijón, Trea, 2007.

Melo, Adrián, *El amor de los muchachos: homosexualidad y literature*, Lea, Buenos Aires, 2005.

Mercer, Jeremy, *Time Was Soft There: A Paris Sojourn at Shakespeare and Co.*, St. Martin's Press, New York, 2005.

Michaud, Joseph A., *Booking in Iowa: The Book Trade In and Around Iowa City. A Look Back*, The Bookery and The Press of the Camp Pope Bookshop, Iowa City, 2009.

Mogel, Leonard, *Making It in Book Publishing*, Arco, New York, 1996.

Monnier, Adrienne, *Rue de l'Odéon*, Albin Michel, Paris, 1960.

—*The Very Rich Hours of Adrienne Monnier*, translated, with an introduction and commentary by Richard McDougall, University of Nebraska Press, Lincoln, NE, 1996.

Montaigne, Michel de, *The Complete Essays*, translated by M. A. Screech, Penguin Classics, London, 1991. English translation copyright © M. A. Screech 1987, 1991, 2003. Reproduced by permission of Penguin Ltd.

Montroni, Romano, *Vendere l'anima: Il mestiere del libraio*, GLF Editore, Laterza, Rome, 2006.

Morand, Paul, *Venices*, translated by Euan Cameron, Pushkin Press, London, 2002.

Moretti, Franco, *Atlas of the European Novel 1800–1900*, Verso, London, 1998.

Morgan, Bill, *Beat Generation in New York: A Walking Tour of Jack Kerouac's City*, City Lights Books, San Francisco, 1997.

—*Jack Kerouac and Allen Ginsberg: The Letters*, edited by Bill Morgan and David Stanford, Viking, New York, 2010. Excerpt from Allen Ginsberg © 2011 by Allen Ginsberg, used by permission of The Wylie Agency (UK) Limited.

Muyal, Rachel, *My Years in the Librairie des Colonnes*, Khbar Bladna, Tangier, 2012.

Nancy, Jean Luc, *On the Commerce of Thinking: of Books and Bookstores*, translated by David Mills, Fordham University Press, New York, 2008.

Nooteboom, Cees, *All Souls Day*, translated by Susan Massotty, Picador, London, 2001. © Cees Nooteboom 1998, English translation © Susan Massotty 2001. First published by Atlas Uitgeverij as *Allerzeilen* in 1998. Reproduced by permission of Pan Macmillan via PLSclear.

Ordóñez, Marcos, *Un jardín abandonado por los pájaros*, El Aleph, Barcelona, 2013.

Osorgin, Mikhail, Alexei Remizov and Marina Tsvetaeva, *La Librería de los Escritores*, translated by Selma Ancira, Edicions de La Central/Sexto Piso, 2007.

Ortiz, Renato, *Modernidad y espacio: Benjamin en París*, translated by María Eugenia Contursi and Fabiola Ferro, Norma, Buenos Aires, 2000.

Otlet, Paul, *Traité de Documentation: le libre sur le libre, théorie et pratique*, Editions Mundaneum, Brussels, 1934.

Palmquist, Peter, and Thomas Kailbourn, *Pioneer Photographers of the Far West: A Biographical Dictionary, 1840–1865*, Stanford UP, 2006.

Parish, Nina, Henri Michaux, *Experimentation with Signs*, Rodopi, Amsterdam 2007.

Pascual, Carlos, Paco Puche and Antonio Rivero, *Memoria de la Librería*, Trama Editorial, Madrid, 2012.

Paz, Octavio, *The Monkey Grammarian*, translated by Helen R. Lane, Peter Owen Publishers, London, 1989.

Petroski, Henry, *The Book on the Bookshelf*, Vintage Books, London, 2000.

Pirandello, Luigi, *Cuentos para un año*, translated by Marilena de Chiara, Nórdica Madrid, 2011.

Ponte, Antonio José, *Un seguidor de Montaigne mira La Habana / Las comidas profundas*, Verbum, Matanzas, 1985.

Primera, Maye, "La librería del exilio cubano cierra sus puertas", El País, April 26, 2013.

Ramírez, Antonio, "Imagining the bookshop of the future", Huffington Post, September 18, 2012.

Reyes, Alfonso, and Pedro Henríquez Ureña, *Correspondencia 1907–1914*, edited by José Luis Martínez, Fondo de Cultura Económica, Mexico City, 1986.

Rice, Ronald, *My Bookstore: Writers Celebrate Their Favorite Places to Browse, Read, and Shop*, Black Dog & Leventhal Publishers, New York, 2012. Excerpt from "Green Apple Books, San Francisco. CA" by Dave Eggers. Copyright © 2012 Dave Eggers, used by permission of The Wylie Agency (UK) Limited.

Rushdie, Salman, *Joseph Anton: A Memoir*, Jonathan Cape, London, 2012. Copyright © Salman Rushdie 2012. Reproduced by permission of The Random House Group Ltd.

Saint Phalle, Nathalie, *Hoteles literarios: Viaje alrededor de la Tierra*, translated by Esther Benítez, Alfaguara, Madrid, 1993.

Sansieviero, Chachi, "La librería limeña El Virrey", Cuadernos Hispanoamericanos, n. 691, December 2008.

Schiffrin, André, *Words and Money*, Verso Books, London, 2010.

Scott, Anne, *18 Bookshops*, Sandstone Press, Dingwall, 2013.

Sebald, W. G., *The Rings of Saturn*, translated by Michael Hulse, Vintage Books, London, 2002.

—*Austerlitz*, translated by Anthea Bell, (Hamish Hamilton 2001, Penguin Books 2002), London 2002. Copyright © The Estate of W.G. Sebald 2001. English translation © Anthea Bell 2001. Reproduced by permission of Penguin Books Ltd.

Sennett, Richard, *The Craftsman*, Penguin Books, London, 2009. Copyright © Richard Sennett, 2008. Reproduced by permission of Penguin Books Ltd.

Serra, Cristóbal, editor, *Apocalipsis*, Siruela, Madrid, 2003.

Service, Robert, *Lenin: A Biography*, Macmillan, London, 2000. © Robert Service 2000. Reproduced with permission of Pan Macmillan via PLSclear.

—*Stalin: A Biography*, Macmillan, London, 2004.

Shakespeare, Nicholas, *Bruce Chatwin*, Vintage, London, 2000.

Smith, Gibbs M., *The Art of the Bookstore: The Bookstore Paintings of Gibbs M. Smith*, Gibbs Smith, Layton, UT, 2009.

Sontag, Susan, *I, etcetera*, Farrar, Straus, Giroux, New York, 1978.

Sorrel, Patricia and Fréderique Leblanc, *Histoire de la librairie française*, Paris, Editions du Cercle de la Librairie, 2008.

Steiner, George, *Extraterritorial: Papers on language and the language revolution*, Athenaeum, New York, 1971. Copyright © 1968, 1969, 1970, 1971 by George Steiner. Reprinted by permission of Georges Borchardt, Inc., on behalf of the author.

Steloff, Frances, *In Touch with Genius: Memoirs of a Bookseller*, Marian Seldes, Direct Cinema Ltd, Los Angeles, 1987.

Sterne, Laurence, *A Sentimental Journey Through France and Italy*, Lanham Start Classics, 2014.

Talese, Gay, *A Writer's Life*, Knopf, New York, 2006. Copyright © 2006 by Gay Talese. Reproduced by permission of Random House Ltd.

Thorpe Nicholson, Joyce, and Daniel Wrixon Thorpe, *A Life of Books. The Story of D.W. Thorpe PTY LTD 1921–1987*, Courtyard Press, Middle Park, 2000.

Unwin, Sir Stanley, *The Truth about Publishing*, Macmillan, London, 1960.

Verne, Jules, *The Lighthouse at the End of the World*, translated by William Butcher, Nebraska University Press, 2007.

Vila-Matas, Enrique, *Never Any End to Paris*, translated by Anne McLean, Harvill Secker, London, 2014. Copyright © Enrique Vila-Matas 2003. English Translation copyright © Anne McLean, 2011. Reproduced by permission of The Random House Group Ltd.

Vitkine, Antoine, *"Mein Kampf": histoire d'un livre*, Flammarion, Paris, 2009.

Various authors, *El libro de los libros. Guía de librerías de la ciudad de Buenos Aires*, Asunto Impreso Ediciones, Buenos Aires, 2009.

Various authors, *Kerouac en la carretera. Sobre el rollo mecanografiado original y la generación beat*, translated by Antonio Prometeo Moya, Anagrama, Barcelona, 2010.

Various authors, *El origen del narrador: Actas completas de los juicios a Baudelaire y Flaubert*, Mardulce, Buenos Aires, 2011.

Vollmann, William T., *The Royal Family*, New York, Penguin Books, New York 2000. Copyright © William T. Vollmann, 2000.

—*Central Europe*, Alma Books, 2006.

Walser, Robert, *The Walk and Other Stories*, translated by Christopher Middleton, Serpent's Tail, 2013.

Weiss, Jason, *The Lights of Home: A Century of Latin American Writers in Paris*, Routledge, New York, 2003.

Whitman, George, *The Rag and Bone Shop of the Heart*, Shakespeare and Company, Paris, 2000.

Williamson, Edwin, *Borges: A Life*, Viking, New York, 2004.

Yánover, Héctor, *Memorias de un librero*, Anaya & Mario Muchnik, Buenos Aires 1994.

—*El regreso del Librero Establecido*, Taller de Mario Muchnik, Madrid, 2003.

Zweig, Stefan, *The World of Yesterday*, translated by Anthea Bell. Pushkin Press, London, 2009.

—"Mendel the Bibliophile," *The Collected Stories of Stefan Zweig*, translated by Anthea Bell, Pushkin Press, London, 2013. Translation © Anthea Bell, reproduced by permission from Pushkin Press.

INDEX

10 Corso Como, Milan, 23, 236–7
"2001: Space Odyssey", Arthur C. Clarke, 124

A. H. Wheeler & Co., chain, 196–7
Abbey's, Sydney, 93, 239
Achar, Mauricio, 192
Acqua Alta, Venice, 222–4
Aínsa, Fernando, 153
Aira, César, 158, 214, 242
Akhmatova, Anna, 84
Ak'abal, Humberto, 23
Alberdi, Juan Bautista, 48
Alborta, Freddy, 100
Alexander the Great, 104
Alexandria 332 BC, Caracas, 153
Alemián, Ezequiel, 242
Alexis, 36
    Linos, 36
Alfred Hitchcock and the Three Investigators, 247
Alibri, Barcelona, 252
Allende, Salvador, 156, 162
Alonso, Dámaso, 178
Altaïr, Barcelona, 28–9, 249, 252
Alvear, Elvira, 68
Amazon, 203–4, 206–7, 272–4
American University, Cairo, 118
Amicis, Edmundo de, 57
Anderson, Sherwood, 67, 134
Angus & Robertson, Western Australia, 239
Another Country, Berlin, 225
Antonio Machado, Madrid, 244,
Arenas, Reinaldo, 101, 271
    Before Night Falls, 101
    Singing from the Well,
Argonaut, the, San Francisco, 144
Arkham Comics, Barcelona, 249
Arlt, Roberto, 158
Artemis Edinter, Guatemala City, 23
Astaire, Fred, 139
Asturias, Miguel Ángel, 68
Atahualpa, Inca, 154

Ateneo, el, Rosario, 244
Ateneo Grand Splendid, Buenos Aires, 277, 228–9
Atrectus, 38
Atticus, 37
Au Vieux Campeur, Paris, 32
Auden, W. H., 126
Aunós, Eduard, 256
Auster, Paul, 187
Autorenbuchhandlung, Berlin, 85, 225, 228
Avellaneda, Nicolás, 48, 182
Ávila, Miguel Ángel, 48

Bábel, Isaak, 280
Baedeker, Karl, 195
Balafrej, Si Ahmed, 111
Ballena Blanca, The, Mérida, 20, 242
Balzac, Honoré de, 202
Banerjee, T. K., 196–7
Barbey d'Aurevilly, Jules, 257
Barbier, Frédéric,
    Histoire du livre, 198
Barbusse, Henri, 157
Barea, Arturo,
    Making of a Rebel, The, 267
Baricco, Alessandro, 58, 275
    Barbarians, The, 274
Barnes, family, 192
Barnes & Noble, 192, 203, 273–4
Barter Books, Alnwick, 239
Barthes, Roland, 173
Bass, Benjamin, 132
Bass, Fred, 132
Bass, Nancy, 132
Batalla del Ebro, Mexico, 148
Batlló, José, 252
Baudelaire, Charles, 63–4, 120
    Fleurs du Mal, Les, 63–4, 182
Beach, Sylvia, 127–8, 180, 186–9, 208, 224
    Shakespeare and Company, 65
Bechdel, Alison, 129
    Are You My Mother? 129

Beckett, Samuel, 72, 66, 178, 190
"Before Sunrise", Richard Linklater, 140
Beijing Book Building, Beijing, 97
Bellatin, Mario, 163, 214
Ben–Gurión, David, 95
Ben Jelloun, Tahar, 176
Benda, Julien, 69
Benjamin, Walter, 17, 61, 65, 85, 120
    Arcades Project, The, 61–2
    One Way Street, 85
Bellow, Saul, 133–4
Bergamín, José, 177
Bergé, Pierre, 111
Bernadas, Josep, 29
+Bernat, Barcelona, 253
Berthe Trépat, 172
Bertolucci, Bernardo, 107
Bertrand Livreiros, chain, 50, 59
Bertrand Martin, João Augusto, 60
Beuf, Antonio, 56
Bizzio, Sergio, 242
Blackwell's, Oxford, 241
Blagg, Kim, 274
Blanc, Patrick, 232
"Blonde on Blonde", Bob Dylan, 124
Boccaccio, Giovanni, 131
Boekehuis, Johannesburg, 213, 220
Boekhandel Selexyz Dominicanen, Maastrich, 226
Bolaño, Roberto, 151, 155–8 160, 165, 168–9, 171, 177, 230, 250, 271
    2666, 156, 249
    Advice from a Follower of Morrison to a Fan of Joyce, 171
    Between Parentheses, 170
    "Dance Card", 157
    Distant Star, 160
    Insufferable Gaucho, The, 250
    Last Evenings on Earth, 172
    Nazi Literature in America, 156, 169
    Night in Chile, 160
    Savage Detectives, The, 147, 158, 267
    Skating Rink, The,

"Vagaries of the Literature of Doom, The", 156
Bookàbar, Rome, 234
Book Bazaar, Istanbul, 114, 244
Book City, Hollywood, 144
Book Gallery, Athens, 44
Book Lounge, The, Cape Town, 21, 213, 215, 228
Bookmall, Shanghai, 118
Books Inc., San Francisco, 136
Bookshop 41, Jarkov, 271
Bookworm, Beijing, 234
Bonaparte, Napoleón 39
Booth, Richard, 220
Borders, chain, 203, 207–8
Borges, Jorge Luis, 11–2, 14–5, 72, 85, 143, 156–8, 168–9, 171, 177, 272, 277
    Aleph, The, 12, 14–5
    Library of Babel, The, 12, 14, 132, 169
    Obra Poetica, 171
Borràs, Manuel, 262
Boswell, James, 271
Boulaich, Abdeslam, 107
Boumediane el Metni, Rajae, 176
Bourdieu, Pierre,
    Distinction: A Social Critique of the Judgment of Taste, 66
Bowles, Jane, 107–8, 175, 271
Bowles, Paul, 107–11, 117, 174–6, 186–7, 212
    Travels, 212
Bozzi, Mario, 56
Bozzi, Tonino, 56
Braque, George, 125
Bravo, Claudio, 107
Brecht, Bertolt, 82
Brentano's, 238
Breton, André, 65, 127, 180
    Nadja, 184
Bridges, E. Lucas, 218
Brink, André,
    Praying Mantis, 213
Brock, Jack, 90
Brod, Max, 183

Bryson, Bill, 32
Bücherbogen, Berlin, 225
Bukowski, Charles, 77
Burke, Peter, 276
Burrito Blanco, El, Montevideo, 154
Burroughs, William S., 79, 107,
    124–5, 173, 183, 223
    Naked Lunch, The, 124, 183–4
Buscón, El, Caracas, 237
Bush, George W., 58
Bussola, La, Turin, 62
Byron, Lord, 36, 214

Caellas, Marc, 250
Cai Lun, 120
Cairns, Huntington, 128–9
Callao, Buenos Aires, 228
Callejas, Mariana, 160
Callejón de los Milagros, El, Mexico,
    151
Calvino, Italo,
    Invisible Cities, 85
Camacho, Jorge, 271
Camarasa, Paco, 252
Camus, Albert, 20
Canet, Figueras, 271
Canetti, Elias,
    Auto da Fé, 248
    Voices of Marrakesh, The, 105
Capote, Truman, 107
Capriolo, Ettore, 93
Cardoso Pires, José, 45
Carey, Peter, 211
    *True History of the Kelly Gang,
    The*, 211
Carpentier, Alejo, 68
Casa del Libro, 273
Casanova, Francesco, 57–8
Casanova, Pascale, 71, 186
Castellanos, Rafael Ramón, 151, 167
Castellanos, Rómulo, 151, 167
Castillo, Abelardo, 165
Castro, Fidel, 98–9
Castro, Raúl, 101
Catalònia, Barcelona, 259–60
Catullus, 37

Catunda, Márcio, 145
Cavafy, Constantino, 41
Cella, Jack, 133
Central, La, Barcelona, 229, 249, 252
Central de Callao, La, Madrid, 229,
    231
Central, La, Museum of the History
    of the City, Barcelona, 254
Central del Raval, La, Barcelona, 229
Central del Reina Sofía, La, Madrid,
    244
Cepeda Samudio, Álvaro, 266
Cervantes Saavedra, Miguel de, 20,
    182, 252, 257, 274
    Don Quixote, 118, 182
Chapters, 201, 203
Chartier, Roger,
    *Inscription and Erasure, Written
    Culture and Literature from the
    Eleventh to the Eighteenth Cen-
    tury*, 268
Chartoprateia, Bizancio, 114
Chateaubriand, François–René, 52,
    70
    Genius of Christianity, The, 52
    Memories from Beyond the Tomb,
    70
Chatwin, Bruce, 29–33, 198, 209, 212,
    217–8
    Anatomy of Restlessness, 217
    In Patagonia, 218
    Songlines, The, 29, 204
Chatwins, Berlin, 29
Chejfec, Sergio, 214
"Chelsea Girls, The", Andy Warhol,
    125
"Chelsea Hotel", Leonard Cohen,
    124
Chih Cheng, Lo,
    Bookstore in a Dream, 263
Chomsky, Noam, 77
Churchill, Winston S., 30, 95
Cicciolina, 81
Cícero, Antônio, 146
Cicero, 37
City Lights, San Francisco, 136–7,
    224

Clásica y Moderna, Buenos Aires, 165–6, 228
Clavel, Vicente, 256
Cocteau, Jean, 272
    Opium, 169
Cody's, Berkeley, 92
Coelho, Paulo, 215–6
Coetzee, J. M., 134, 214–6
    Diary of a Bad Year, 216
    Disgrace, 214, 216
Cole, Teju, 176
    Open City, 176
Collet's, London, 92
Colombo, Alberto, 56
Compagnie, Paris, 178–9
Conte, Alberto, 167
Cook & Book, Brussels, 234
Cordero, Diómedes, 242
Corso, Gregory, 77, 110, 124–6
Cortázar, Julio, 101, 158, 160, 168–9, 184–5
    Hopscotch 158, 188, 183–5, 252
    Nicaragua tan violentamente dulce 169
Corte Inglés, El, 231, 258, 263
Cozarinsky, Edgardo, 173–4, 177, 244
    Urban Voodoo, 177
Cruzet, Josep Maria, 262
Cuadros, Ricardo, 160
Cúpula, La, Guatamala City, 21, 23

Dahl, Svend, 48, 62
    A History of the Book, 48
Daunt Books, London, 32, 204. 206
Davies, Tom, 271
De Cabo, Marina P., 246
Debord, Guy, 178
Del Valle, Aristóbulo, 48
Delacroix, Eugène, 105
DeMarco, Eileen S.,
    Reading and Riding, 195
Desnivel, Madrid, 29
Di Benedetto, Antonio, 158
Díaz Plaja, Guillermo, 256
Dickens, Charles, 194
Diderot, Denis, 64, 130

    L'Encyclopédie, 64, 130, 194
    Jacques the Fatalist, 130
    Letter on the Book Trade, 272
    Letter on the Deaf and Mute, 130
Didi–Huberman, Georges,
    Atlas: How to carry the world on your back, 25
    Before Time, 17
Didion, Joan, 214
Dillons, 93, 203
Disney, Walt, 122
Documenta, Barcelona, 252
Donoso, José, 132
    "A New York Obsession", 132
Dòria Llibres, Mataró, 263
Dos Passos, John, 186
Drieu La Rochelle, Pierre, 68
Drummond de Andrade, Carlos, 145
Dubuisson, Sylvain, 179
Duchamp, Marcel, 127
Dugdale, Edgar, 95
Dukhan, Nihad,
    Contemporary Arabic Calligraphy, 118
Dumas, Alexandre, 202
Duras, Marguerite, 178
Durrell, Lawrence, 128, 190
    Alexandria Quartet, The, 190

Eberhard, Hermann, 217
Eça de Queirós, José Maria, 45
L'Écume des Pages, Paris, 21, 178–9, 190
Edwards, Jorge,
    Persona non grata: A memoir of disenchantment with the Cuban Revolution, 101
Eggers, Dave, 263
Eliot, T. S., 30, 127
Elzevir, family, 194
Embryo Concepts, Los Angeles, 139
Eminem, 90
Énard, Mathias,
    Street of Thieves, 176
Ennis, Garth, & Robertson, Darick,
    Boys, The, 142

Ernst, Max, 179
Escari, Raúl, 242
Estrada, José Manuel, 48
Eterna Cadencia, Buenos Aires, 21,
    86, 215, 228

Fabre, Luis Felipe, 273
Family Christian Stores, 193
"Fantômes de Tanger", Edgardo
    Cozarinsky, 173
Fargue, Léon–Paul, 65, 68
Faulkner, William, 271
Feltrinelli, chain, 33, 35, 206, 244
Ferlinghetti, Lawrence, 77, 79, 125,
    136, 187, 208, 271
Fermor, Patrick Leigh, 30
Ferreiro, Rosa, 165
Fischer, Bram, 213
Fitzgerald, F. Scott, 65, 186, 225
Flaubert, Gustave, 63–4, 104
    Madame Bovary, 63, 182, 271
Fnac, chain, 201, 203, 228, 231, 258,
    263, 269
Foix, J. V., 20
Fondo de Cultura Económica, chain,
    231
Fondo de Cultura Económica, San-
    tiago, 156
Forbes, Malcolm, 107–8
Fortuny, Mariano, 106
Foucault, Michel, 173
Foyle, Christina, 30–1, 94
Foyle, William, 30, 94–5
Foyles, chain, 30–2, 94
Fraga Iribarne, Manuel, 257
Franck, Dan,
    Bohemians, 79
Franco, Francisco, 257
Freund, Gisèle, 68
Frizzo, Luigi, 222
Frost, Robert, 134
Fuck You, magazine, 125
Fuenmayor, Alfonso, 266
Fuentes, Antonio, 106
Fuentes, Carlos, 157, 242

"Funny Face", S. Donen, 129
Galeano, Eduardo, 153
Gallardo, Damià, 246
Gandhi, Buenos Aires,
Gandhi, Rajiv, 92
Gapers Block magazine, 133
Garamona, Francisco, 242
García Madero, Juan, 147
García Márquez, Gabriel, 215–6, 231,
    264, 266–7
Garcilaso de la Vega, Inca, 257
Genet, Jean, 107, 109, 125, 173–4
Gerardi, Juan, Bishop, 21
Gerofi, sisters, 107–11
Gerofi, Robert, 107–8
Gheerbrant, Bernard, 180
Gide, André, 65, 107
Gigamesh, Barcelona, 251
Ginsberg, Allen, 58, 77–8, 86, 110,
    124–6, 173, 183, 187
    Howl, 77, 183
Girod, Patrice, 226
Girodias, Maurice, 183
Gleebooks, Sydney, 209, 211
Goethe, Johann Wolfgang von, 51,
    71, 74, 237, 270
Goffman, Ken,
    Counterculture through the ages:
    From Abraham to Acid House, 79
Goldsboro Books, London 26–7
González de Léon, Teodoro, 232
Gotham Book Mart, 122, 127–9, 179
Goytisolo, Juan, 107, 109, 116, 173–4,
    176
    Cock–Eyed Comedy, A, 109
    Ottoman Istanbul, 116
    Realms of Strife, In, 109
Gran Pulpería del Libro, La, 151, 167
Grass, Günter, 86
Green Apple Books, San Francisco,
    20, 136–7, 139, 263
Gris, Juan, 124
Groussac, Paul, 48
Guadalquivir, Buenos Aires, 228
Guarino, Gustavo, 245

"Guatemala: Never Again", 21, 24
Guerrero Mathineitz, Hugo, 169
Guevara, Ernesto Che, 99–100, 156
Guggenheim, Peggy, 123, 127, 179
Guillén, Nicolás, 99
Guirao, Maribel, 230
Gutenberg, Johannes, 120

Hachette, 43, 195–7
Hachette, Louis, 43, 195
Haines, Robert D., 144
Hamelin, Simon–Pierre, 111
Hamri, Mohamed, 107
Haro Ibars, Eduardo, 109
Harris, Jim, 134
Hart, Michael S., 274
Hatchard, John, 47
Hatchards, chain, 47, 50, 204
Heaney, Seamus, 134
Heker, Liliana, 165
Hellas, Turín, 58
Hemingway, Ernest, 33, 65,67, 101,
    178, 186–7, 225
    Moveable Feast, A, 67
Hemingway, Margaux, 190
Hendrix, Jan, 232
Henríquez Ureña, Pedro, 100
Hériz, Enrique de, 211
Hernández, Felisberto, 153, 267
Hernández, José, 106
Hill of Content, Melbourne, 212, 215
Hitchcock, Alfred, 144
Hitler, Adolf, 87, 94–7, 157
    Mein Kampf, 95–6, 102
Hollande, François, 208
Homer, 37, 40
    The Illiad, 186
Hopper, Edward, 124
Horacio, Mexico, 148
Hudson Group, 200
Hudson News, 200
"Hugo", Martin Scorsese, 143
Hugo, Victor, 88, 98, 186, 202
    Year Ninety–Three, The, 88
La Hune, Paris, 178–80, 190, 230

Ianos, Athens, 42

Ibáñez Langlois, José Miguel, 160,
    169
    Marxism: Critical Vision, 160
Igarashi, Hitoshi, 93
Iglesias, Josep Maria, 29
India Today, 91
Indian Express, 197
Index of Banned Books, The, 102
Inframundo, Mexico, 151

Jenkins, Henry, 90
Jiménez, Juan Ramón, 177, 278
John Sandoe Books, London, 21,
    222–3
Johns, Adrian,
    Nature of the Book, The, 243
Johnson, Samuel, 271
Jones, Patrick, 204
Joyce, James, 47, 65, 69, 71–3, 128,
    180, 184, 223, 225, 271
    Dubliners, 47
    Finnegans Wake, 67, 127
    Ulysses, 47, 66–7, 73, 102, 139, 171,
        178, 183–4, 271
"Julie & Julia", N. Ephron, 141

Kabacali, Alpay,
    Through the Eyes of Turkish
    Travellers, 114
Kafka, Franz, 143, 157, 183
    Metamorphosis, 143
Kahlo, Frida, 43, 124
Karl Marx Buchhandlung, Berlin, 82
Katchadjian, Pablo, 82
Kedros, 34
Kerouac, Jack, 79, 125, 174, 183–4, 187
    On the Road, 184
Kingsley, Charles, 45
Kipling, Rudyard, 197
    Jungle Book, The, 197
    Kim, 197
Kiš, Danilo, 11, 13–5, 45, 84, 101
    Encyclopedia of the Dead, The,
        11, 13, 85

Komikova, Alexandra, 84
Krishnan, Shekhar, 197
Kubizek, August, 96
Kurosawa, Akira, 272

Laberinto, El, Mexico, 151
Lackington, James, 50
Laddaga, Reinaldo, 214–6
  Estética de laboratorio, 214
Langlois, Ibáñez, 160, 169
Laguna, Fernanda, 242
Laie, Barcelona, 86, 223, 228, 230,
  249, 252
Laie, Madrid, 246
Lalou, René,
  *Histoire de la littérature française
  contemporaine*, 73
Lamborghini, Osvaldo, 158
Lange, Monique, 109
Last Bookstore, The, Los Angeles,
  233
Lawrence, D. H., 102, 128
  Lady Chatterley's Lover, 93, 102,
  129
Layachi, Larbi, 107
Lefebvre, Henri, 172
Lello, António, 56
Lello, José, 56
Lenin, Vladimir, 84
Lessing, Doris, 182
  Golden Notebook, The, 182
Levertov, Denise, 77
Levrero, Mario, 214
Lezama Lima, José, 148
  Paradiso, 148
Li Dazhao, 97
Librairie des Colonnes, Tangiers,
  106–9, 111–2, 173, 176, 224
Librairie du Donjon, Béchrel, 220
Librairie Espagnole, Paris, 177
Librairie Espagnole Léon Sánchez
  Cuesta, Paris, 177
Librairie Kauffmann, Athens, 43
Librairie Papeterie de Mlle. El
  Ghazzali Amal, Marrakesh, 112
Libreria Bozzi, Genova, 56

Libreria Casanova, 57
Libreria Colonnese, Naples, 245
Librería de Ávila, Buenos Aires, 47,
  49, 224
Librería de Historia, Caracas, 167
Librería del Colegio, Buenos Aires,
  48, 50
Librería del Pensativo, Guatemala
  City, 21
Librería del Sur, 98
Librería Mundo, Barranquilla, 266
Librería Norte, Buenos Aires, 168
Librería Rayuela, de la Casa de las
  Américas, Havana, 102
Librería Rosario Castellanos,
  Mexico, 232
Libro Books, Tokyo, 118
Libros Prólogo, Santiago, 158, 161–2,
  164
Lihn, Enrique, 155–7
Lispector, Clarice,
  "Covert Joy", 279
Literanta, Palma de Mallorca, 21,
  246
Livingstone, David, 32
Livraria Bertrand, Lisbon, 33, 45, 56
Livraria Internacional de Ernesto
  Chardron, Oporto, 56
Livraria Lello, Oporto, 57, 143
Livraria Leonardo da Vinci, Río de
  Janeiro, 146
London Review Bookshop, 23
López, Josep, 262
"Lord Jim", Richard Brooks, 107
Lovecraft, H. P.,
  "Battle that Ended the Century,
  The", 142
Lowry, Malcolm, 183
Ludens, Caracas, 153
Lugan, Mathieux, 56
Lukas, Paul, 107
Luna Park, magazine, 107
Lupa, La, Montevideo, 21, 245
Luxemburg, Turin, 57–8
Lyons, Martyn
  Books: A Living History, 120

Maalouf, Amin, 108
MacCannell, Dean, 181
Macmillan, 238
Madbouly, Cairo, 117
Madonna, 124
Maestro, Domingo, 150, 167, 169
Mahfouz, Naguib, 117
Maison des Amis des Livres, La,
    Paris, 26, 65, 69, 75, 80
Mallarmé, Stéphane, 55, 69, 187
Malraux, André, 43
Manguel, Alberto,
    History of Reading, A, 41, 94
Mao, Tse-tung, 97
Markson, David, 279-80
    Loneliness of the Reader, The, 280
    This is Not a Novel, 279-80
Marquez, Gabriel García, 215-6, 231,
    264, 266-7
One Hundred Years of Solitude, 183,
    263
Martínez Rus, Ana, 178
    "San León Librero", las empresas
    culturales de Sánchez Cuesta, 178
Maruzen, Tokyo, 272
Marx, Karl, 87, 98
    Capital, 88
    Communist Manifesto, The, 98
Matisse, Henri, 33, 108
Mayer, Johann Jakob, 36
McNally, Sarah, 207-8
McNally Jackson Books, New York,
    23, 207
McPhillips, Joseph, 110
Melville, Herman,
    Bartleby the Scrivener, 280
Mercer, Jeremy, 76
    Time Was Soft There: A Paris
    Sojourn at Shakespeare & Co., 190
Mercurio, El, 160
Meskis, Joyce, 134-5
Mexicana, Mexico, 148
Michaux, Henri, 179-80
Milla, Benito, 152
Milla, Leonardo, 153
Milla, Ulises, 151-2, 167

Miller, Henry, 76, 102, 128-9, 190
    Tropic of Cancer, 76, 102, 128-9, 183
Miłosz, Czeslaw, 134
Milton, Mexico, 148
Minnelli, Liza, 166
Miró, Joan, 233
Michaux, Henri, 72, 179-80
    Miserable miracle, 180
Mistral, Le, Paris, 76
Monnier, Adrienne, 26, 65, 67-70, 73,
    75
Montaigne, Michel de, 122, 267
Montané, Bruno, 172
Monti, François, 220
Moore, Alan,
    Neonomicon, 142
Morand, Paul, 108
Moreau, Émile, 196-7
Moreno, Francisco P., 48
Moretti, Franco, 202, 203
    Atlas of the European Novel 1800-
    1900, 202, 214
Morrison, Toni, 134
Moschos, Myrsine, 66
Mrabet, Mohammed, 107
El Mundo, Mexico, 148
Murakami, Haruki, 118
Muret, Theodore, 61
    L'Histoire par le theater, 61
Muyal, Rachel, 111-2, 173-4, 176
    My Years in the Librairie des
    Colonnes, 111

Nabokov, Vladimir, 72
    Lolita, 93, 183
Le Navire d'Argent, 69
Negra y Criminal, Barcelona, 252,
    254
Neruda, Pablo, 156-8, 160, 169, 171
New York Times, 92, 200, 207
Nieto, Amalia, 154
Nightingale, Florence, 32
Nin, Anaïs, 127-8, 190
Nodo & Nodo, Milan, 33
Noel, Eugenio, 257

Nooteboom, Cees, 86, 278
  All Souls Day, 86
"Notting Hill", R. Mitchell, 139
Nygaard, William, 93

Obama, Barack, 134
Obregón, Alejandro, 266
Ocampo, Victoria, 68, 267
Onetti, Juan Carlos, 152
Orpheus, 37
Orozco, Mexico, 148
Ortega y Gasset, José, 68
Ortiz, Renato, 199
Otlet, Paul,
  Traité de Documentation, 238
Ovid, 37

P&G Wells, Winchester, 46–7
Pacelli, Eugenio, Pius XII, 102
Padrol, Albert, 29
Padrón, Alejandro, 242
El País, 154
Palahniuk, Chuck, 134–5
Palladio, Andrea, 50–1, 71
Pamuk, Orhan, 116, 134
Pandora, Istanbul, 262–3
Panero, Leopoldo María, 110
Papirvm, Barcelona, 254
Paris–France, 186
Parker, Dorothy, 122
Parra, Nicanor, 156–7, 160, 169
Parra, Teresa de la, 257
Pascual, Carlos, 5
Pasternak, Boris, 280
Paz, Octavio, 156–8
Peace Eye Bookstore, New York, 126
El Péndulo, chain, 231–2, 240
El Péndulo, Mexico City, 23, 231–2,
  240
Penguin, 92–3, 216
Pensamiento Crítico, 101
Pepys, Samuel, 243–4
Pequod, Barcelona, 252, 254
Peri Rossi, Cristina, 153
Perón, Juan Domingo, 152,
Pessoa, Fernando, 45

Petroski, Henry, 50
  Book on the Bookshelf, The, 50
Pezzana, Angelo, 58–60
Pezzoni, Enrique, 165
Phoenix Bookshop, The, New York,
  125
Piano, Renzo, 36
Picasso, Pablo, 33, 67–8, 125, 187,
Piglia, Ricardo, 158
Pinard, Ernest, 64
Pinner, H. L., 37
Pinochet, Augusto, 160
Pius XI, 102
Piraccini, Vanna, 1 45, 166–7
Pirandello, Luigi, 11, 13–14
  "World of Paper", 11, 13–14
Pivano, Fernanda, 58
Pla, Josep, 271
Plant, Ricardo, 166
Plinio el Joven, 147–8
Plinio el Joven, Mexico, 147–8
Poblet, Emilio, 165
Poblet, Francisco, 165
Poblet, Natu, 165–6, 168
Poblet, Paco, 165
Poblet Brothers, chain, 165
Politeia, Athens, 48
Pollock, Jackson, 126
Polo, Marco, 104
Ponte, Antonio José, 99
  *Un sequidor de Montaigne mira La
  Habana*, 99
Porrúa, Francisco, 184–5
Porta, A.G., 171
"Portrait of a Bookstore as an Old
  Man", Sutherland, B. and
  Pichelin, G., 188
Pound, Ezra, 67
Powell's City of Books, Portland,
  134–5
Prairie Lights, Iowa, 134
Presley, Elvis, 122
Prévert, Jacques, 187
Prévost, Jean, 65
Primera, Maye, 100
Primo de Rivera, Miguel, 256

The Protocols of the Elders of Zion, 117
Puche, Francisco, 89
Puig, Manuel, 158
Puro Verso, Montevideo, 278

Quental, Antero de, 45
Quintero, Ednodio, 242

R. Vinas & Co., Barranquilla, 265–6
Rachou, Madame, 124
Rafael Alberti, La, Madrid, 21, 244
Ramírez, Antonio, 230–1
    "Imagining the bookshop of the
    future", 230–1
Ramoneda, Marta, 230
Ray, Man, 67–8
Reader's Feast Bookshop,
    Melbourne, 211
Rebeca Nodier, Mexico, 147–8
Rebolledo, Efrén, 147
La Reduta, Bratislava, 81
"Reservoir Dogs", Quentin
    Tarantino, 135
Reverdy, Pierre, 69
Rey Rosa, Rodrigo, 23
Reyes, Alfonso, 37, 68, 100, 148,
    267–8
    Books and Bookshops in Antiquity,
    267–8
Rhodes, Cecil, 32
Ricci, Franco Maria, 169
Rilke, Rainer Maria, 157
Rivera, Diego, 124
Rivera, Orlando, 266
    Figurita, 266
Robafaves, Mataró, 247–9, 251, 263
Roberts, Julia, 139
Robertson, Darick, 142
Robinson Crusoe, Istanbul, 21, 55,
    86, 116, 228
Rogés Llibres, Mataró, 247, 248, 251
Rolling Stones, The, 107
Romain, Jules, 65
Roman, Anton, 136
Rondón Hederich, Jorge, 266–7
Roosevelt, Franklin D., 95

Ross Bookshop, Rosario, 244

Ross, Harold, 122
Roth, Samuel, 129
Rousseau, Jean–Jacques,
    Social Contract, The, 131
Roussel, Raymond, 178
Rowling, J. K.,
    Harry Potter series, 90, 143, 188
Rucar, Georgette, 178
Ruedo Ibérico, Paris, 177
Rulfo, Juan, 157
Rushdie, Salman, 90–94
    Joseph Anton, 91–4
Ryan, Meg, 141

Sacristán, José, 166
Sagarra, Josep Maria de, 257
Said, Edward, 177
Sala Aquilino Ribeiro, Lisbon, 45
Salinas, Pedro, 177
Salmona, Rogelio, 232
Sanders, Ed, 125–6
Sandburg, Carl, 134
Sandro, 166
Sano, Riki, 272
Sanseviero, Chachi, 154–5, 167
Sanseviero, Eduardo, 167
Sanseviero, Malena, 154–5, 167
Santo Domingo, Julio Mario, 266
Sarmiento, Domingo Faustino, 48
Sartre, Jean–Paul, 99
Satie, Erik, 67
    "Socrate", 67
Savoy, Richard, 138
Scott, Robert, 32
Scott, Walter, 194, 202
Scribner's, 238
Sebald, W. G., 209, 214, 246
    Austerlitz, 209, 246
Sebreli, Juan José, 165
Secundus, 37
Sefer Ve Sefel, Jerusalem, 117
Seminary Co-op Bookstore,
    Chicago, 133, 216, 244
Semprún, Jorge, 86

Sennett, Richard, 53
  Craftsman, The, 53
Serao, Matilde, 57
Serra, Crsitóbal, 246
Serrano, Montse, 253
Service, Robert, 87–8
"Sex", 124
Shakespeare, Nicholas, 217
Shakespeare, William 26, 198, 257
Shakespeare and Company, chain, 73–6, 187, 192
Shakespeare and Company, Paris, 26, 61, 65–80, 125, 127, 140, 171, 172, 178, 188, 190, 192, 223, 224
Shasta Book Store, Shasta City, 136
Shaw, George Bernard, 27, 30
Sherwood, Robert, 67
Shestov, Lev, 68
Sitin, St Petersberg, 84
Smith, William Henry, 198,
Sociedade José Pinto Sousa Lello & Irmão, 56
Solís, César, 246
Solzhenitsyn, Aleksandr, 84
  Gulag Archipelago, 84
Sontag, Susan, 86, 99
Sophos, Guatemala City, 2 3, 279
Soria, Carmelo, 160
Soriano, Antonio, 177
Soriano Osvaldo, 178
Sosii, brothers, 37–8
Sótano, Mexico, 148
Der Spiegel, 83
Stalin, Joseph Vissarionovich, 87–8, 95, 157, 280
Stanfords, London, 30–32
Stein, Gertrude, 67, 107, 186
Steiner, George, 72, 143
Steloff, Frances, 127, 129, 208, 224
  In Touch with Genius: Memoirs of a Bookseller, 127–8
Stendhal, 202
Sterne, Laurence, 51
Strand, New York, 131–2, 135, 141, 144, 280

Sur, 155
Taifa, Barcelona, 252
Talese, Gay, 129–30
Tamir Books, Jerusalem, 117
Tampax, 58
Tarantino, Quentin, 135
Tattered Cover, Denver, 134–5
Temple of the Muses, London, 50, 238
Thackeray, William, 45, 194
Thesiger, Wilfred, 32
Thomas, Dylan, 124
Thompson, Hunter S., 138
  Open Letter, 138
Thorpe, Daniel Wrixton, 239
Thorpe Nicholson, Joyce, 239
  A Life of Books, 239
Tipos Infames, Madrid, 224
Tolstoy, Leo, 140
Tooley, John Peter, 122
Topping & Company, Bath, 54
Townley, Michael, 160
Travel Book Company, 139
Tropismes, Brussels, 278
Troyes, Chrétien de, 220
Türkmenoglou, Burak, 166
Twain, Mark, 124, 134

Ulysses, Paris, 29
Universal, Miami, 100
Uslar, Pietri, Arturo, 68

Valéry, Paul, 27, 65, 68
Valle–Inclan, Ramón María, 151
  Bohemian Lights, 151
Vallianos, brothers, 35–6
Van Damme, Andries, 274
Van Gogh, Vincent, 33, 187
La Vanguardia Española, 257
Vargas, Germán, 266
Vargas Llosa, Mario, 271
Vásquez, Juan Gabriel, 266
Vásquez, Ángel, 106
  La vida perra de Juanita Narboni, 106

Verbitsky, Horacio, 165
Verga, Giovanni, 57
Verghese, Abraham, 134
"Vertigo", Alfred Hitchcock, 144
Vicéns de la Llave, Juan, 177–8
Vidal, Gore, 108
El Viejo Topo, 171
Viejo y Raro, Caracas, 167
Vila–Matas, Enrique, 57, 177–8, 258,
    272
    Never Any End to Paris, 177
Vinyes, Ramon, 265
Viñas, David, 165
Virgil, 186, 194
    Aenied, 186
Virrey, El, Lima, 154
Vitkine, Antoine, 95
Vitruvius, 51
Voces, 265
Vollmann, William T., 83–4, 101, 137
    Central Europe, 83–4
    Royal Family, The, 137
Vulgate, 254

Walcott, Derek, 134
Walk A Crooked Mile Books,
    Philadelphia, 239
Walser, Robert, 250–1, 257
    Walk, The, 250–1
Warhol, Andy, 123–5, 144, 187
Waterstone, Tim, 203
Waterstones, chain, 47, 203–7
We Moderns 1920–1940, anthology,
    127
Weber, Max, 98
Wells, H. G., 30
    War of the Worlds, The, 183

Wheeler, Arthur Henry, 196–7
Whitman, George, 76–7, 188
Whitman, Sylvia Beach, 189
WHSmith, chain, 92, 198, 201, 203,
    206, 207
Wilde, Oscar, 33, 63–4
Wilkins, John, 143
Williams, Tennessee, 107
Williams, William Carlos, 77
Williamson, Edwin, 169
Wilson, Edmund, 122
Winch, Tara June, 211–2
Woolf, Virginia, 68, 143
    Orlando, 143
World's Biggest Bookstore, Ontario,
    132,
Wyden, Ava Rose, 132
Wyden, William Peter, 132

Yacoubi, Ahmed, 107
Yaday, Lalu Prasad, 197
Yánover, Débora, 168
Yánover, Héctor, 167–8
    Memorias de un librero, 167–8
Yenny, chain, 228
Yourcenar, Marguerite, 108
Yüksel, Rasim, 116

Zafón, Carlos Ruiz, 140
    Shadow of the Wind, The, 140
Zamora, Crispín, 148
Zeus, 186
Zombie International, 58
Zondervan, brothers, 193
Zurita, Raúl, 169
Zweig, Stefan, 9–17, 61, 98, 274

JORGE CARRIÓN is a writer and literary critic. He studied at the University of Pompeu Fabra, where he now teaches literature and creative writing. His published works include essays, novellas, novels and travel writing, and his articles have appeared in *National Geographic* and *Lonely Planet* Magazine. *Bookshops* was a finalist in the Premio Anagrama de Ensayo, 2013.

PETER BUSH is an academic and translator of French, Catalan, Portuguese and Spanish. He has previously translated works by Federico García Lorca, Pedro Almodóvar and Joan Sales. He was awarded La Creu de Sant Jordi for his translation and promotion of Catalan literature in 2015.